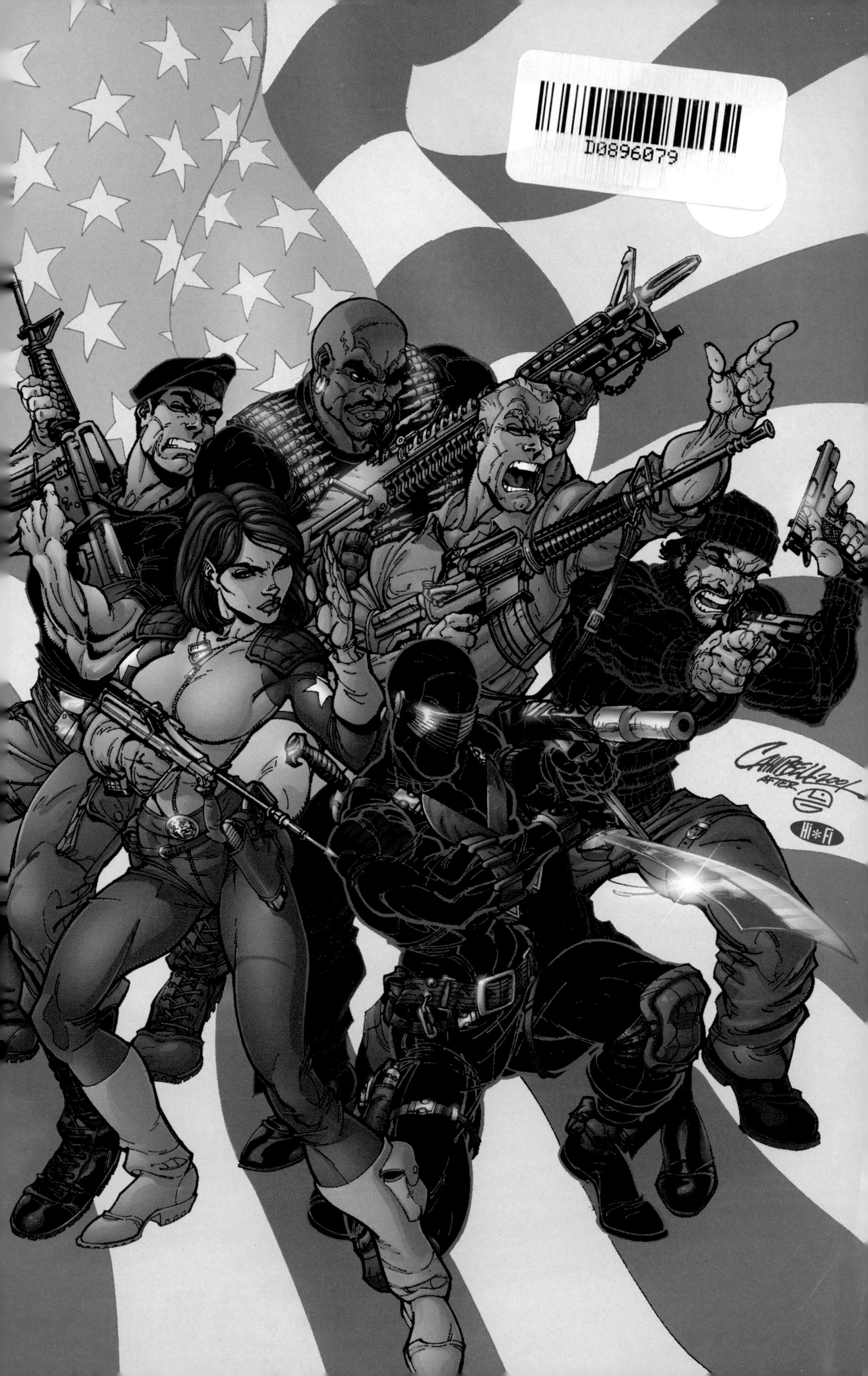
CAMPBELL 2001
AFTER
Hi*Fi

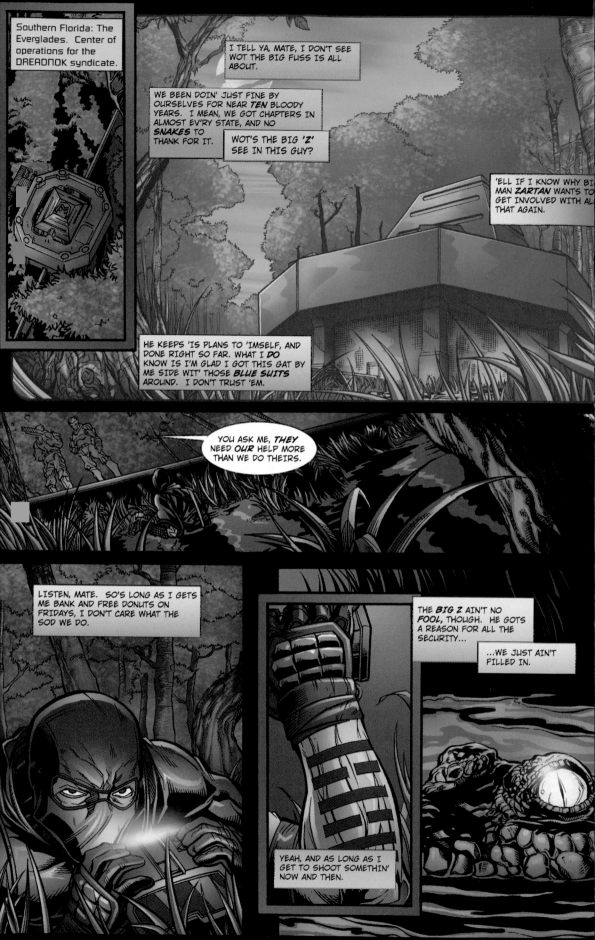

Southern Florida: The Everglades. Center of operations for the DREADNOK syndicate.

I TELL YA, MATE, I DON'T SEE WOT THE BIG FUSS IS ALL ABOUT.

WE BEEN DOIN' JUST FINE BY OURSELVES FOR NEAR TEN BLOODY YEARS. I MEAN, WE GOT CHAPTERS IN ALMOST EV'RY STATE, AND NO SNAKES TO THANK FOR IT.

WOT'S THE BIG 'Z' SEE IN THIS GUY?

'ELL IF I KNOW WHY BI[G] MAN ZARTAN WANTS TO GET INVOLVED WITH AL[L] THAT AGAIN.

HE KEEPS 'IS PLANS TO 'IMSELF, AND DONE RIGHT SO FAR. WHAT I DO KNOW IS I'M GLAD I GOT THIS GAT BY ME SIDE WIT' THOSE BLUE SUITS AROUND. I DON'T TRUST 'EM.

YOU ASK ME, THEY NEED OUR HELP MORE THAN WE DO THEIRS.

LISTEN, MATE. SO'S LONG AS I GETS ME BANK AND FREE DONUTS ON FRIDAYS, I DON'T CARE WHAT THE SOD WE DO.

THE BIG Z AIN'T NO FOOL, THOUGH. HE GOTS A REASON FOR ALL THE SECURITY...

...WE JUST AIN'T FILLED IN.

YEAH, AND AS LONG AS I GET TO SHOOT SOMETHIN' NOW AND THEN.

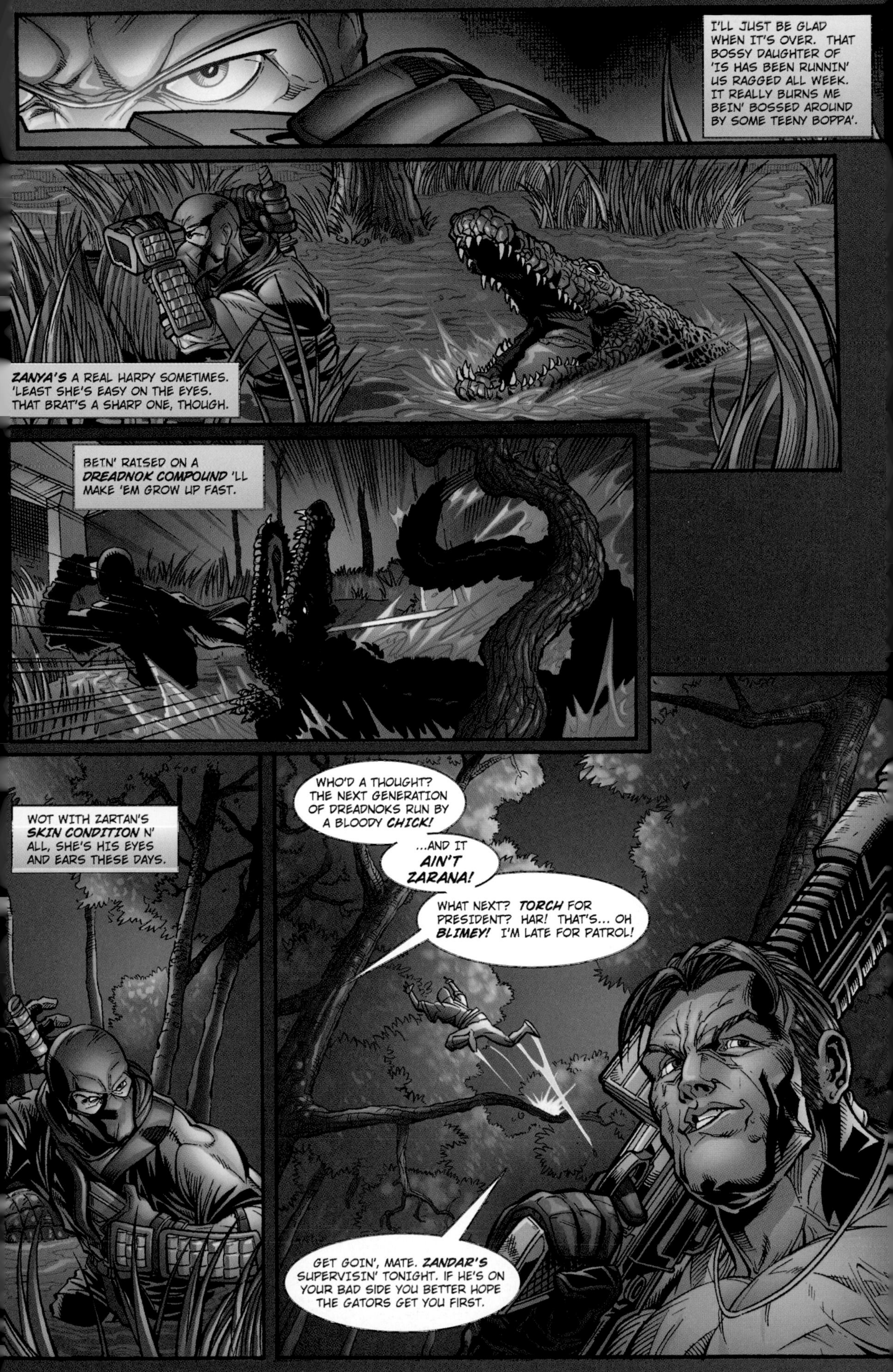
I'LL JUST BE GLAD WHEN IT'S OVER. THAT BOSSY DAUGHTER OF 'IS HAS BEEN RUNNIN' US RAGGED ALL WEEK. IT REALLY BURNS ME BEIN' BOSSED AROUND BY SOME TEENY BOPPA'.
ZANYA'S A REAL HARPY SOMETIMES. 'LEAST SHE'S EASY ON THE EYES. THAT BRAT'S A SHARP ONE, THOUGH.
BEIN' RAISED ON A DREADNOK COMPOUND 'LL MAKE 'EM GROW UP FAST.
WOT WITH ZARTAN'S SKIN CONDITION N' ALL, SHE'S HIS EYES AND EARS THESE DAYS.
WHO'D A THOUGHT? THE NEXT GENERATION OF DREADNOKS RUN BY A BLOODY CHICK!
...AND IT AIN'T ZARANA!
WHAT NEXT? TORCH FOR PRESIDENT? HAR! THAT'S... OH BLIMEY! I'M LATE FOR PATROL!
GET GOIN', MATE. ZANDAR'S SUPERVISIN' TONIGHT. IF HE'S ON YOUR BAD SIDE YOU BETTER HOPE THE GATORS GET YOU FIRST.

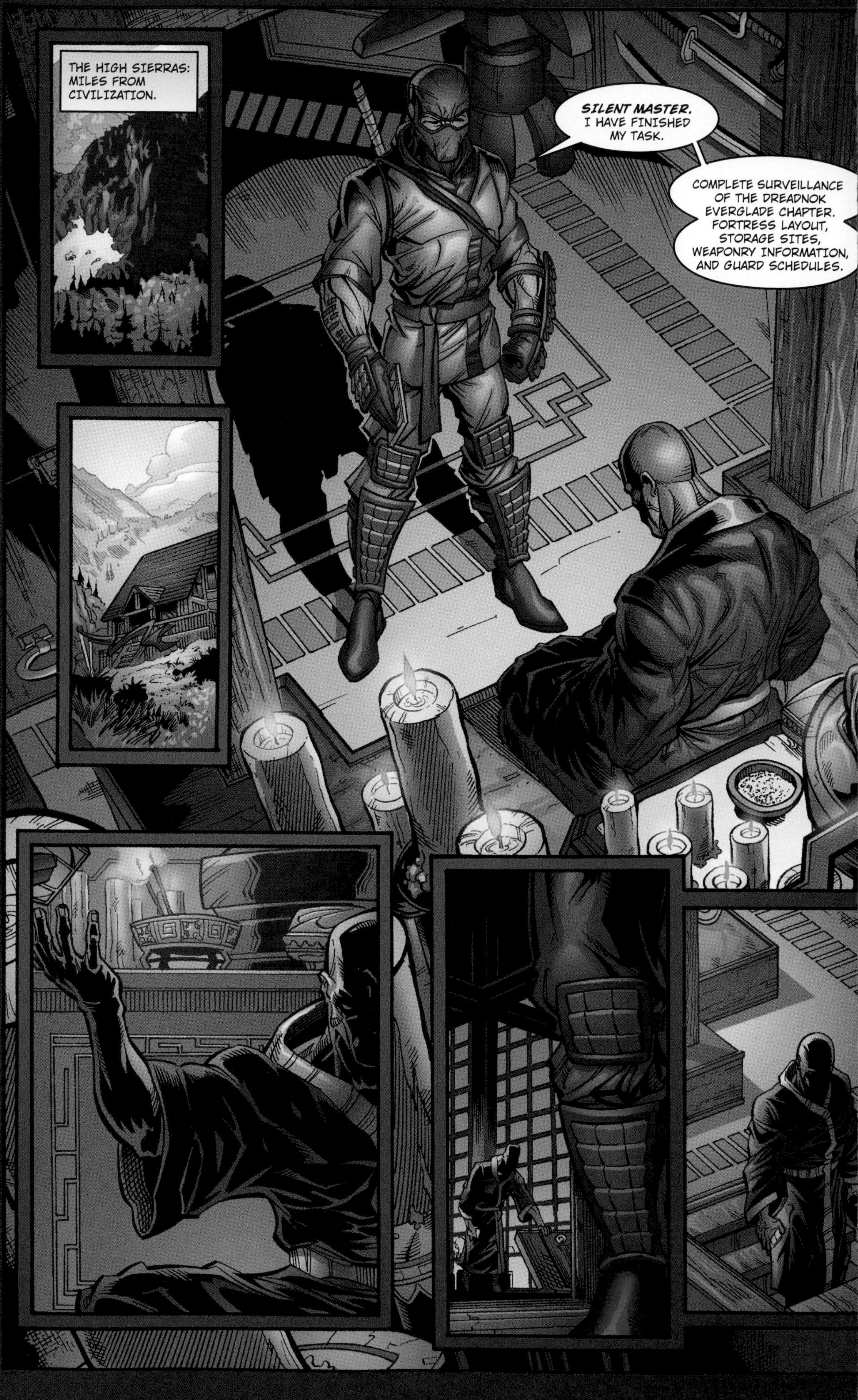
THE HIGH SIERRAS: MILES FROM CIVILIZATION.
SILENT MASTER. I HAVE FINISHED MY TASK.
COMPLETE SURVEILLANCE OF THE DREADNOK EVERGLADE CHAPTER. FORTRESS LAYOUT, STORAGE SITES, WEAPONRY INFORMATION, AND GUARD SCHEDULES.

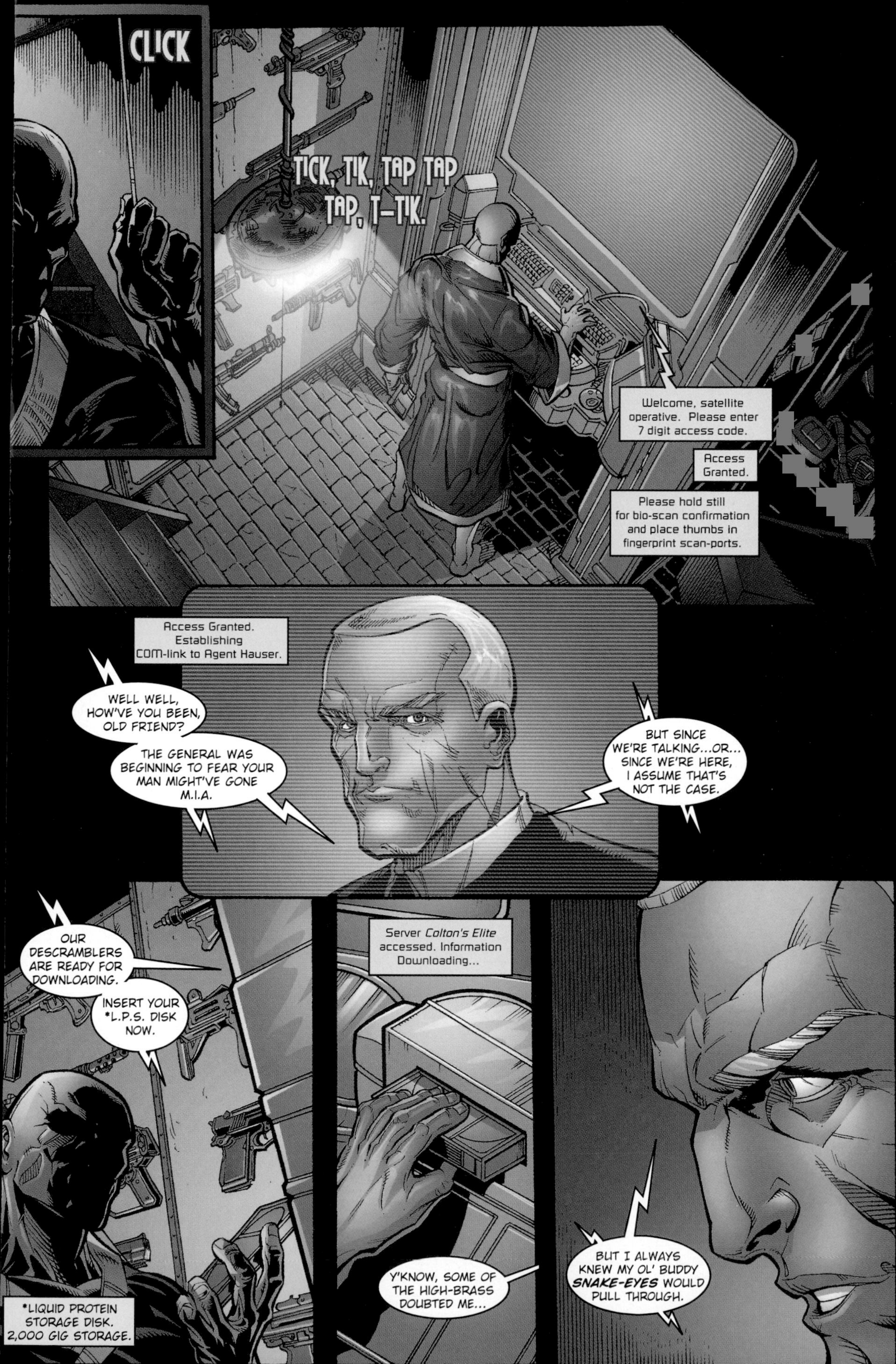
CLICK
TICK, TIK, TAP TAP TAP, T-TIK.
Welcome, satellite operative. Please enter 7 digit access code.
Access Granted.
Please hold still for bio-scan confirmation and place thumbs in fingerprint scan-ports.
Access Granted. Establishing COM-link to Agent Hauser.
WELL WELL, HOW'VE YOU BEEN, OLD FRIEND?
THE GENERAL WAS BEGINNING TO FEAR YOUR MAN MIGHT'VE GONE M.I.A.
BUT SINCE WE'RE TALKING...OR... SINCE WE'RE HERE, I ASSUME THAT'S NOT THE CASE.
OUR DESCRAMBLERS ARE READY FOR DOWNLOADING.
INSERT YOUR *L.P.S. DISK NOW.
*LIQUID PROTEIN STORAGE DISK. 2,000 GIG STORAGE.
Server *Colton's Elite* accessed. Information Downloading...
Y'KNOW, SOME OF THE HIGH-BRASS DOUBTED ME...
BUT I ALWAYS KNEW MY OL' BUDDY **SNAKE-EYES** WOULD PULL THROUGH.

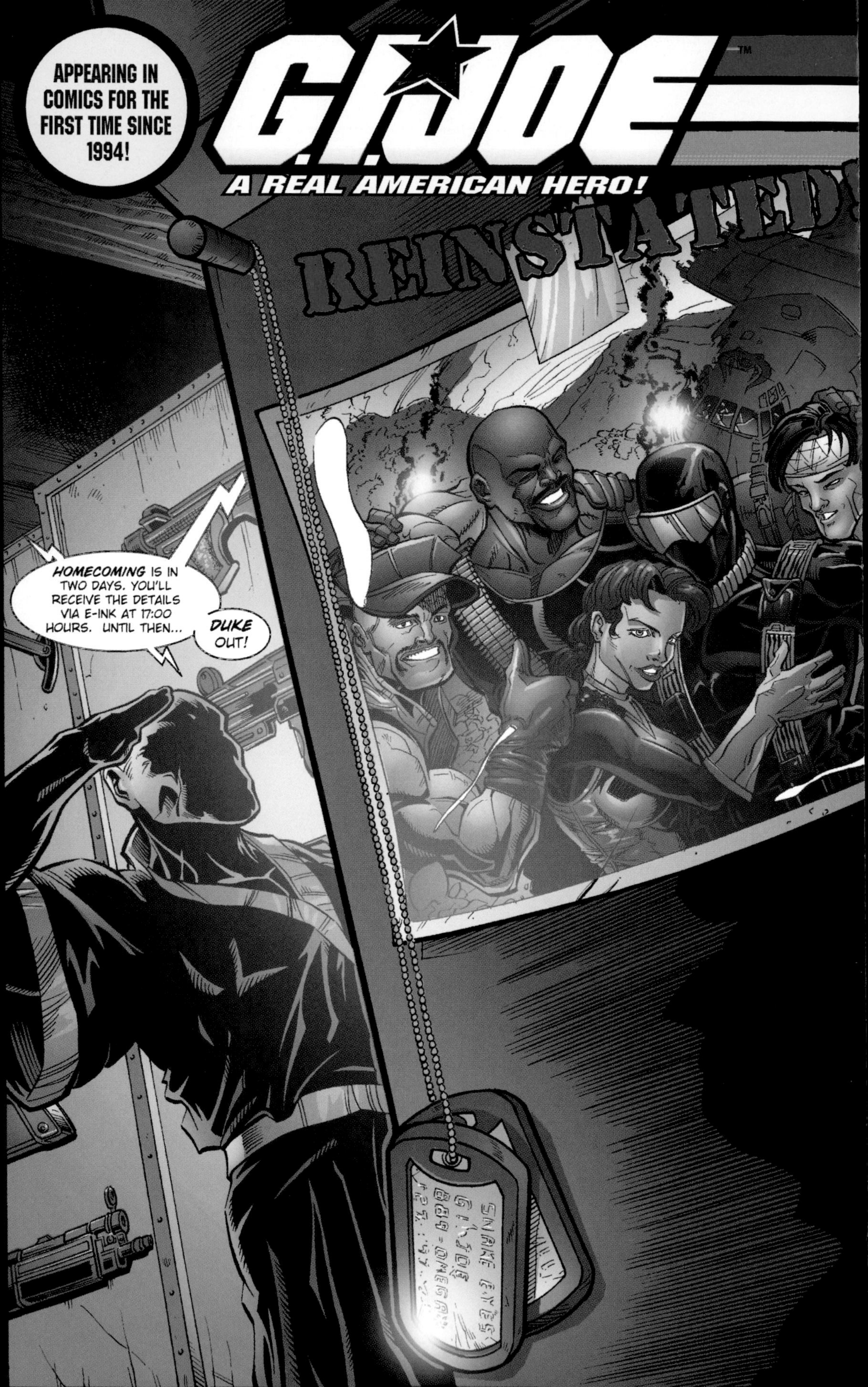
APPEARING IN COMICS FOR THE FIRST TIME SINCE 1994!
G.I. JOE™
A REAL AMERICAN HERO!
REINSTATED!
HOMECOMING IS IN TWO DAYS. YOU'LL RECEIVE THE DETAILS VIA E-INK AT 17:00 HOURS. UNTIL THEN...
DUKE OUT!
SNAKE EYES
G.I. JOE

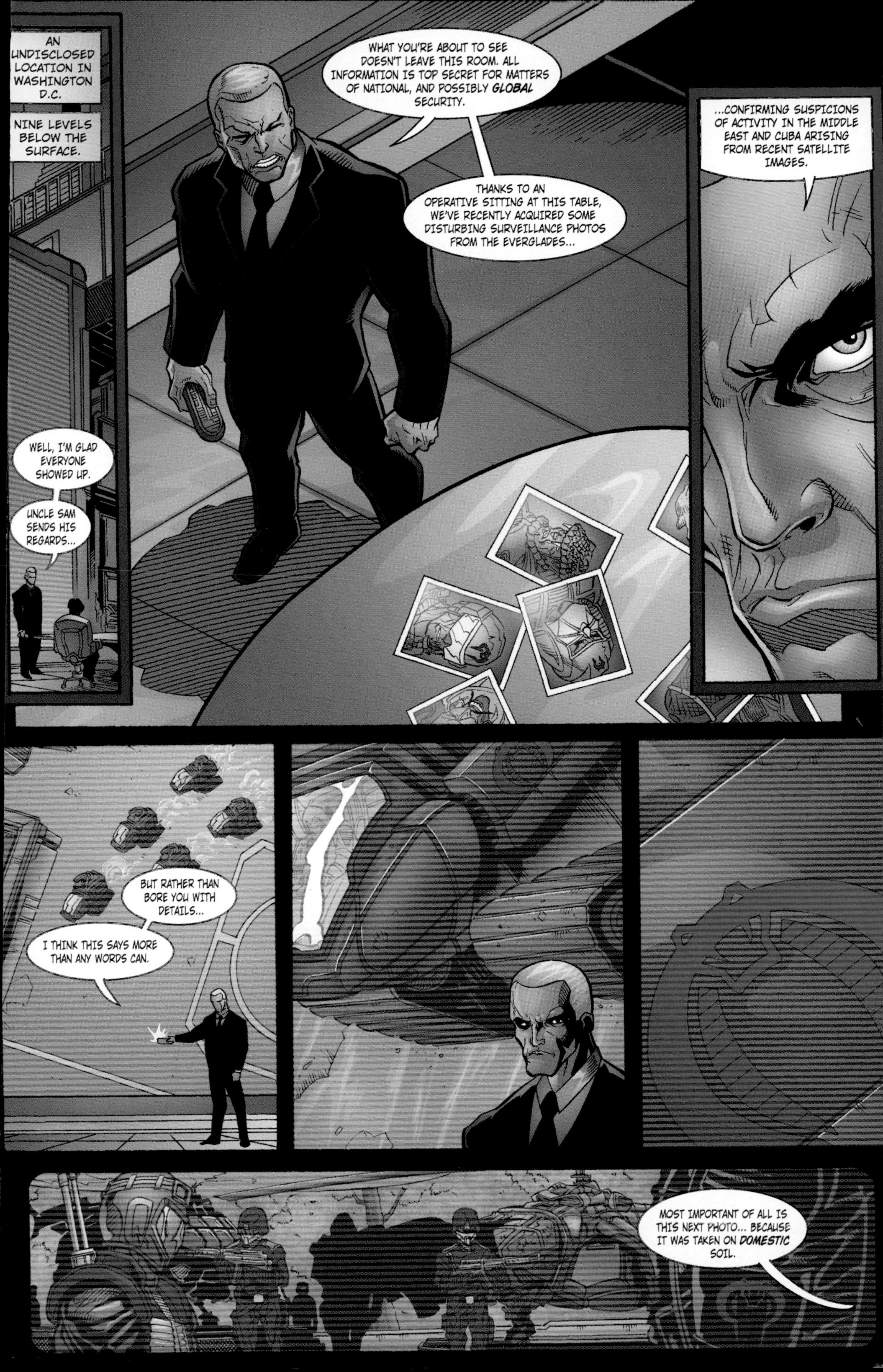
AN UNDISCLOSED LOCATION IN WASHINGTON D.C.
NINE LEVELS BELOW THE SURFACE.
WHAT YOU'RE ABOUT TO SEE DOESN'T LEAVE THIS ROOM. ALL INFORMATION IS TOP SECRET FOR MATTERS OF NATIONAL, AND POSSIBLY GLOBAL SECURITY.
THANKS TO AN OPERATIVE SITTING AT THIS TABLE, WE'VE RECENTLY ACQUIRED SOME DISTURBING SURVEILLANCE PHOTOS FROM THE EVERGLADES...
...CONFIRMING SUSPICIONS OF ACTIVITY IN THE MIDDLE EAST AND CUBA ARISING FROM RECENT SATELLITE IMAGES.
WELL, I'M GLAD EVERYONE SHOWED UP.
UNCLE SAM SENDS HIS REGARDS...
BUT RATHER THAN BORE YOU WITH DETAILS...
I THINK THIS SAYS MORE THAN ANY WORDS CAN.
MOST IMPORTANT OF ALL IS THIS NEXT PHOTO... BECAUSE IT WAS TAKEN ON DOMESTIC SOIL.

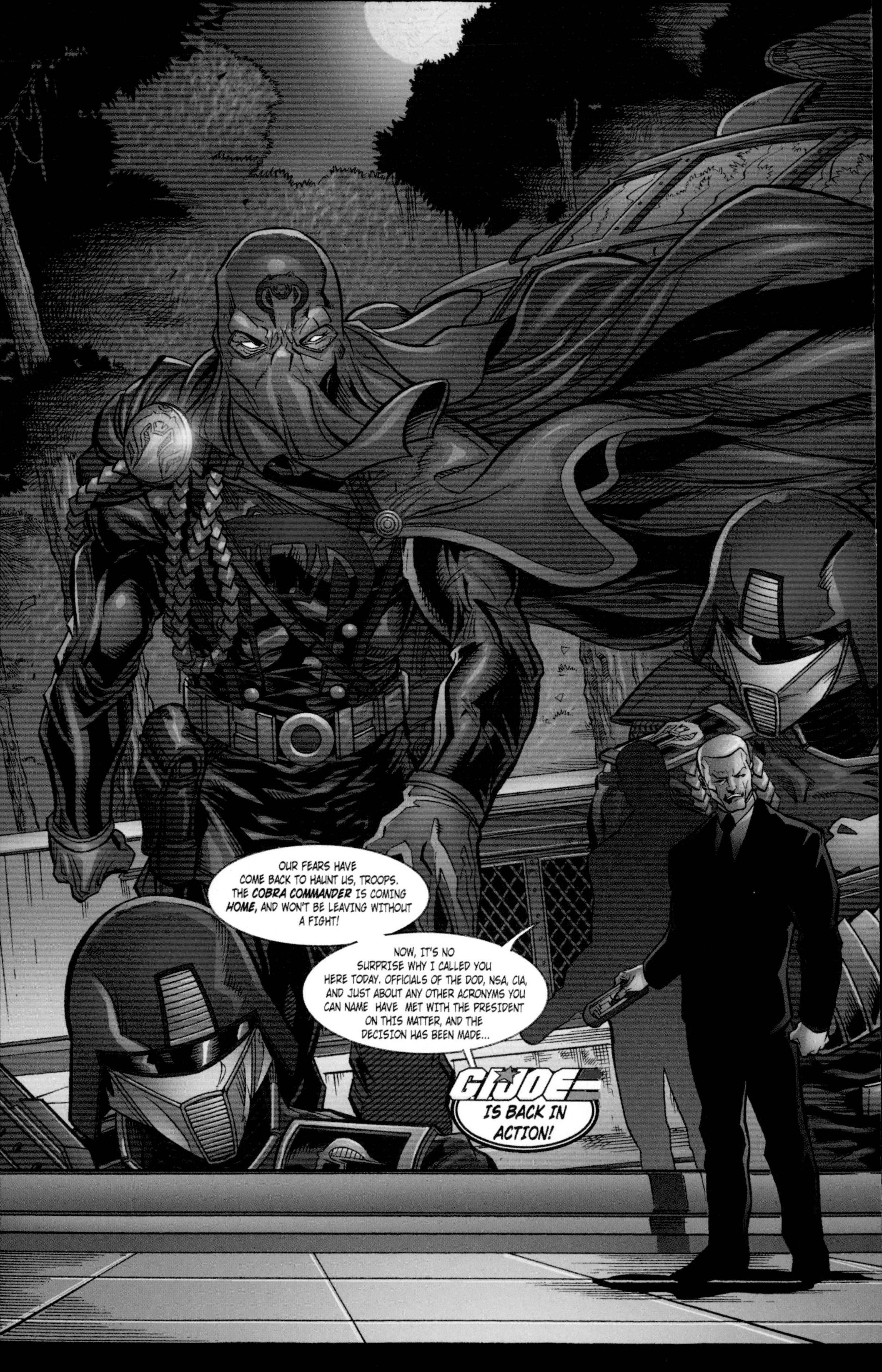
OUR FEARS HAVE COME BACK TO HAUNT US, TROOPS. THE COBRA COMMANDER IS COMING HOME, AND WON'T BE LEAVING WITHOUT A FIGHT!
NOW, IT'S NO SURPRISE WHY I CALLED YOU HERE TODAY. OFFICIALS OF THE DOD, NSA, CIA, AND JUST ABOUT ANY OTHER ACRONYMS YOU CAN NAME HAVE MET WITH THE PRESIDENT ON THIS MATTER, AND THE DECISION HAS BEEN MADE...
G.I. JOE IS BACK IN ACTION!

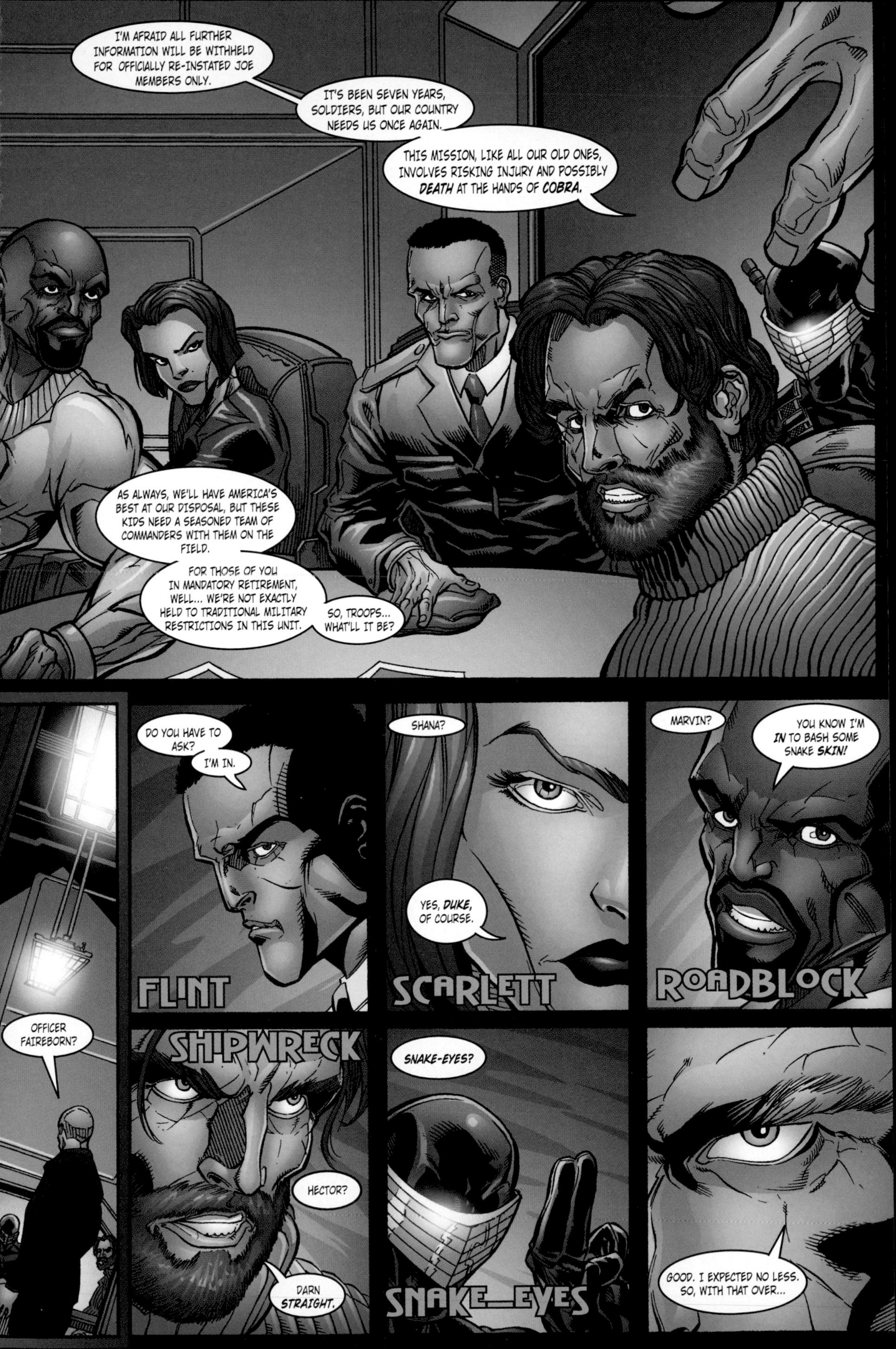
I'M AFRAID ALL FURTHER INFORMATION WILL BE WITHHELD FOR OFFICIALLY RE-INSTATED JOE MEMBERS ONLY.
IT'S BEEN SEVEN YEARS, SOLDIERS, BUT OUR COUNTRY NEEDS US ONCE AGAIN.
THIS MISSION, LIKE ALL OUR OLD ONES, INVOLVES RISKING INJURY AND POSSIBLY DEATH AT THE HANDS OF COBRA.
AS ALWAYS, WE'LL HAVE AMERICA'S BEST AT OUR DISPOSAL, BUT THESE KIDS NEED A SEASONED TEAM OF COMMANDERS WITH THEM ON THE FIELD.
FOR THOSE OF YOU IN MANDATORY RETIREMENT, WELL... WE'RE NOT EXACTLY HELD TO TRADITIONAL MILITARY RESTRICTIONS IN THIS UNIT.
SO, TROOPS... WHAT'LL IT BE?
DO YOU HAVE TO ASK?
I'M IN.
FLINT
SHANA?
YES, DUKE, OF COURSE.
SCARLETT
MARVIN?
YOU KNOW I'M IN TO BASH SOME SNAKE SKIN!
ROADBLOCK
OFFICER FAIREBORN?
SHIPWRECK
HECTOR?
DARN STRAIGHT.
SNAKE-EYES?
SNAKE-EYES
GOOD. I EXPECTED NO LESS. SO, WITH THAT OVER...

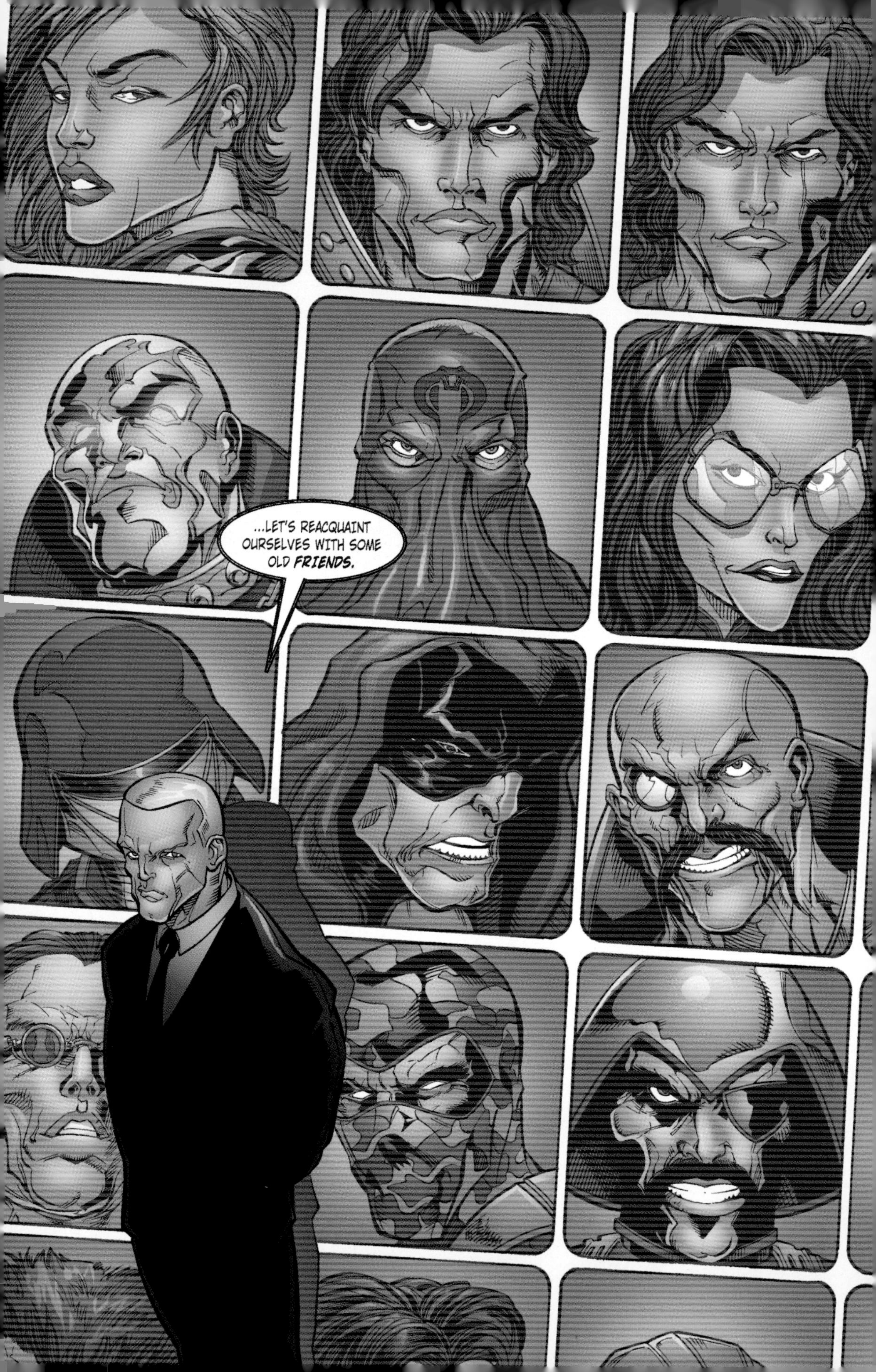
...LET'S REACQUAINT OURSELVES WITH SOME OLD FRIENDS.

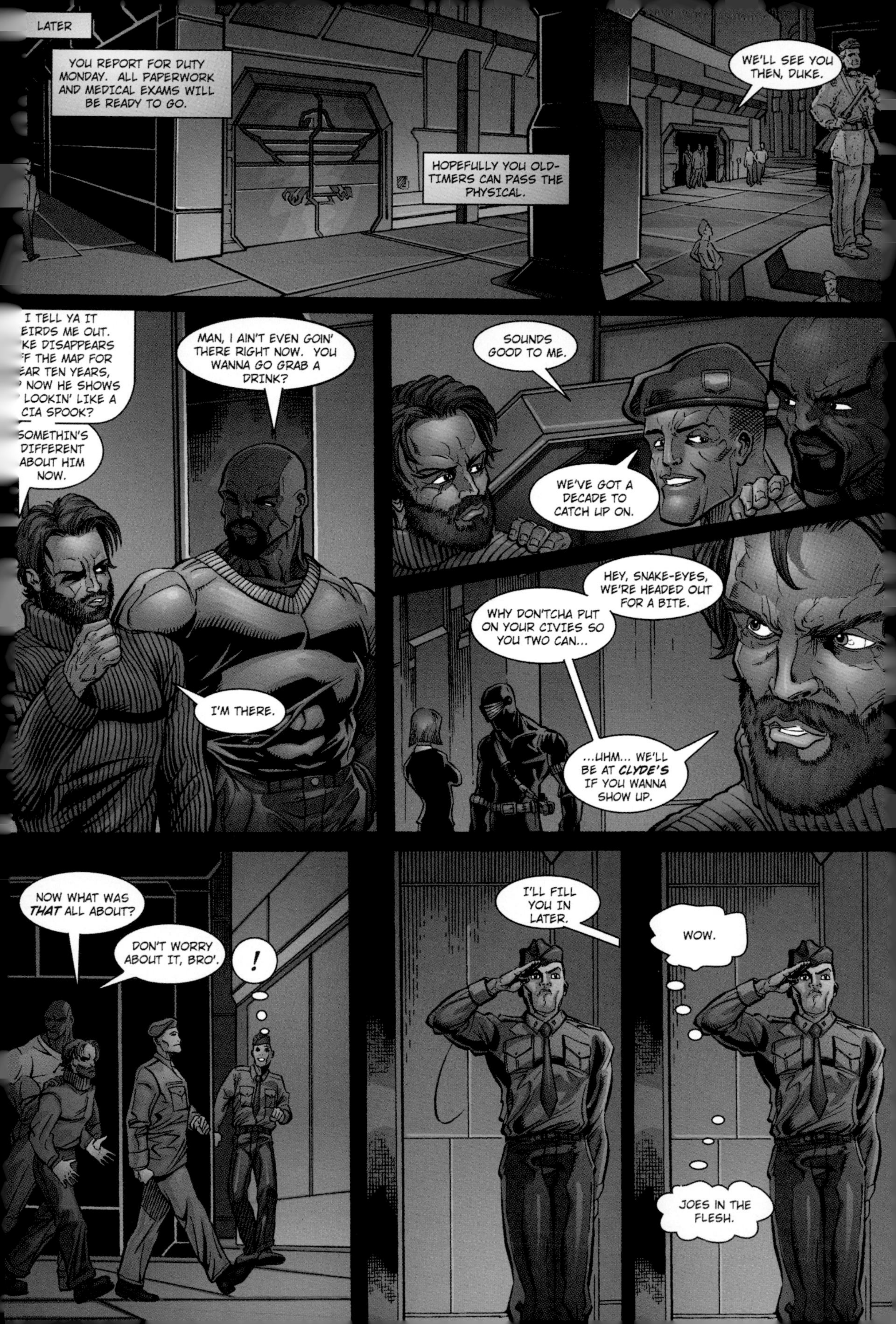
LATER
YOU REPORT FOR DUTY MONDAY. ALL PAPERWORK AND MEDICAL EXAMS WILL BE READY TO GO.
HOPEFULLY YOU OLD-TIMERS CAN PASS THE PHYSICAL.
WE'LL SEE YOU THEN, DUKE.
I TELL YA IT EIRDS ME OUT. KE DISAPPEARS F THE MAP FOR EAR TEN YEARS, NOW HE SHOWS LOOKIN' LIKE A CIA SPOOK?
SOMETHIN'S DIFFERENT ABOUT HIM NOW.
MAN, I AIN'T EVEN GOIN' THERE RIGHT NOW. YOU WANNA GO GRAB A DRINK?
I'M THERE.
SOUNDS GOOD TO ME.
WE'VE GOT A DECADE TO CATCH UP ON.
HEY, SNAKE-EYES, WE'RE HEADED OUT FOR A BITE.
WHY DON'TCHA PUT ON YOUR CIVIES SO YOU TWO CAN...
...UHM... WE'LL BE AT ***CLYDE'S*** IF YOU WANNA SHOW UP.
NOW WHAT WAS ***THAT*** ALL ABOUT?
DON'T WORRY ABOUT IT, BRO'.
!
I'LL FILL YOU IN LATER.
WOW.
JOES IN THE FLESH.

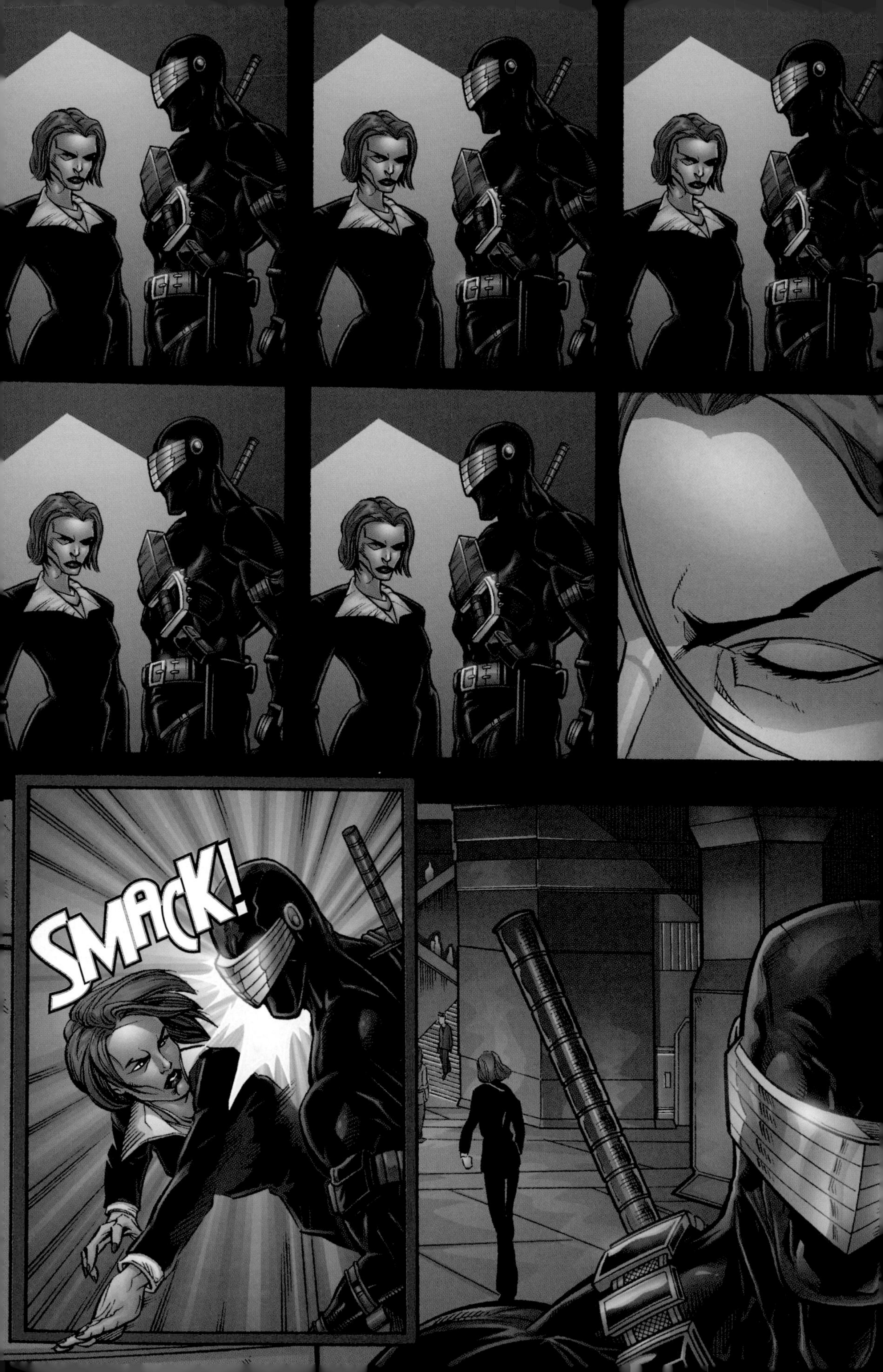
SMACK!

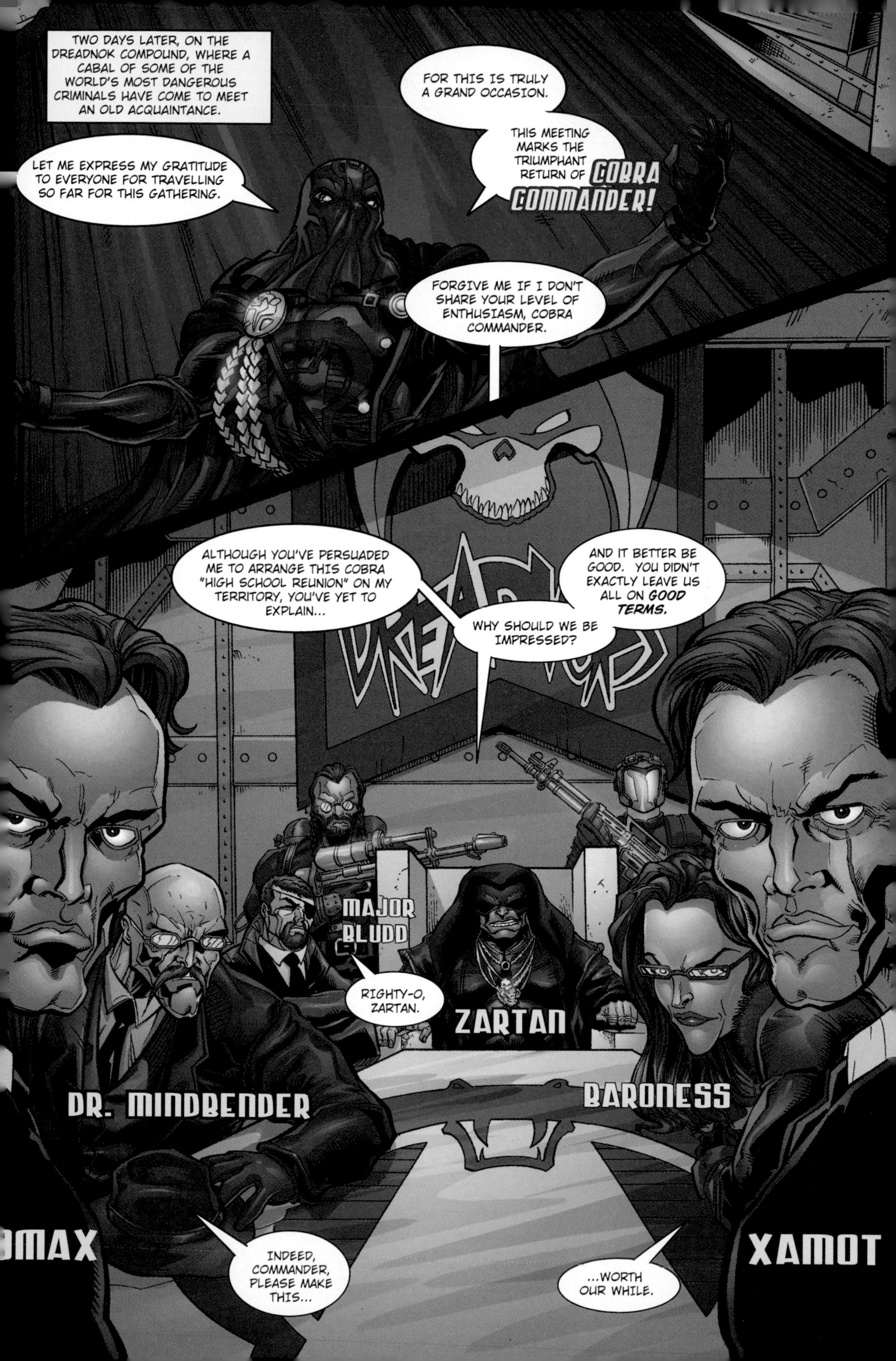
TWO DAYS LATER, ON THE DREADNOK COMPOUND, WHERE A CABAL OF SOME OF THE WORLD'S MOST DANGEROUS CRIMINALS HAVE COME TO MEET AN OLD ACQUAINTANCE.
LET ME EXPRESS MY GRATITUDE TO EVERYONE FOR TRAVELLING SO FAR FOR THIS GATHERING.
FOR THIS IS TRULY A GRAND OCCASION.
THIS MEETING MARKS THE TRIUMPHANT RETURN OF COBRA COMMANDER!
FORGIVE ME IF I DON'T SHARE YOUR LEVEL OF ENTHUSIASM, COBRA COMMANDER.
ALTHOUGH YOU'VE PERSUADED ME TO ARRANGE THIS COBRA "HIGH SCHOOL REUNION" ON MY TERRITORY, YOU'VE YET TO EXPLAIN...
WHY SHOULD WE BE IMPRESSED?
AND IT BETTER BE GOOD. YOU DIDN'T EXACTLY LEAVE US ALL ON GOOD TERMS.
MAJOR BLUDD
RIGHTY-O, ZARTAN.
ZARTAN
DR. MINDBENDER
BARONESS
MAX
INDEED, COMMANDER, PLEASE MAKE THIS...
...WORTH OUR WHILE.
XAMOT

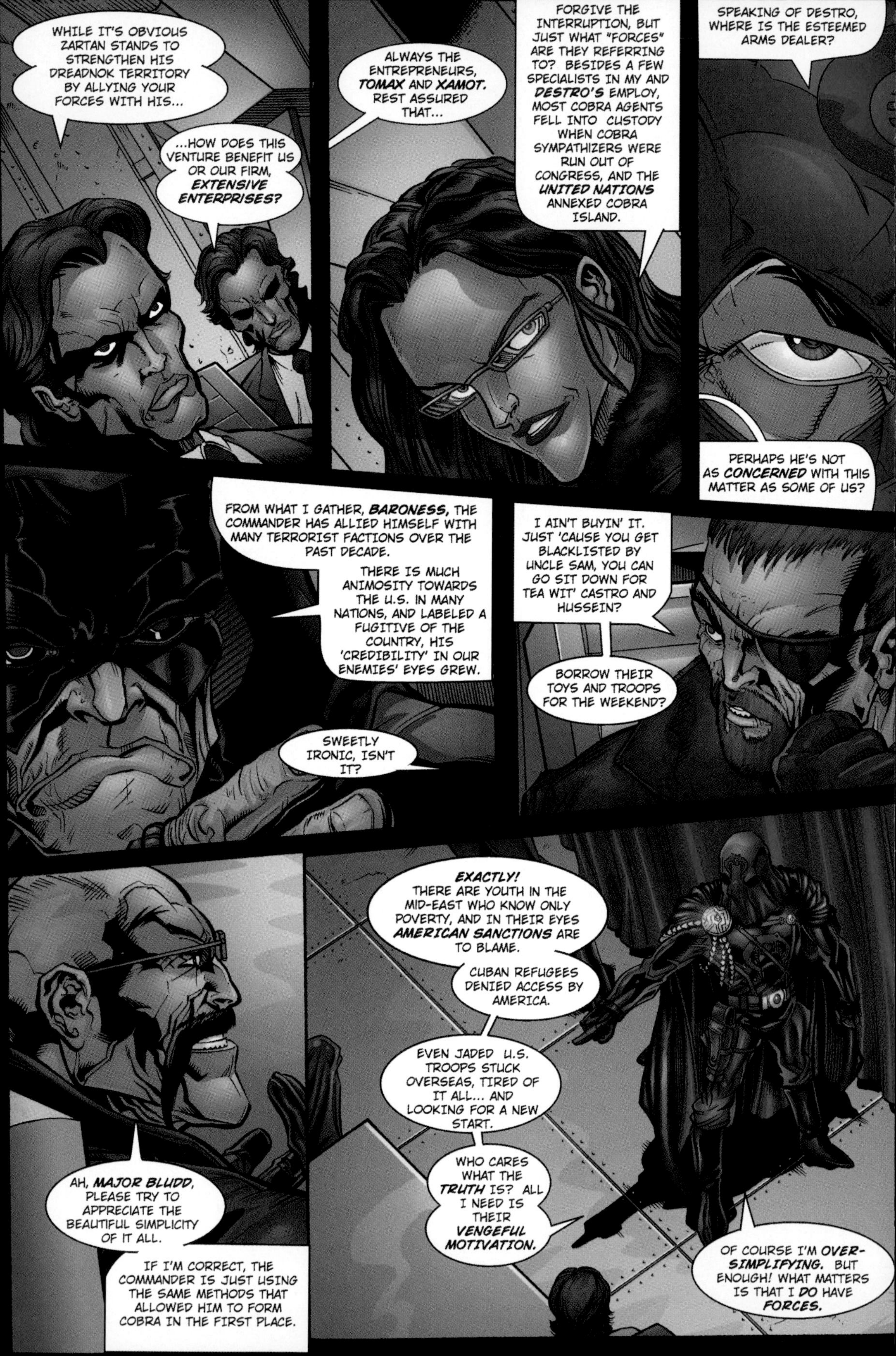
WHILE IT'S OBVIOUS ZARTAN STANDS TO STRENGTHEN HIS DREADNOK TERRITORY BY ALLYING YOUR FORCES WITH HIS...
...HOW DOES THIS VENTURE BENEFIT US OR OUR FIRM, EXTENSIVE ENTERPRISES?
ALWAYS THE ENTREPRENEURS, TOMAX AND XAMOT. REST ASSURED THAT...
FORGIVE THE INTERRUPTION, BUT JUST WHAT "FORCES" ARE THEY REFERRING TO? BESIDES A FEW SPECIALISTS IN MY AND DESTRO'S EMPLOY, MOST COBRA AGENTS FELL INTO CUSTODY WHEN COBRA SYMPATHIZERS WERE RUN OUT OF CONGRESS, AND THE UNITED NATIONS ANNEXED COBRA ISLAND.
SPEAKING OF DESTRO, WHERE IS THE ESTEEMED ARMS DEALER?
PERHAPS HE'S NOT AS CONCERNED WITH THIS MATTER AS SOME OF US?
FROM WHAT I GATHER, BARONESS, THE COMMANDER HAS ALLIED HIMSELF WITH MANY TERRORIST FACTIONS OVER THE PAST DECADE.
THERE IS MUCH ANIMOSITY TOWARDS THE U.S. IN MANY NATIONS, AND LABELED A FUGITIVE OF THE COUNTRY, HIS 'CREDIBILITY' IN OUR ENEMIES' EYES GREW.
SWEETLY IRONIC, ISN'T IT?
I AIN'T BUYIN' IT. JUST 'CAUSE YOU GET BLACKLISTED BY UNCLE SAM, YOU CAN GO SIT DOWN FOR TEA WIT' CASTRO AND HUSSEIN?
BORROW THEIR TOYS AND TROOPS FOR THE WEEKEND?
AH, MAJOR BLUDD, PLEASE TRY TO APPRECIATE THE BEAUTIFUL SIMPLICITY OF IT ALL.
IF I'M CORRECT, THE COMMANDER IS JUST USING THE SAME METHODS THAT ALLOWED HIM TO FORM COBRA IN THE FIRST PLACE.
EXACTLY! THERE ARE YOUTH IN THE MID-EAST WHO KNOW ONLY POVERTY, AND IN THEIR EYES AMERICAN SANCTIONS ARE TO BLAME.
CUBAN REFUGEES DENIED ACCESS BY AMERICA.
EVEN JADED U.S. TROOPS STUCK OVERSEAS, TIRED OF IT ALL... AND LOOKING FOR A NEW START.
WHO CARES WHAT THE TRUTH IS? ALL I NEED IS THEIR VENGEFUL MOTIVATION.
OF COURSE I'M OVER-SIMPLIFYING. BUT ENOUGH! WHAT MATTERS IS THAT I DO HAVE FORCES.

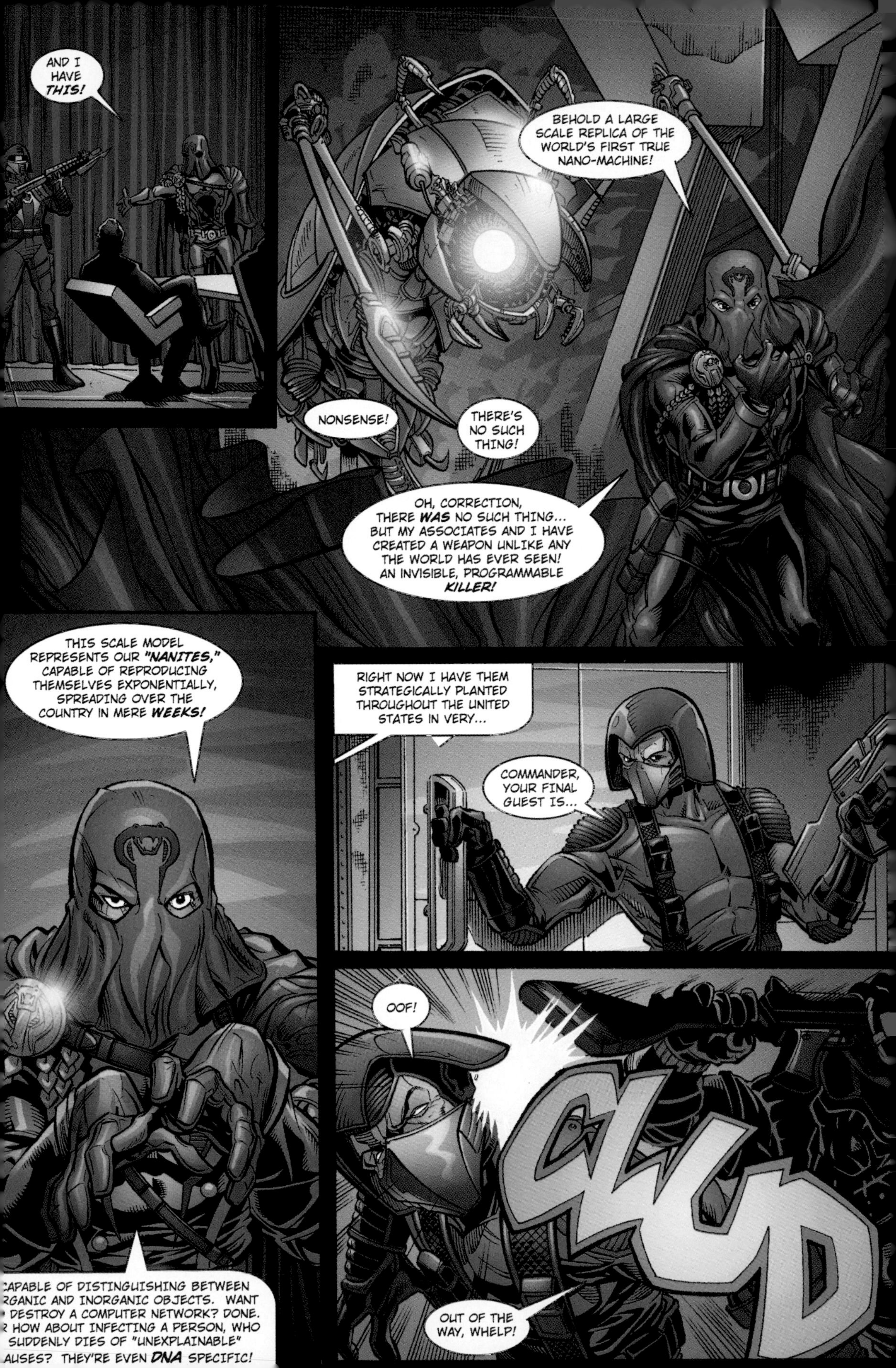
AND I HAVE THIS!
BEHOLD A LARGE SCALE REPLICA OF THE WORLD'S FIRST TRUE NANO-MACHINE!
NONSENSE!
THERE'S NO SUCH THING!
OH, CORRECTION, THERE WAS NO SUCH THING... BUT MY ASSOCIATES AND I HAVE CREATED A WEAPON UNLIKE ANY THE WORLD HAS EVER SEEN! AN INVISIBLE, PROGRAMMABLE KILLER!
THIS SCALE MODEL REPRESENTS OUR "NANITES," CAPABLE OF REPRODUCING THEMSELVES EXPONENTIALLY, SPREADING OVER THE COUNTRY IN MERE WEEKS!
CAPABLE OF DISTINGUISHING BETWEEN RGANIC AND INORGANIC OBJECTS. WANT DESTROY A COMPUTER NETWORK? DONE. R HOW ABOUT INFECTING A PERSON, WHO SUDDENLY DIES OF "UNEXPLAINABLE" AUSES? THEY'RE EVEN DNA SPECIFIC!
RIGHT NOW I HAVE THEM STRATEGICALLY PLANTED THROUGHOUT THE UNITED STATES IN VERY...
COMMANDER, YOUR FINAL GUEST IS...
OOF!
OUT OF THE WAY, WHELP!

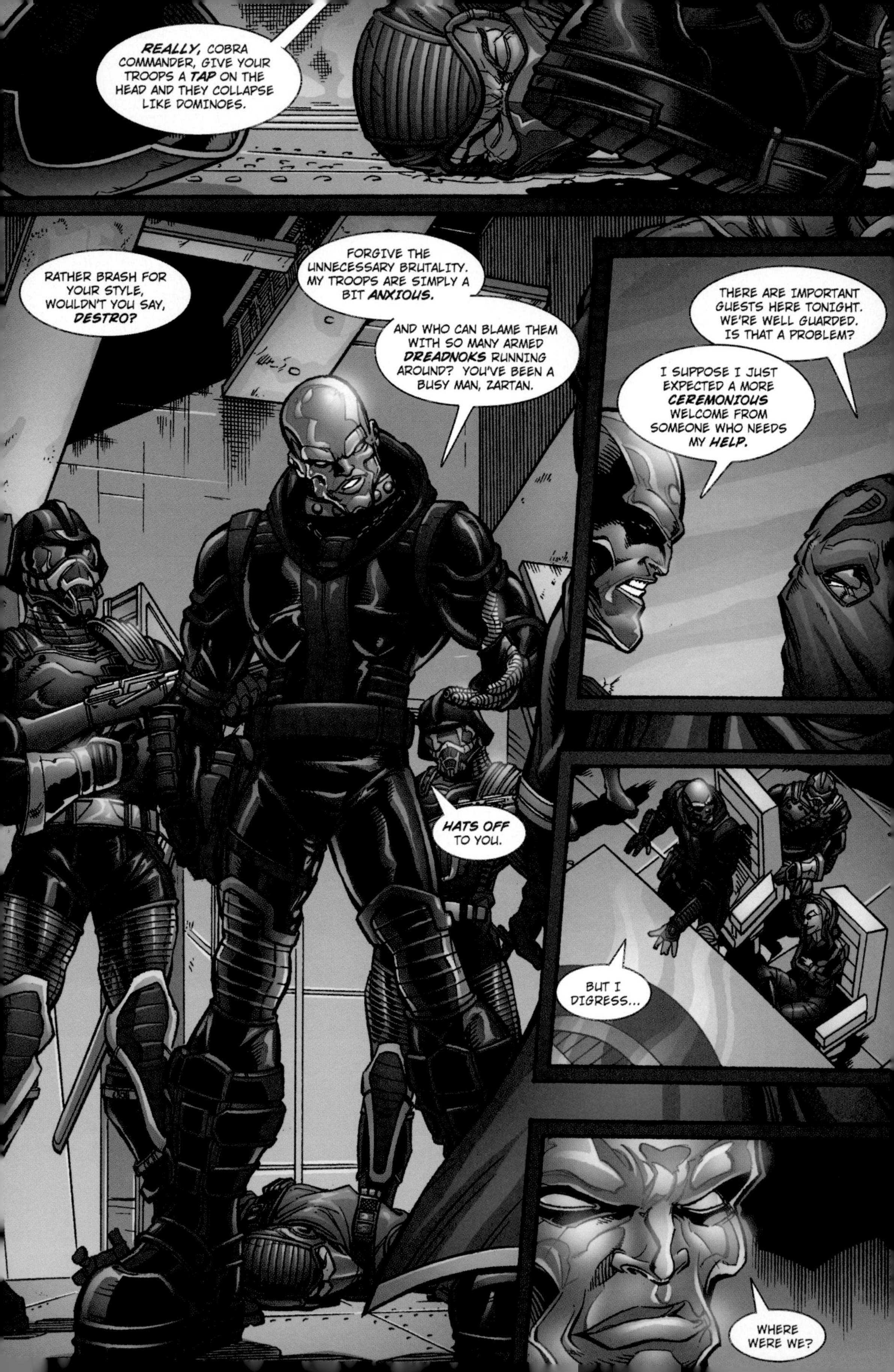
REALLY, COBRA COMMANDER, GIVE YOUR TROOPS A *TAP* ON THE HEAD AND THEY COLLAPSE LIKE DOMINOES.
RATHER BRASH FOR YOUR STYLE, WOULDN'T YOU SAY, *DESTRO?*
FORGIVE THE UNNECESSARY BRUTALITY. MY TROOPS ARE SIMPLY A BIT *ANXIOUS.*
AND WHO CAN BLAME THEM WITH SO MANY ARMED *DREADNOKS* RUNNING AROUND? YOU'VE BEEN A BUSY MAN, ZARTAN.
HATS OFF TO YOU.
THERE ARE IMPORTANT GUESTS HERE TONIGHT. WE'RE WELL GUARDED. IS THAT A PROBLEM?
I SUPPOSE I JUST EXPECTED A MORE *CEREMONIOUS* WELCOME FROM SOMEONE WHO NEEDS MY *HELP.*
BUT I DIGRESS...
WHERE WERE WE?

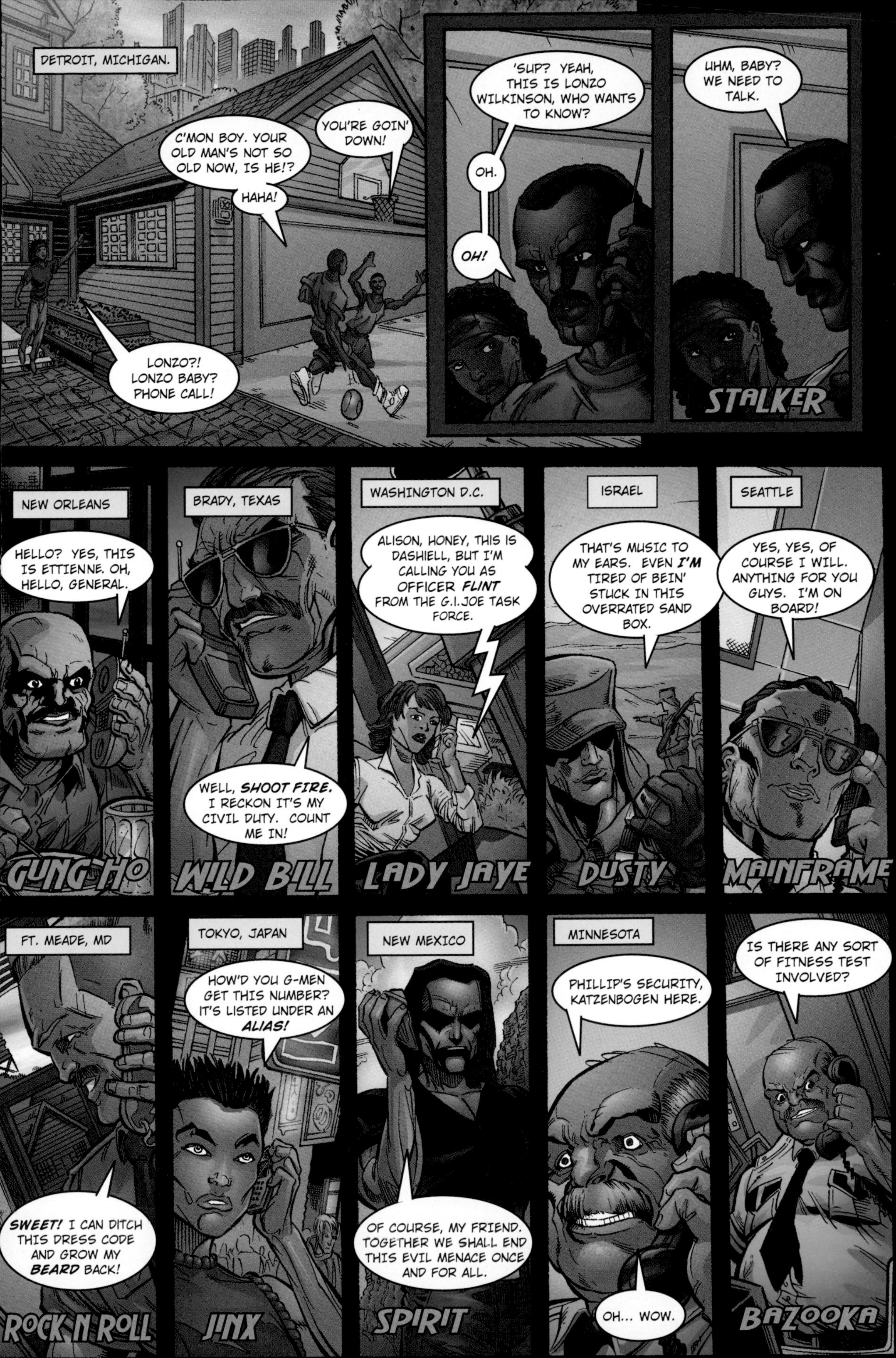
DETROIT, MICHIGAN.
C'MON BOY. YOUR OLD MAN'S NOT SO OLD NOW, IS HE!?
HAHA!
YOU'RE GOIN' DOWN!
LONZO?! LONZO BABY? PHONE CALL!
'SUP? YEAH, THIS IS LONZO WILKINSON, WHO WANTS TO KNOW?
OH.
OH!
UHM, BABY? WE NEED TO TALK.
STALKER
NEW ORLEANS
HELLO? YES, THIS IS ETTIENNE. OH, HELLO, GENERAL.
GUNG HO
BRADY, TEXAS
WELL, SHOOT FIRE. I RECKON IT'S MY CIVIL DUTY. COUNT ME IN!
WILD BILL
WASHINGTON D.C.
ALISON, HONEY, THIS IS DASHIELL, BUT I'M CALLING YOU AS OFFICER FLINT FROM THE G.I.JOE TASK FORCE.
LADY JAYE
ISRAEL
THAT'S MUSIC TO MY EARS. EVEN I'M TIRED OF BEIN' STUCK IN THIS OVERRATED SAND BOX.
DUSTY
SEATTLE
YES, YES, OF COURSE I WILL. ANYTHING FOR YOU GUYS. I'M ON BOARD!
MAINFRAME
FT. MEADE, MD
SWEET! I CAN DITCH THIS DRESS CODE AND GROW MY BEARD BACK!
ROCK N ROLL
TOKYO, JAPAN
HOW'D YOU G-MEN GET THIS NUMBER? IT'S LISTED UNDER AN ALIAS!
JINX
NEW MEXICO
OF COURSE, MY FRIEND. TOGETHER WE SHALL END THIS EVIL MENACE ONCE AND FOR ALL.
SPIRIT
MINNESOTA
PHILLIP'S SECURITY, KATZENBOGEN HERE.
OH... WOW.
IS THERE ANY SORT OF FITNESS TEST INVOLVED?
BAZOOKA

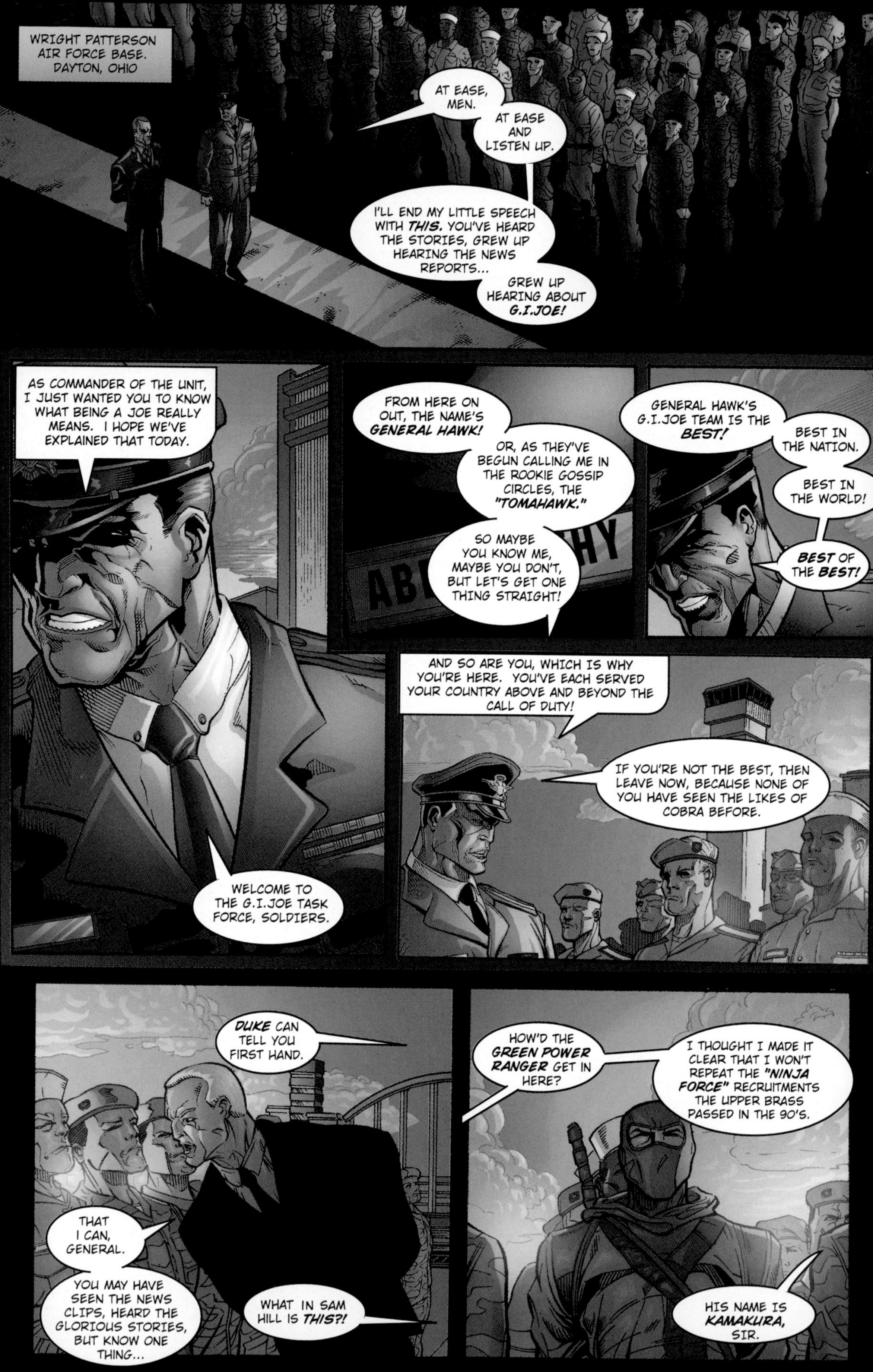
WRIGHT PATTERSON AIR FORCE BASE. DAYTON, OHIO
AT EASE, MEN.
AT EASE AND LISTEN UP.
I'LL END MY LITTLE SPEECH WITH *THIS.* YOU'VE HEARD THE STORIES, GREW UP HEARING THE NEWS REPORTS...
GREW UP HEARING ABOUT *G.I.JOE!*
AS COMMANDER OF THE UNIT, I JUST WANTED YOU TO KNOW WHAT BEING A JOE REALLY MEANS. I HOPE WE'VE EXPLAINED THAT TODAY.
FROM HERE ON OUT, THE NAME'S *GENERAL HAWK!*
OR, AS THEY'VE BEGUN CALLING ME IN THE ROOKIE GOSSIP CIRCLES, THE *"TOMAHAWK."*
SO MAYBE YOU KNOW ME, MAYBE YOU DON'T, BUT LET'S GET ONE THING STRAIGHT!
GENERAL HAWK'S G.I.JOE TEAM IS THE *BEST!*
BEST IN THE NATION.
BEST IN THE WORLD!
BEST OF THE *BEST!*
AND SO ARE YOU, WHICH IS WHY YOU'RE HERE. YOU'VE EACH SERVED YOUR COUNTRY ABOVE AND BEYOND THE CALL OF DUTY!
IF YOU'RE NOT THE BEST, THEN LEAVE NOW, BECAUSE NONE OF YOU HAVE SEEN THE LIKES OF COBRA BEFORE.
WELCOME TO THE G.I.JOE TASK FORCE, SOLDIERS.
DUKE CAN TELL YOU FIRST HAND.
THAT I CAN, GENERAL.
YOU MAY HAVE SEEN THE NEWS CLIPS, HEARD THE GLORIOUS STORIES, BUT KNOW ONE THING...
WHAT IN SAM HILL IS *THIS?!*
HOW'D THE *GREEN POWER RANGER* GET IN HERE?
I THOUGHT I MADE IT CLEAR THAT I WON'T REPEAT THE *"NINJA FORCE"* RECRUITMENTS THE UPPER BRASS PASSED IN THE 90'S.
HIS NAME IS *KAMAKURA,* SIR.

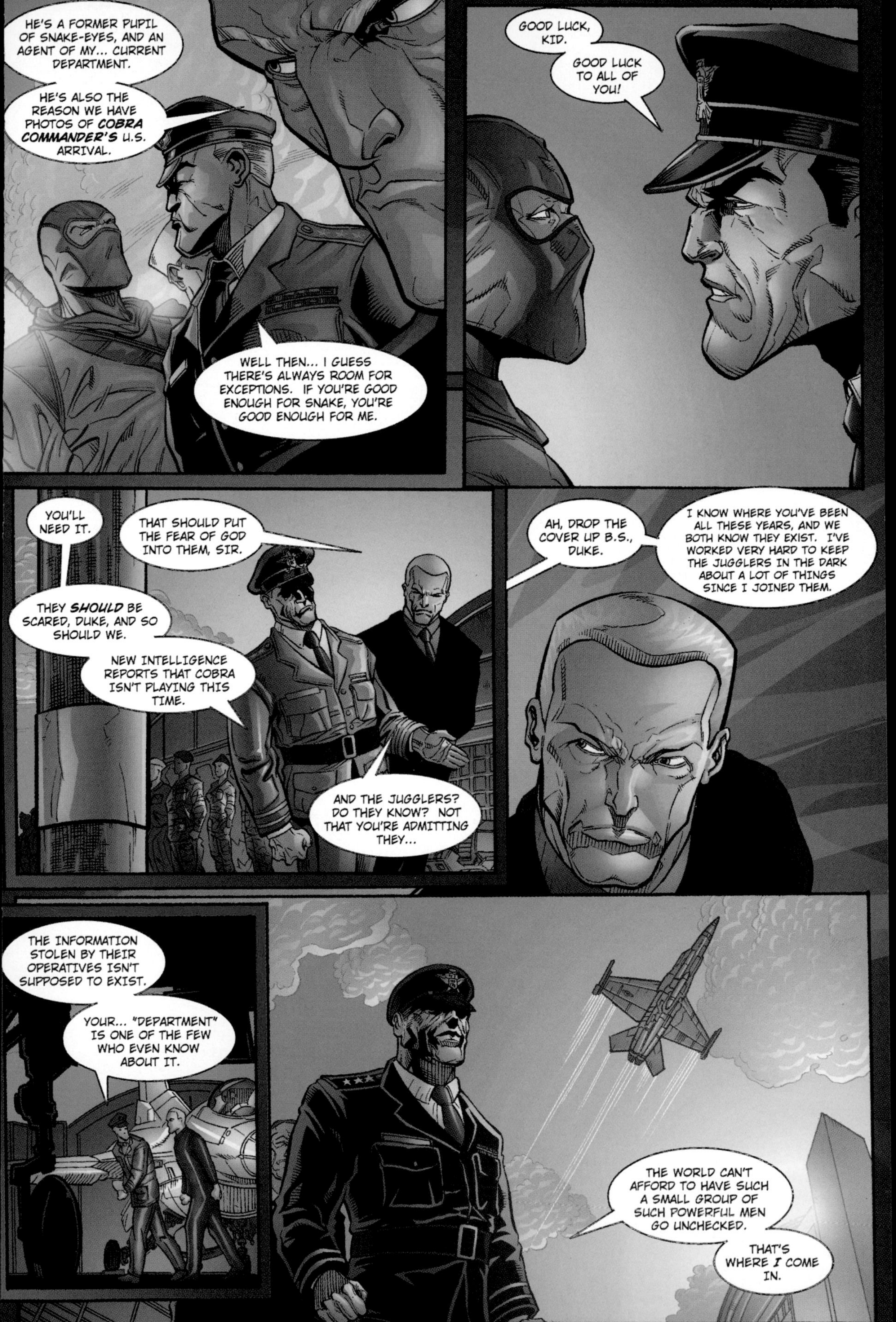
HE'S A FORMER PUPIL OF SNAKE-EYES, AND AN AGENT OF MY... CURRENT DEPARTMENT.
HE'S ALSO THE REASON WE HAVE PHOTOS OF COBRA COMMANDER'S U.S. ARRIVAL.
WELL THEN... I GUESS THERE'S ALWAYS ROOM FOR EXCEPTIONS. IF YOU'RE GOOD ENOUGH FOR SNAKE, YOU'RE GOOD ENOUGH FOR ME.
GOOD LUCK, KID.
GOOD LUCK TO ALL OF YOU!
YOU'LL NEED IT.
THAT SHOULD PUT THE FEAR OF GOD INTO THEM, SIR.
THEY SHOULD BE SCARED, DUKE, AND SO SHOULD WE.
NEW INTELLIGENCE REPORTS THAT COBRA ISN'T PLAYING THIS TIME.
AND THE JUGGLERS? DO THEY KNOW? NOT THAT YOU'RE ADMITTING THEY...
AH, DROP THE COVER UP B.S., DUKE.
I KNOW WHERE YOU'VE BEEN ALL THESE YEARS, AND WE BOTH KNOW THEY EXIST. I'VE WORKED VERY HARD TO KEEP THE JUGGLERS IN THE DARK ABOUT A LOT OF THINGS SINCE I JOINED THEM.
THE INFORMATION STOLEN BY THEIR OPERATIVES ISN'T SUPPOSED TO EXIST.
YOUR... "DEPARTMENT" IS ONE OF THE FEW WHO EVEN KNOW ABOUT IT.
THE WORLD CAN'T AFFORD TO HAVE SUCH A SMALL GROUP OF SUCH POWERFUL MEN GO UNCHECKED.
THAT'S WHERE I COME IN.

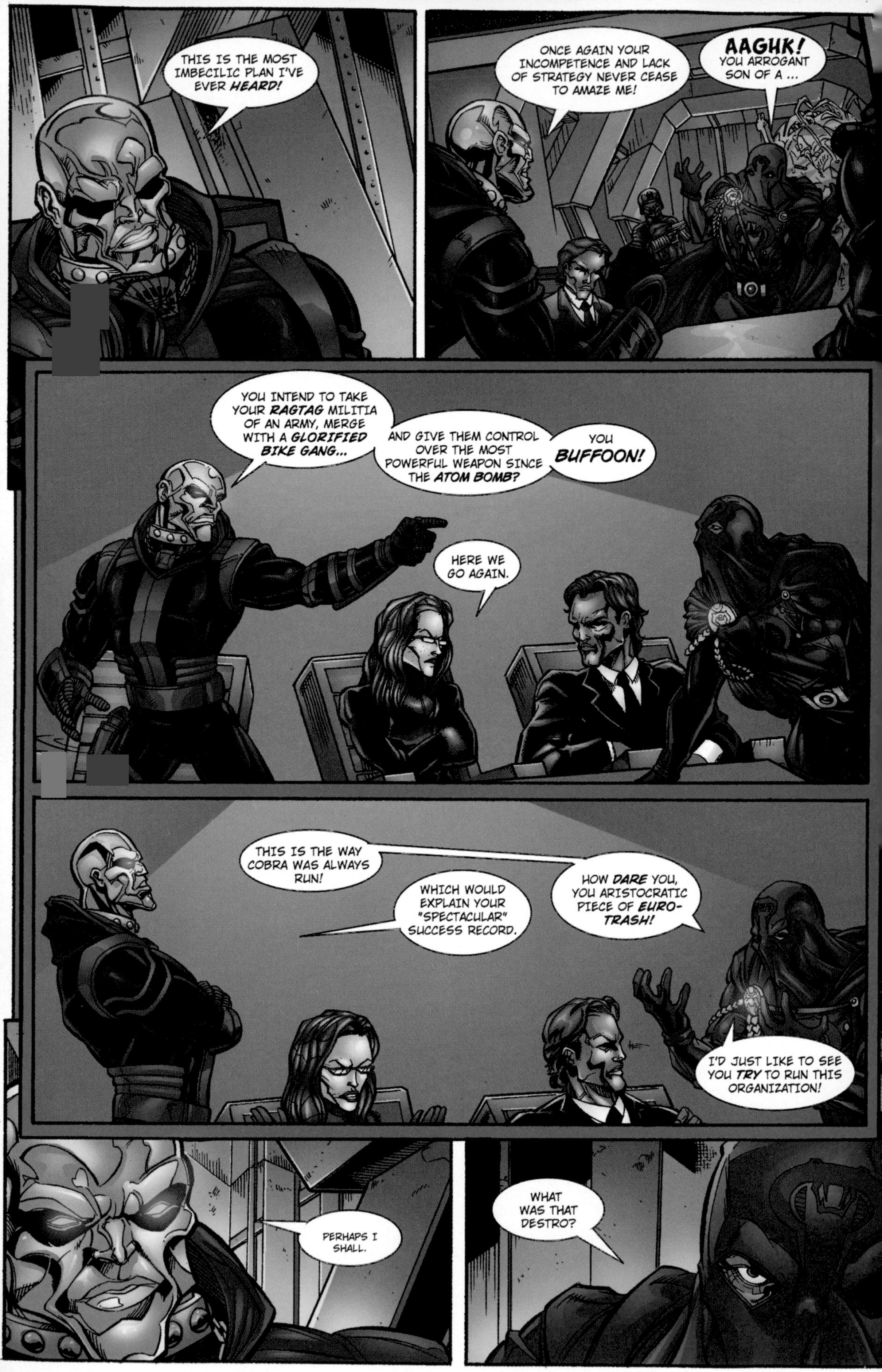
THIS IS THE MOST IMBECILIC PLAN I'VE EVER HEARD!
ONCE AGAIN YOUR INCOMPETENCE AND LACK OF STRATEGY NEVER CEASE TO AMAZE ME!
AAGHK! YOU ARROGANT SON OF A ...
YOU INTEND TO TAKE YOUR RAGTAG MILITIA OF AN ARMY, MERGE WITH A GLORIFIED BIKE GANG...
AND GIVE THEM CONTROL OVER THE MOST POWERFUL WEAPON SINCE THE ATOM BOMB?
YOU BUFFOON!
HERE WE GO AGAIN.
THIS IS THE WAY COBRA WAS ALWAYS RUN!
WHICH WOULD EXPLAIN YOUR "SPECTACULAR" SUCCESS RECORD.
HOW DARE YOU, YOU ARISTOCRATIC PIECE OF EURO-TRASH!
I'D JUST LIKE TO SEE YOU TRY TO RUN THIS ORGANIZATION!
PERHAPS I SHALL.
WHAT WAS THAT DESTRO?

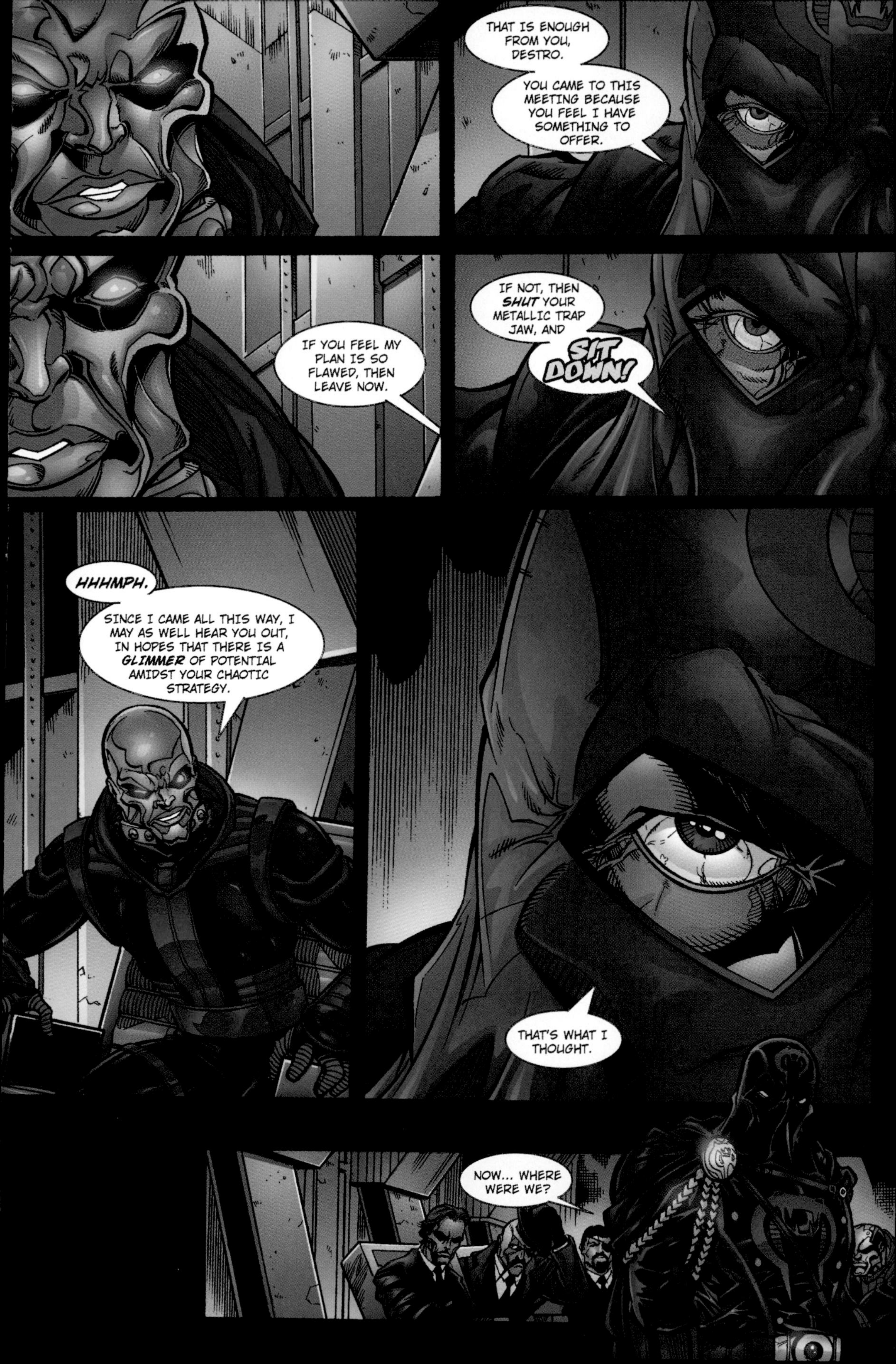

THAT IS ENOUGH FROM YOU, DESTRO.
YOU CAME TO THIS MEETING BECAUSE YOU FEEL I HAVE SOMETHING TO OFFER.
IF YOU FEEL MY PLAN IS SO FLAWED, THEN LEAVE NOW.
IF NOT, THEN SHUT YOUR METALLIC TRAP JAW, AND
SIT DOWN!
HHHMPH.
SINCE I CAME ALL THIS WAY, I MAY AS WELL HEAR YOU OUT, IN HOPES THAT THERE IS A GLIMMER OF POTENTIAL AMIDST YOUR CHAOTIC STRATEGY.
THAT'S WHAT I THOUGHT.
NOW... WHERE WERE WE?

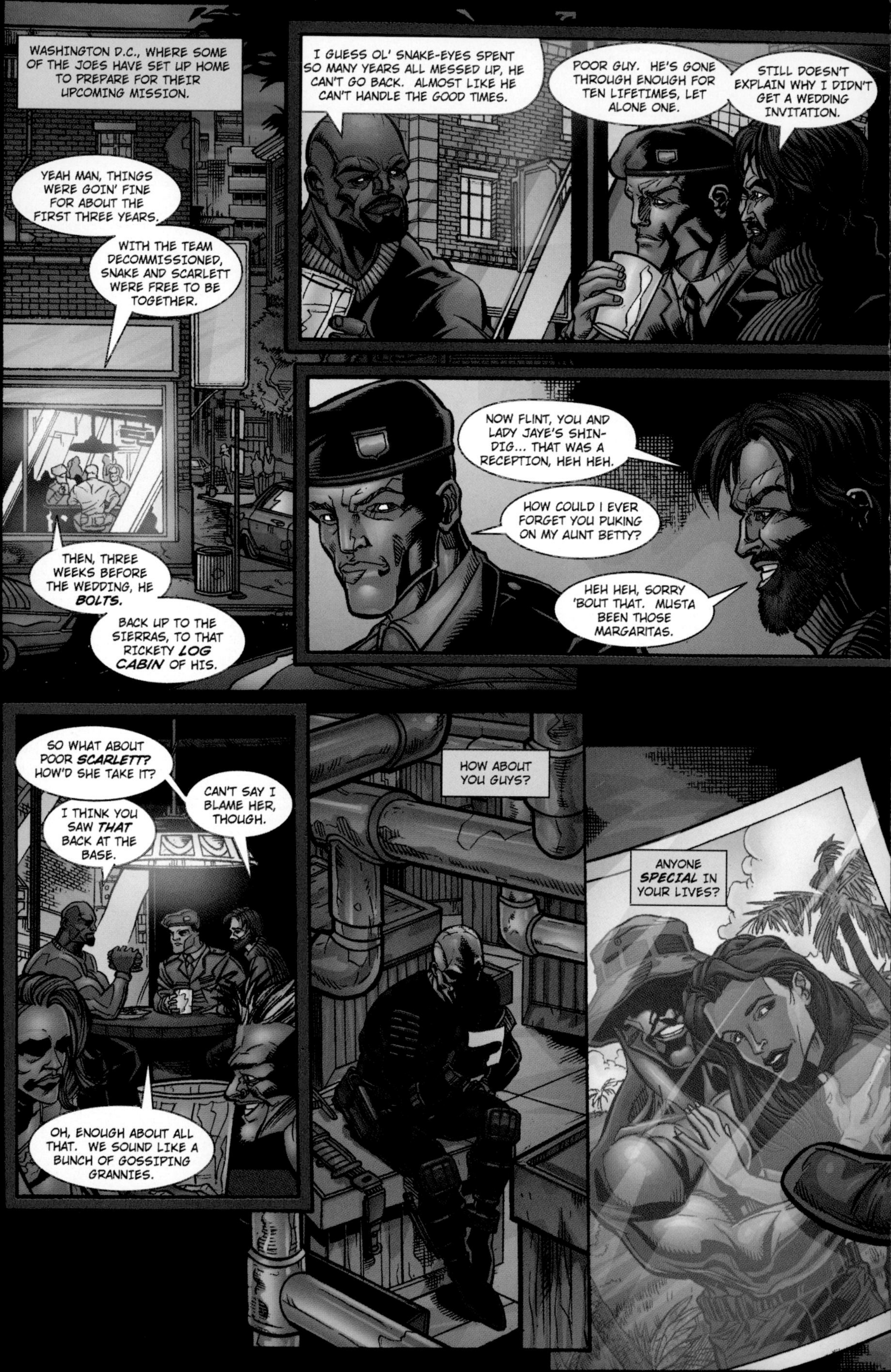
WASHINGTON D.C., WHERE SOME OF THE JOES HAVE SET UP HOME TO PREPARE FOR THEIR UPCOMING MISSION.
YEAH MAN, THINGS WERE GOIN' FINE FOR ABOUT THE FIRST THREE YEARS.
WITH THE TEAM DECOMMISSIONED, SNAKE AND SCARLETT WERE FREE TO BE TOGETHER.
THEN, THREE WEEKS BEFORE THE WEDDING, HE **BOLTS.**
BACK UP TO THE SIERRAS, TO THAT RICKETY **LOG CABIN** OF HIS.
I GUESS OL' SNAKE-EYES SPENT SO MANY YEARS ALL MESSED UP, HE CAN'T GO BACK. ALMOST LIKE HE CAN'T HANDLE THE GOOD TIMES.
POOR GUY. HE'S GONE THROUGH ENOUGH FOR TEN LIFETIMES, LET ALONE ONE.
STILL DOESN'T EXPLAIN WHY I DIDN'T GET A WEDDING INVITATION.
NOW FLINT, YOU AND LADY JAYE'S SHIN-DIG... THAT WAS A RECEPTION, HEH HEH.
HOW COULD I EVER FORGET YOU PUKING ON MY AUNT BETTY?
HEH HEH, SORRY 'BOUT THAT. MUSTA BEEN THOSE MARGARITAS.
SO WHAT ABOUT POOR **SCARLETT?** HOW'D SHE TAKE IT?
I THINK YOU SAW **THAT** BACK AT THE BASE.
CAN'T SAY I BLAME HER, THOUGH.
OH, ENOUGH ABOUT ALL THAT. WE SOUND LIKE A BUNCH OF GOSSIPING GRANNIES.
HOW ABOUT YOU GUYS?
ANYONE **SPECIAL** IN YOUR LIVES?

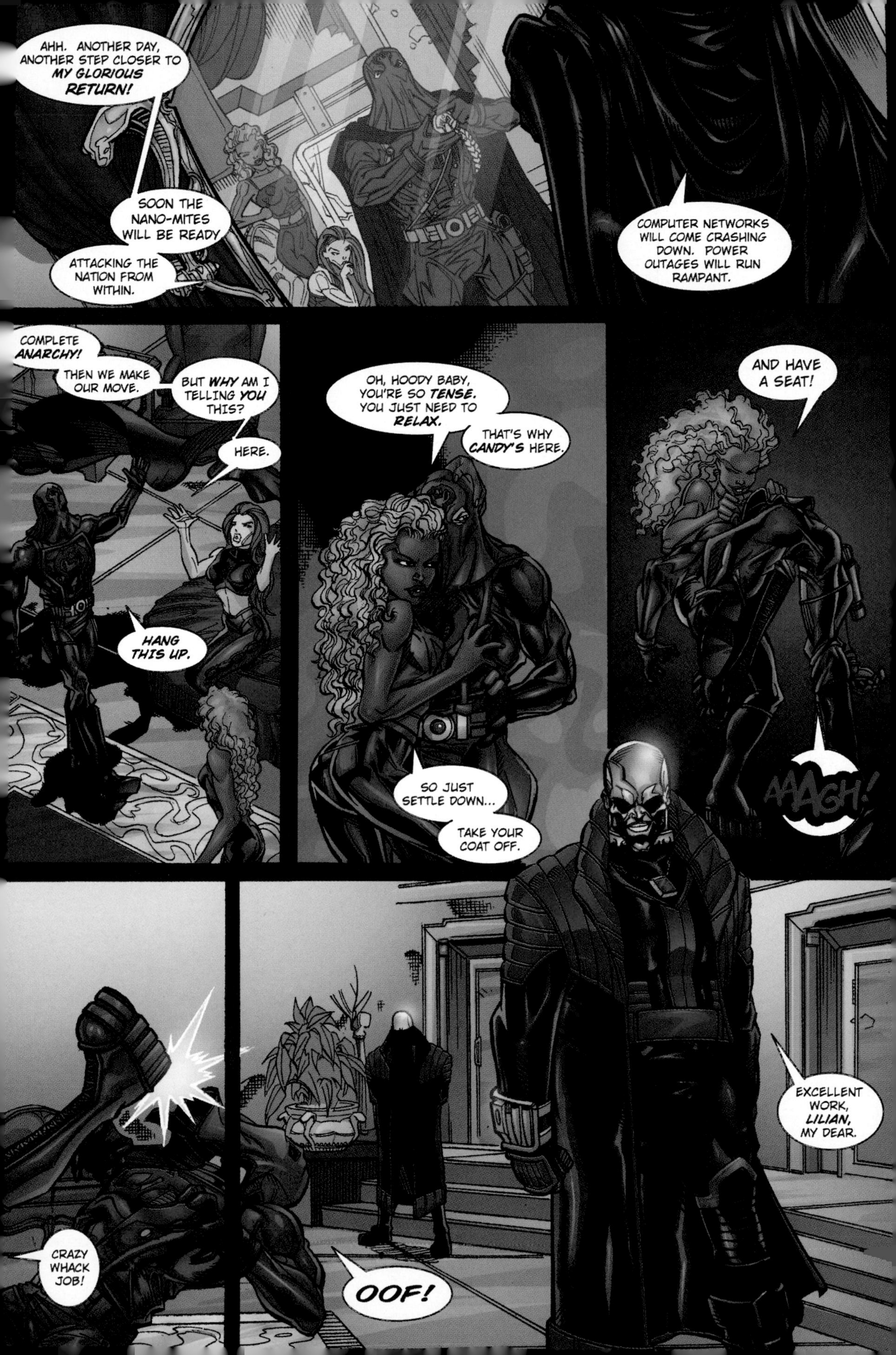
AHH. ANOTHER DAY, ANOTHER STEP CLOSER TO MY GLORIOUS RETURN!
SOON THE NANO-MITES WILL BE READY.
ATTACKING THE NATION FROM WITHIN.
COMPUTER NETWORKS WILL COME CRASHING DOWN. POWER OUTAGES WILL RUN RAMPANT.
COMPLETE ANARCHY!
THEN WE MAKE OUR MOVE.
BUT WHY AM I TELLING YOU THIS?
HERE.
HANG THIS UP.
OH, HOODY BABY, YOU'RE SO TENSE. YOU JUST NEED TO RELAX.
THAT'S WHY CANDY'S HERE.
SO JUST SETTLE DOWN...
TAKE YOUR COAT OFF.
AND HAVE A SEAT!
AAAGH!
CRAZY WHACK JOB!
OOF!
EXCELLENT WORK, LILIAN, MY DEAR.

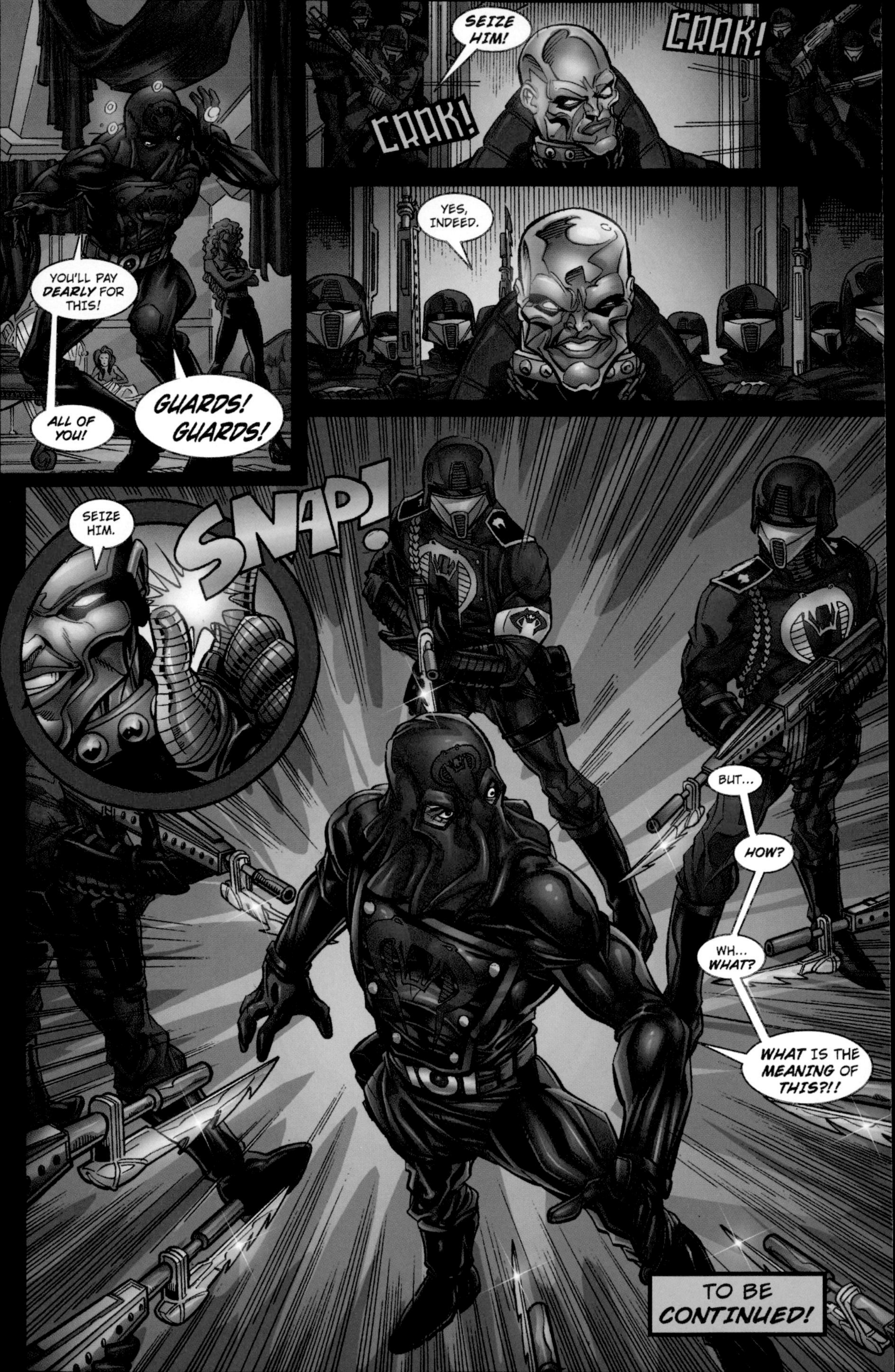
YOU'LL PAY DEARLY FOR THIS!
ALL OF YOU!
GUARDS! GUARDS!
SEIZE HIM!
CRAK!
CRAK!
YES, INDEED.
SEIZE HIM.
SNAP!
BUT...
HOW?
WH... WHAT?
WHAT IS THE MEANING OF THIS?!!
TO BE CONTINUED!

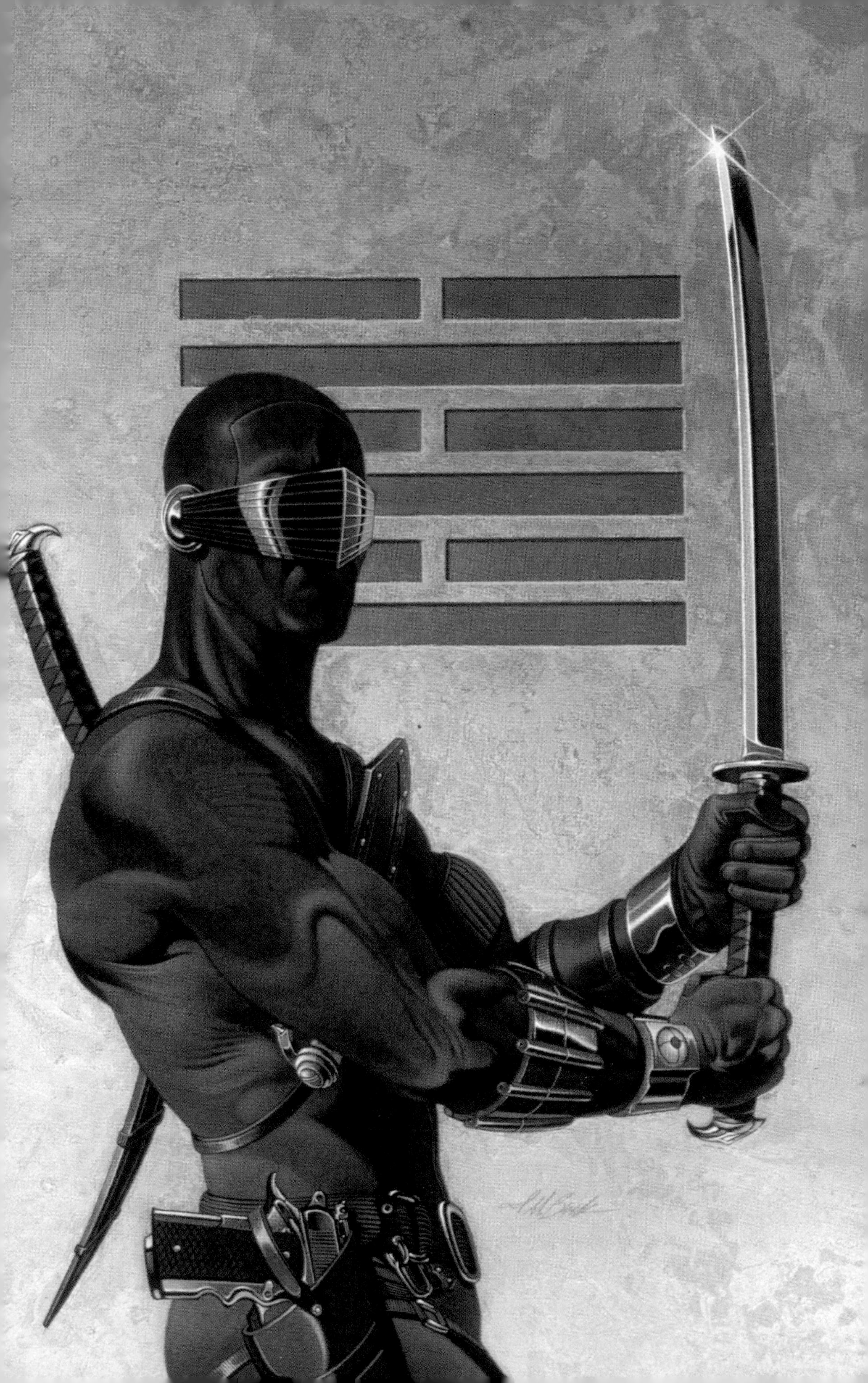

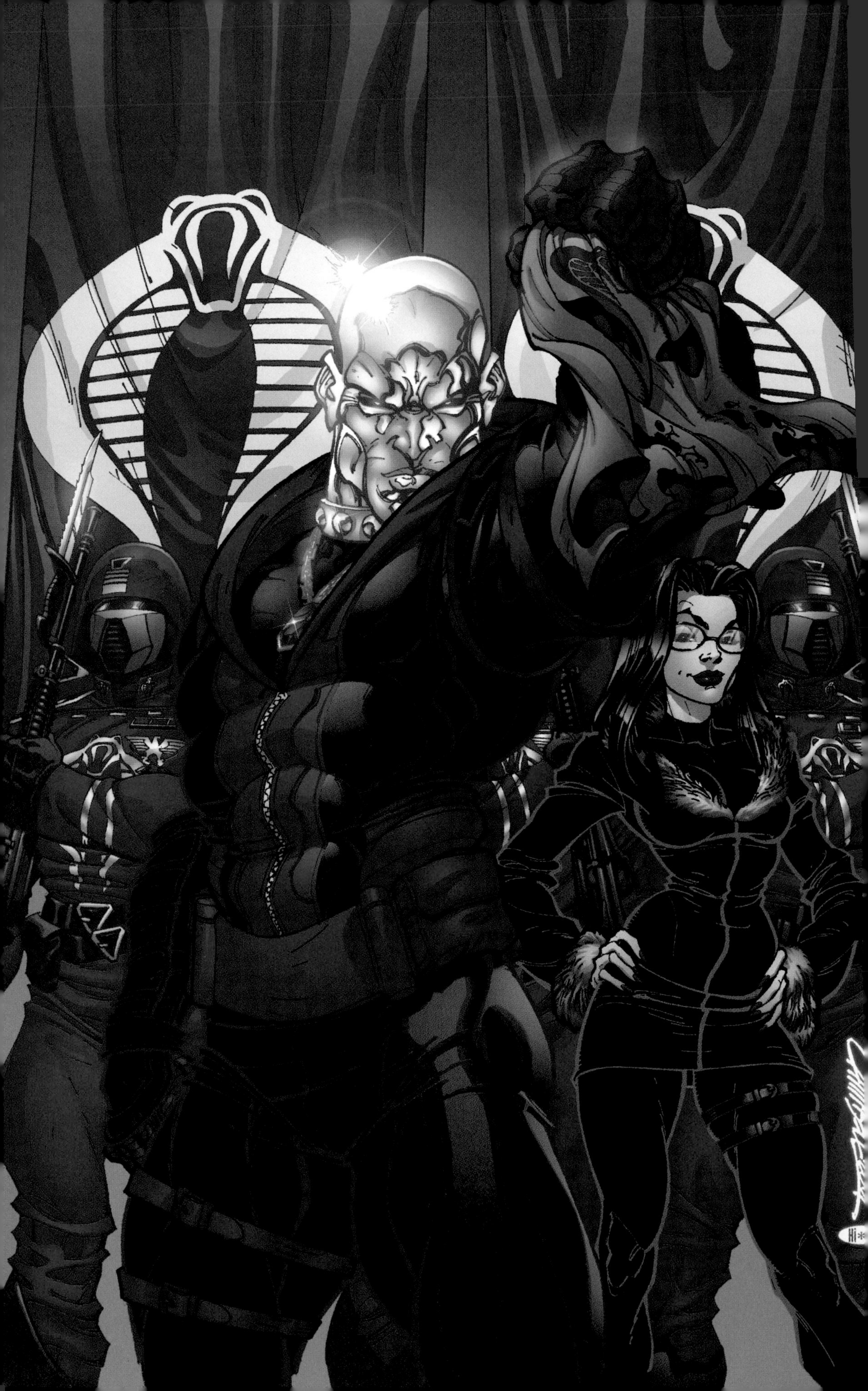

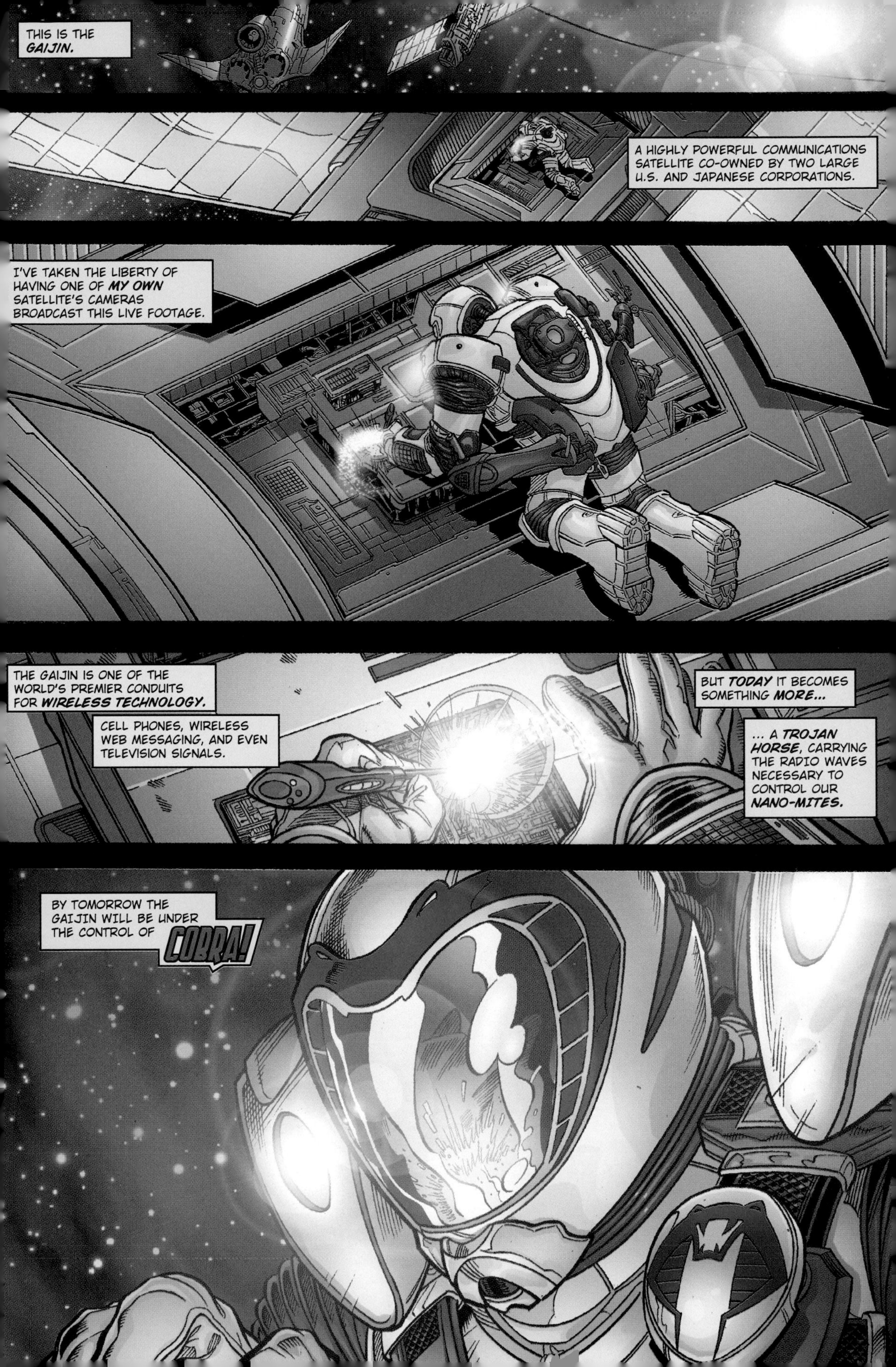
THIS IS THE GAIJIN.
A HIGHLY POWERFUL COMMUNICATIONS SATELLITE CO-OWNED BY TWO LARGE U.S. AND JAPANESE CORPORATIONS.
I'VE TAKEN THE LIBERTY OF HAVING ONE OF MY OWN SATELLITE'S CAMERAS BROADCAST THIS LIVE FOOTAGE.
THE GAIJIN IS ONE OF THE WORLD'S PREMIER CONDUITS FOR WIRELESS TECHNOLOGY.
CELL PHONES, WIRELESS WEB MESSAGING, AND EVEN TELEVISION SIGNALS.
BUT TODAY IT BECOMES SOMETHING MORE...
... A TROJAN HORSE, CARRYING THE RADIO WAVES NECESSARY TO CONTROL OUR NANO-MITES.
BY TOMORROW THE GAIJIN WILL BE UNDER THE CONTROL OF COBRA!

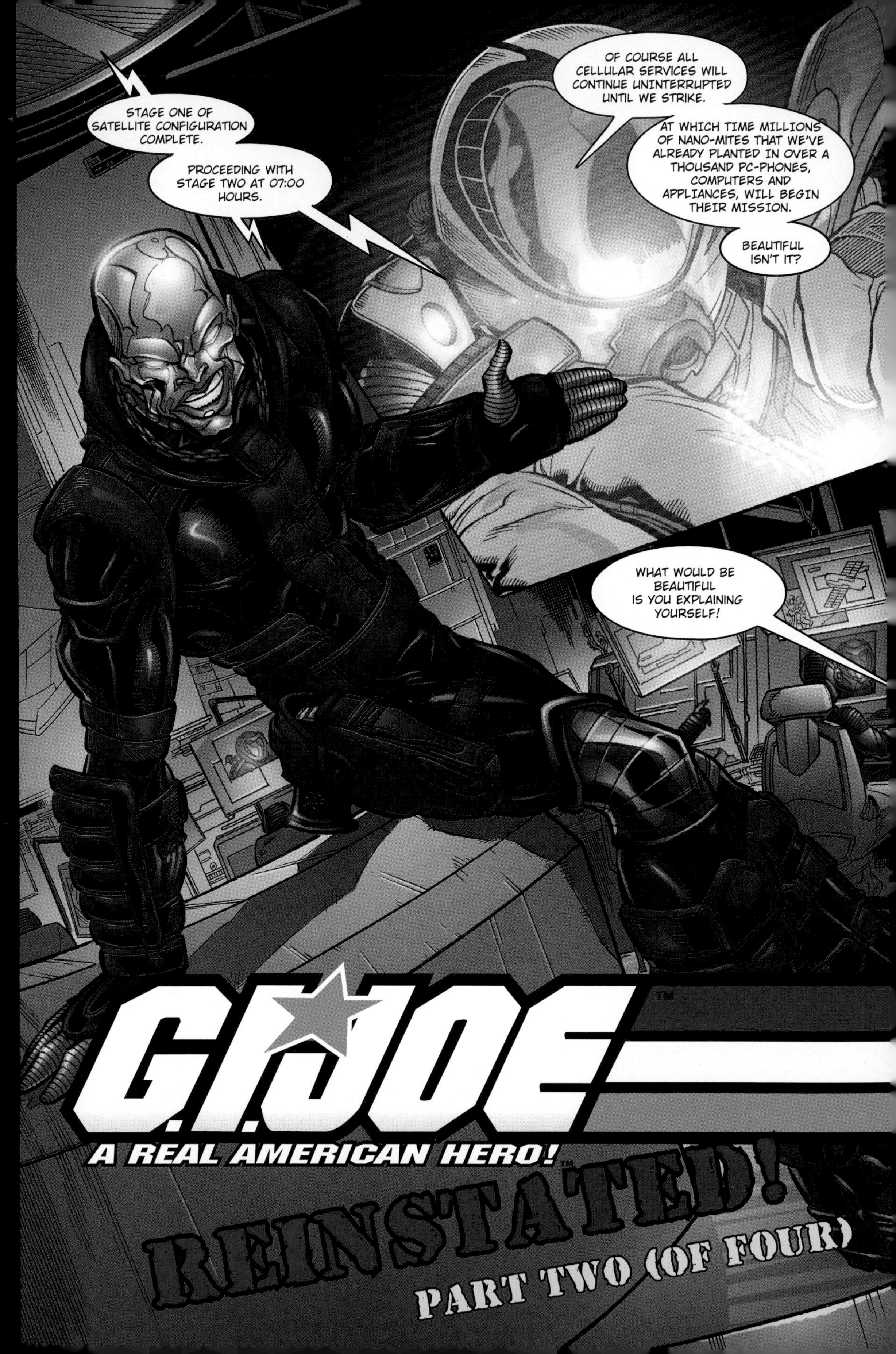
STAGE ONE OF SATELLITE CONFIGURATION COMPLETE.
PROCEEDING WITH STAGE TWO AT 07:00 HOURS.
OF COURSE ALL CELLULAR SERVICES WILL CONTINUE UNINTERRUPTED UNTIL WE STRIKE.
AT WHICH TIME MILLIONS OF NANO-MITES THAT WE'VE ALREADY PLANTED IN OVER A THOUSAND PC-PHONES, COMPUTERS AND APPLIANCES, WILL BEGIN THEIR MISSION.
BEAUTIFUL ISN'T IT?
WHAT WOULD BE BEAUTIFUL IS YOU EXPLAINING YOURSELF!
G.I. JOE™
A REAL AMERICAN HERO!™
REINSTATED!
PART TWO (OF FOUR)

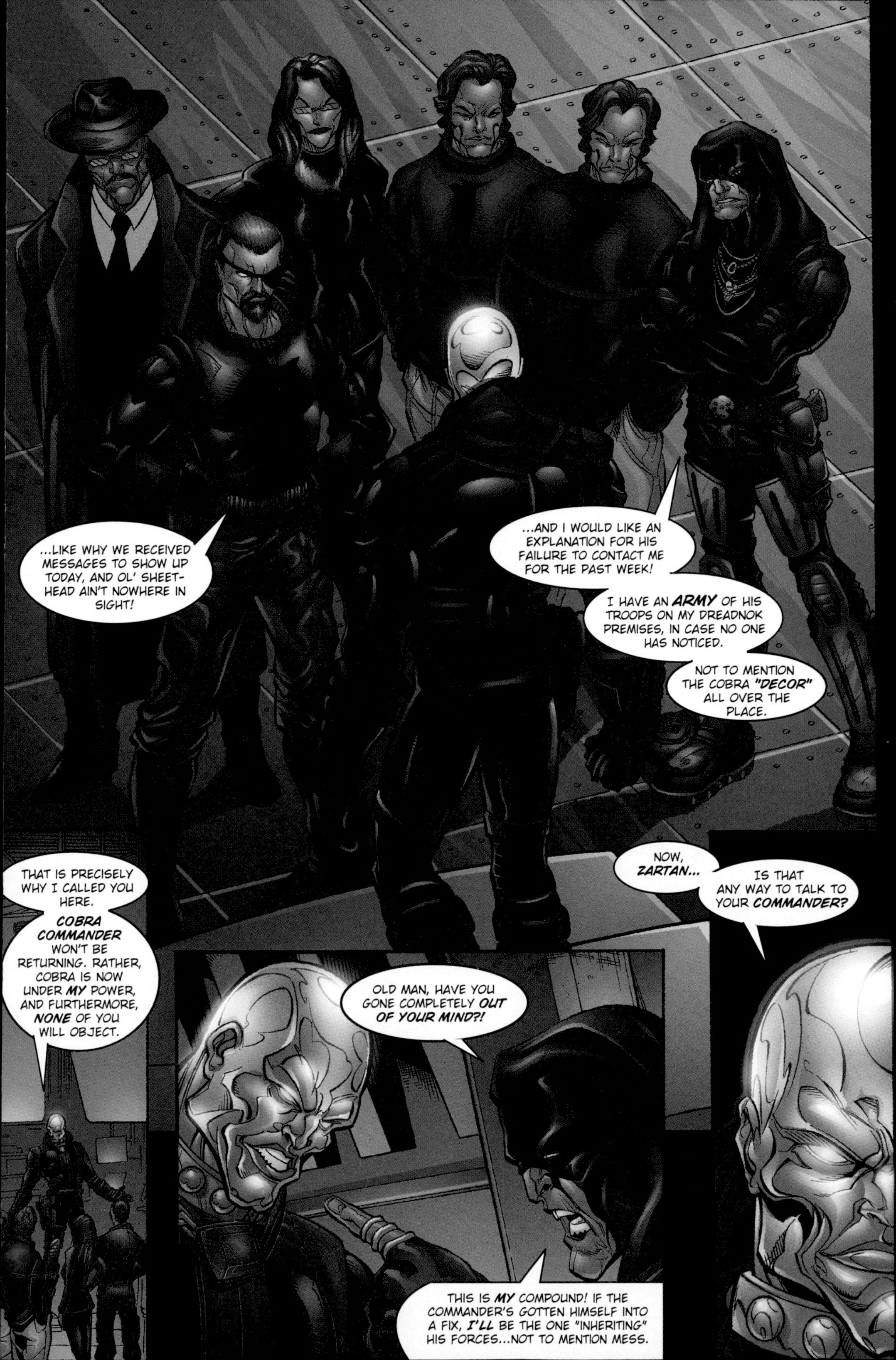
...LIKE WHY WE RECEIVED MESSAGES TO SHOW UP TODAY, AND OL' SHEET-HEAD AIN'T NOWHERE IN SIGHT!
...AND I WOULD LIKE AN EXPLANATION FOR HIS FAILURE TO CONTACT ME FOR THE PAST WEEK!
I HAVE AN ARMY OF HIS TROOPS ON MY DREADNOK PREMISES, IN CASE NO ONE HAS NOTICED.
NOT TO MENTION THE COBRA "DECOR" ALL OVER THE PLACE.
THAT IS PRECISELY WHY I CALLED YOU HERE.
COBRA COMMANDER WON'T BE RETURNING. RATHER, COBRA IS NOW UNDER MY POWER, AND FURTHERMORE, NONE OF YOU WILL OBJECT.
OLD MAN, HAVE YOU GONE COMPLETELY OUT OF YOUR MIND?!
THIS IS MY COMPOUND! IF THE COMMANDER'S GOTTEN HIMSELF INTO A FIX, I'LL BE THE ONE "INHERITING" HIS FORCES...NOT TO MENTION MESS.
NOW, ZARTAN...
IS THAT ANY WAY TO TALK TO YOUR COMMANDER?

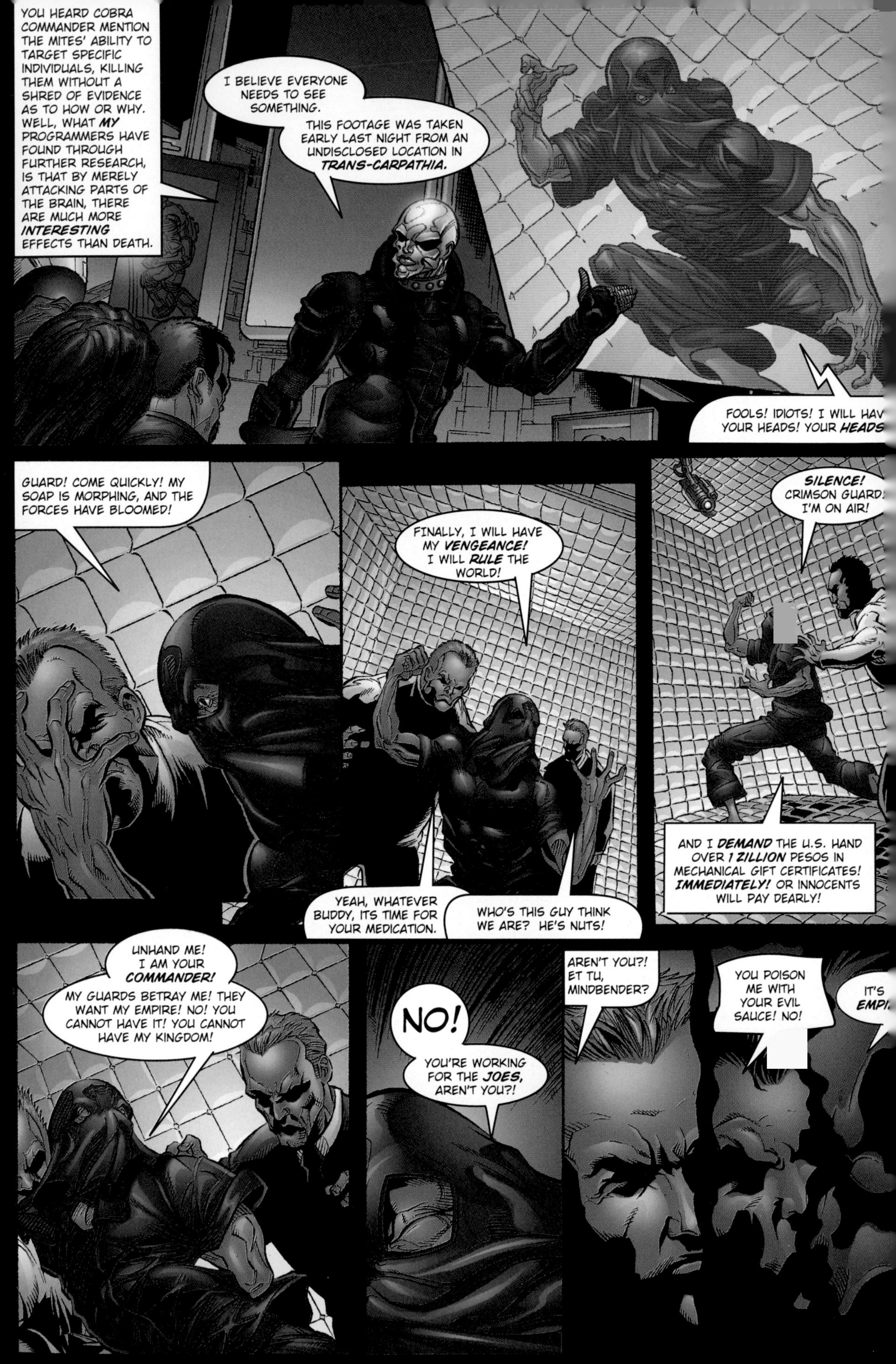
YOU HEARD COBRA COMMANDER MENTION THE MITES' ABILITY TO TARGET SPECIFIC INDIVIDUALS, KILLING THEM WITHOUT A SHRED OF EVIDENCE AS TO HOW OR WHY. WELL, WHAT MY PROGRAMMERS HAVE FOUND THROUGH FURTHER RESEARCH, IS THAT BY MERELY ATTACKING PARTS OF THE BRAIN, THERE ARE MUCH MORE INTERESTING EFFECTS THAN DEATH.
I BELIEVE EVERYONE NEEDS TO SEE SOMETHING.
THIS FOOTAGE WAS TAKEN EARLY LAST NIGHT FROM AN UNDISCLOSED LOCATION IN TRANS-CARPATHIA.
FOOLS! IDIOTS! I WILL HAV
YOUR HEADS! YOUR HEADS
GUARD! COME QUICKLY! MY SOAP IS MORPHING, AND THE FORCES HAVE BLOOMED!
FINALLY, I WILL HAVE MY VENGEANCE! I WILL RULE THE WORLD!
YEAH, WHATEVER BUDDY, ITS TIME FOR YOUR MEDICATION.
WHO'S THIS GUY THINK WE ARE? HE'S NUTS!
SILENCE! CRIMSON GUARD I'M ON AIR!
AND I DEMAND THE U.S. HAND OVER 1 ZILLION PESOS IN MECHANICAL GIFT CERTIFICATES! IMMEDIATELY! OR INNOCENTS WILL PAY DEARLY!
UNHAND ME! I AM YOUR COMMANDER!
MY GUARDS BETRAY ME! THEY WANT MY EMPIRE! NO! YOU CANNOT HAVE IT! YOU CANNOT HAVE MY KINGDOM!
NO!
YOU'RE WORKING FOR THE JOES, AREN'T YOU?!
AREN'T YOU?! ET TU, MINDBENDER?
YOU POISON ME WITH YOUR EVIL SAUCE! NO!
IT'S EMPI

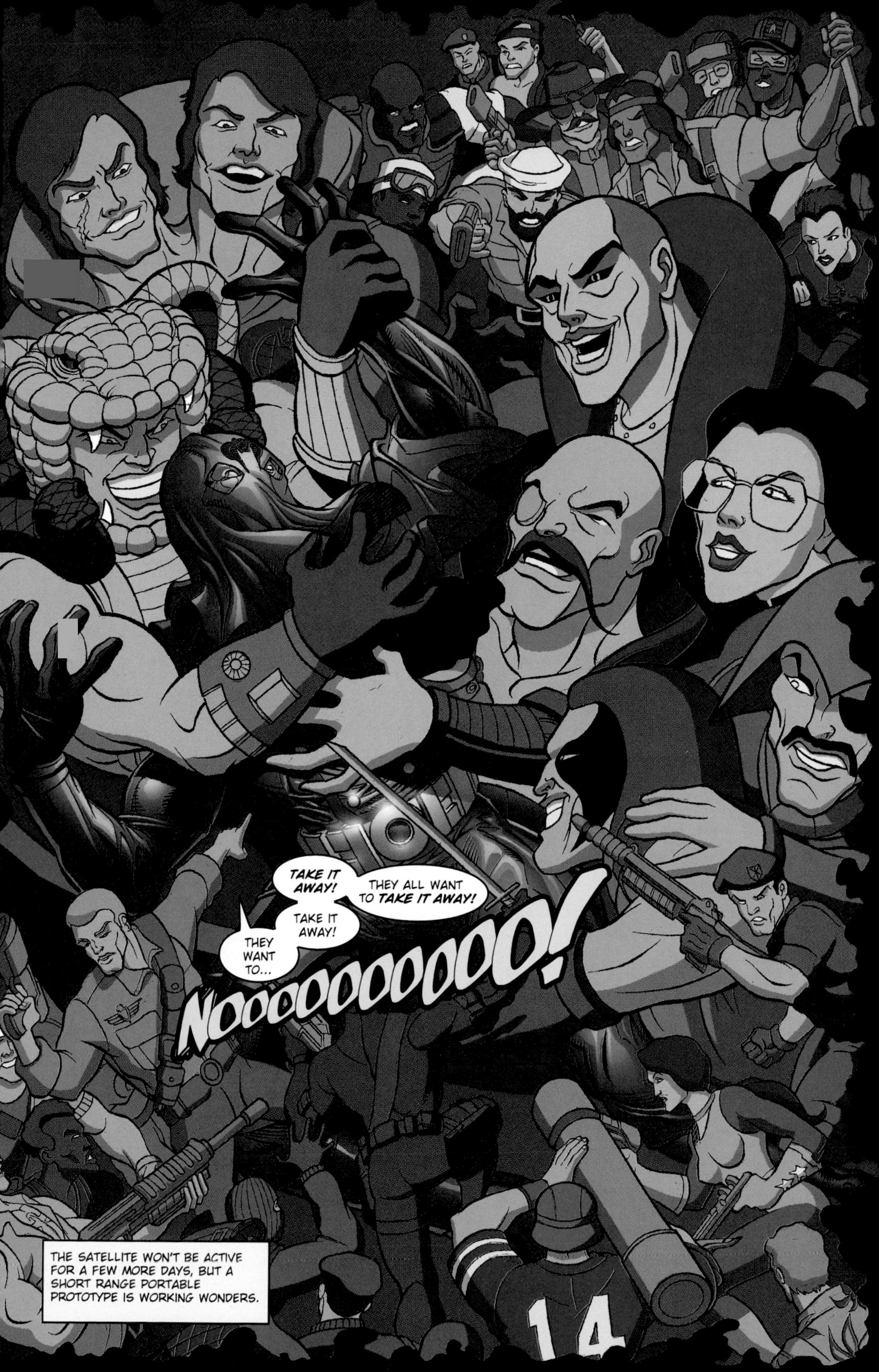
THEY WANT TO...
TAKE IT AWAY!
TAKE IT AWAY!
THEY ALL WANT TO *TAKE IT AWAY!*
NOOOOOOOOOOO!
THE SATELLITE WON'T BE ACTIVE FOR A FEW MORE DAYS, BUT A SHORT RANGE PORTABLE PROTOTYPE IS WORKING WONDERS.

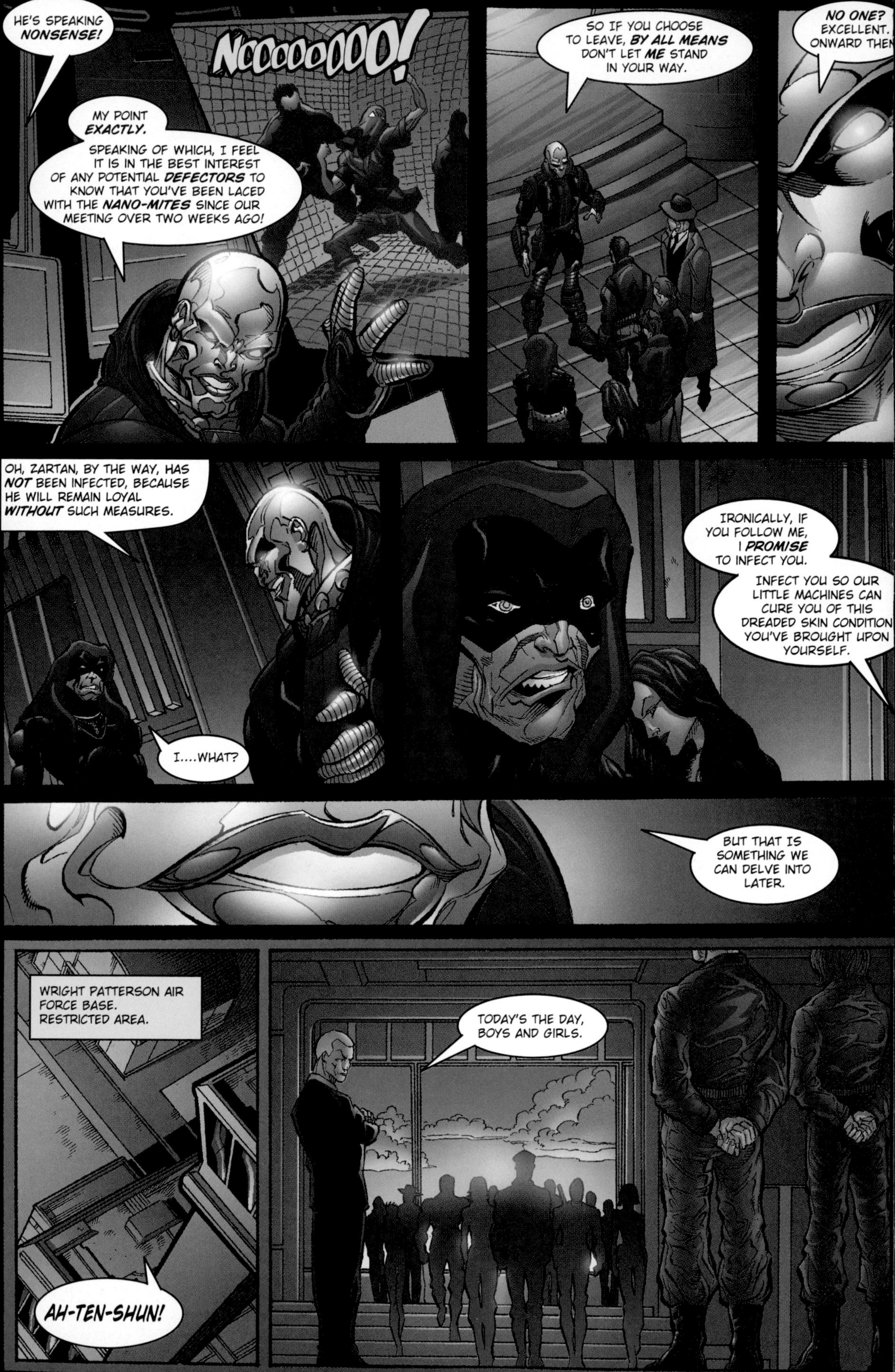
HE'S SPEAKING NONSENSE!
NOOOOOOOOO!
MY POINT EXACTLY.
SPEAKING OF WHICH, I FEEL IT IS IN THE BEST INTEREST OF ANY POTENTIAL DEFECTORS TO KNOW THAT YOU'VE BEEN LACED WITH THE NANO-MITES SINCE OUR MEETING OVER TWO WEEKS AGO!
SO IF YOU CHOOSE TO LEAVE, BY ALL MEANS DON'T LET ME STAND IN YOUR WAY.
NO ONE? EXCELLENT. ONWARD THEN
OH, ZARTAN, BY THE WAY, HAS NOT BEEN INFECTED, BECAUSE HE WILL REMAIN LOYAL WITHOUT SUCH MEASURES.
IRONICALLY, IF YOU FOLLOW ME, I PROMISE TO INFECT YOU.
INFECT YOU SO OUR LITTLE MACHINES CAN CURE YOU OF THIS DREADED SKIN CONDITION YOU'VE BROUGHT UPON YOURSELF.
I....WHAT?
BUT THAT IS SOMETHING WE CAN DELVE INTO LATER.
WRIGHT PATTERSON AIR FORCE BASE. RESTRICTED AREA.
TODAY'S THE DAY, BOYS AND GIRLS.
AH-TEN-SHUN!

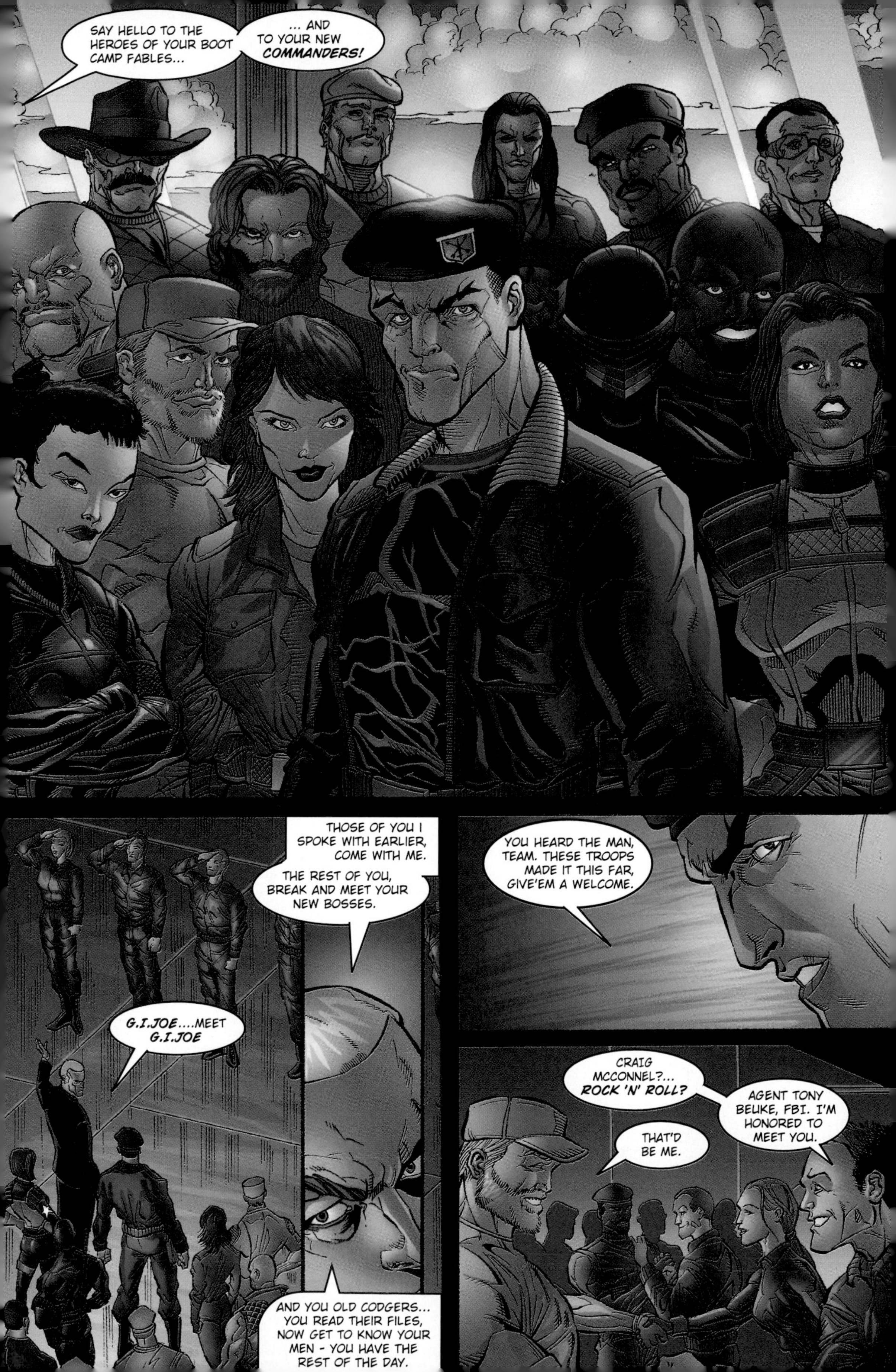
SAY HELLO TO THE HEROES OF YOUR BOOT CAMP FABLES...
... AND TO YOUR NEW COMMANDERS!
THOSE OF YOU I SPOKE WITH EARLIER, COME WITH ME.
THE REST OF YOU, BREAK AND MEET YOUR NEW BOSSES.
G.I.JOE....MEET G.I.JOE
AND YOU OLD CODGERS... YOU READ THEIR FILES, NOW GET TO KNOW YOUR MEN - YOU HAVE THE REST OF THE DAY.
YOU HEARD THE MAN, TEAM. THESE TROOPS MADE IT THIS FAR, GIVE'EM A WELCOME.
CRAIG MCCONNEL?... ROCK 'N' ROLL?
THAT'D BE ME.
AGENT TONY BEUKE, FBI. I'M HONORED TO MEET YOU.

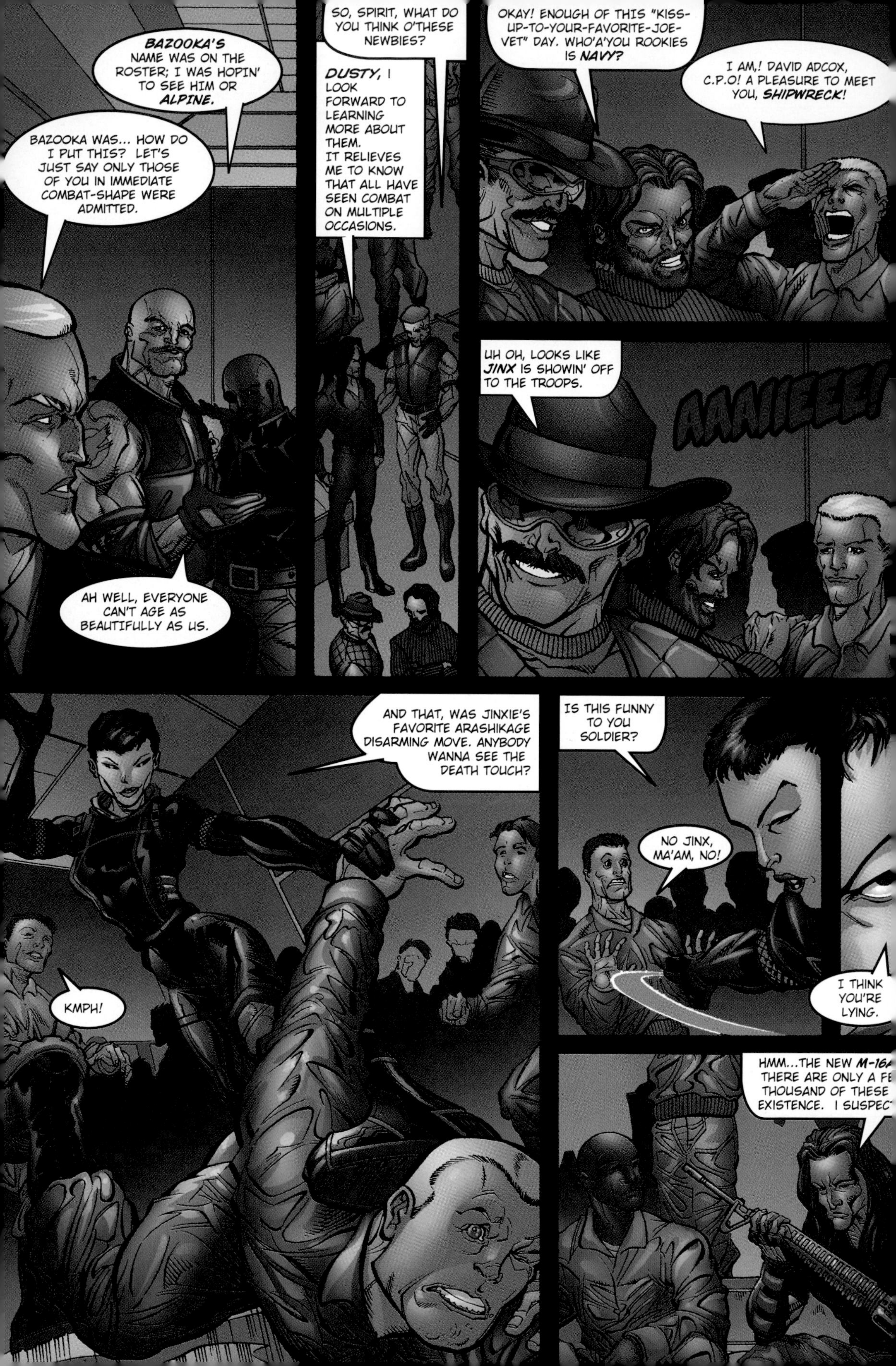
BAZOOKA'S NAME WAS ON THE ROSTER; I WAS HOPIN' TO SEE HIM OR ALPINE.
BAZOOKA WAS... HOW DO I PUT THIS? LET'S JUST SAY ONLY THOSE OF YOU IN IMMEDIATE COMBAT-SHAPE WERE ADMITTED.
AH WELL, EVERYONE CAN'T AGE AS BEAUTIFULLY AS US.
SO, SPIRIT, WHAT DO YOU THINK O'THESE NEWBIES?
DUSTY, I LOOK FORWARD TO LEARNING MORE ABOUT THEM. IT RELIEVES ME TO KNOW THAT ALL HAVE SEEN COMBAT ON MULTIPLE OCCASIONS.
OKAY! ENOUGH OF THIS "KISS-UP-TO-YOUR-FAVORITE-JOE-VET" DAY. WHO'A'YOU ROOKIES IS NAVY?
I AM,! DAVID ADCOX, C.P.O! A PLEASURE TO MEET YOU, SHIPWRECK!
UH OH, LOOKS LIKE JINX IS SHOWIN' OFF TO THE TROOPS.
AAAIIEEE!
AND THAT, WAS JINXIE'S FAVORITE ARASHIKAGE DISARMING MOVE. ANYBODY WANNA SEE THE DEATH TOUCH?
KMPH!
IS THIS FUNNY TO YOU SOLDIER?
NO JINX, MA'AM, NO!
I THINK YOU'RE LYING.
HMM...THE NEW M-16A
THERE ARE ONLY A FE
THOUSAND OF THESE
EXISTENCE. I SUSPECT

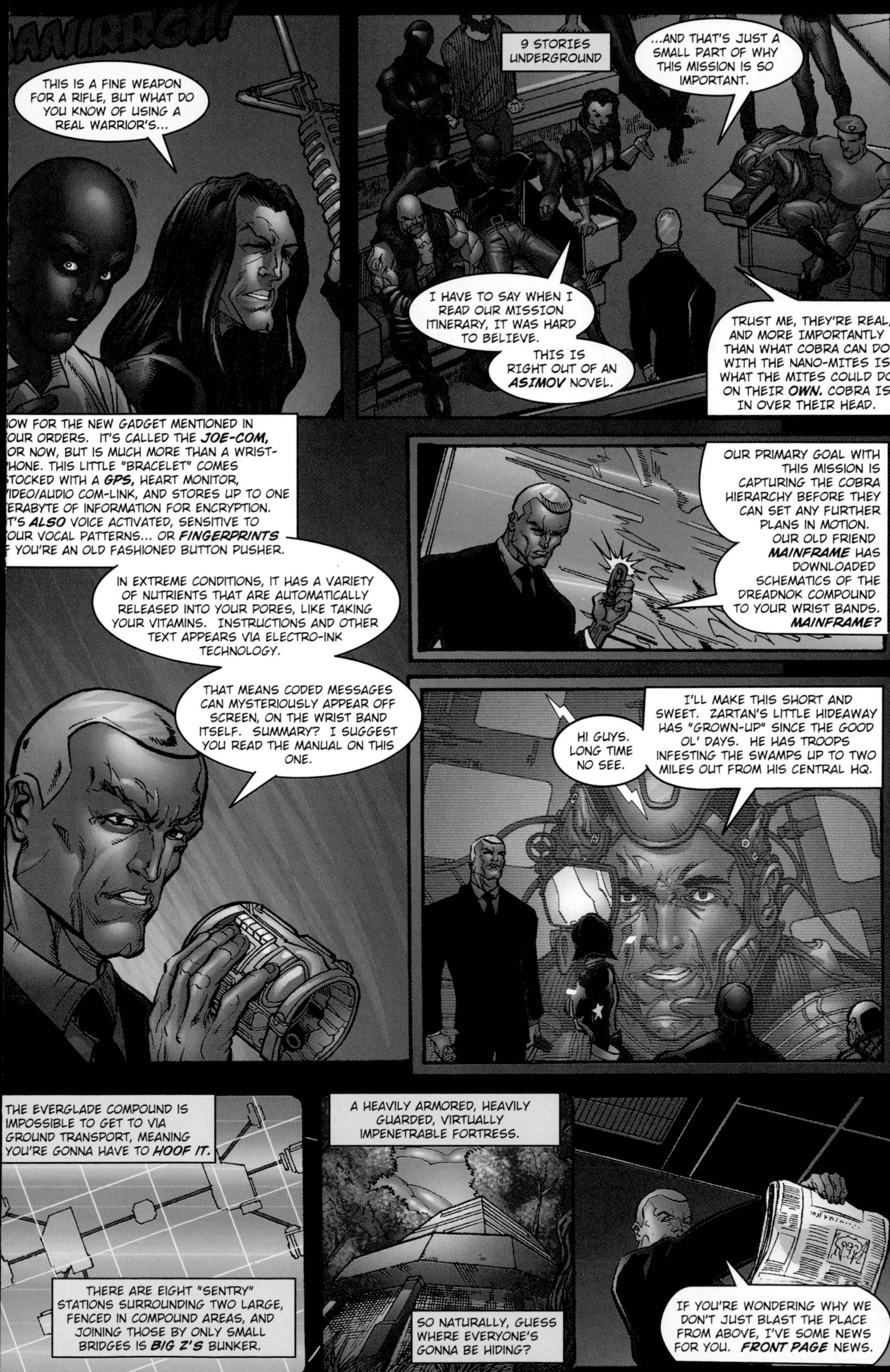

THIS IS A FINE WEAPON FOR A RIFLE, BUT WHAT DO YOU KNOW OF USING A REAL WARRIOR'S...
9 STORIES UNDERGROUND
...AND THAT'S JUST A SMALL PART OF WHY THIS MISSION IS SO IMPORTANT.
I HAVE TO SAY WHEN I READ OUR MISSION ITINERARY, IT WAS HARD TO BELIEVE.
THIS IS RIGHT OUT OF AN ***ASIMOV*** NOVEL.
TRUST ME, THEY'RE REAL, AND MORE IMPORTANTLY THAN WHAT COBRA CAN DO WITH THE NANO-MITES IS WHAT THE MITES COULD DO ON THEIR ***OWN.*** COBRA IS IN OVER THEIR HEAD.
OW FOR THE NEW GADGET MENTIONED IN OUR ORDERS. IT'S CALLED THE ***JOE-COM,*** OR NOW, BUT IS MUCH MORE THAN A WRIST-HONE. THIS LITTLE "BRACELET" COMES TOCKED WITH A ***GPS,*** HEART MONITOR, IDEO/AUDIO COM-LINK, AND STORES UP TO ONE ERABYTE OF INFORMATION FOR ENCRYPTION. T'S ***ALSO*** VOICE ACTIVATED, SENSITIVE TO OUR VOCAL PATTERNS... OR ***FINGERPRINTS*** F YOU'RE AN OLD FASHIONED BUTTON PUSHER.
IN EXTREME CONDITIONS, IT HAS A VARIETY OF NUTRIENTS THAT ARE AUTOMATICALLY RELEASED INTO YOUR PORES, LIKE TAKING YOUR VITAMINS. INSTRUCTIONS AND OTHER TEXT APPEARS VIA ELECTRO-INK TECHNOLOGY.
THAT MEANS CODED MESSAGES CAN MYSTERIOUSLY APPEAR OFF SCREEN, ON THE WRIST BAND ITSELF. SUMMARY? I SUGGEST YOU READ THE MANUAL ON THIS ONE.
OUR PRIMARY GOAL WITH THIS MISSION IS CAPTURING THE COBRA HIERARCHY BEFORE THEY CAN SET ANY FURTHER PLANS IN MOTION. OUR OLD FRIEND ***MAINFRAME*** HAS DOWNLOADED SCHEMATICS OF THE DREADNOK COMPOUND TO YOUR WRIST BANDS. ***MAINFRAME?***
HI GUYS. LONG TIME NO SEE.
I'LL MAKE THIS SHORT AND SWEET. ZARTAN'S LITTLE HIDEAWAY HAS "GROWN-UP" SINCE THE GOOD OL' DAYS. HE HAS TROOPS INFESTING THE SWAMPS UP TO TWO MILES OUT FROM HIS CENTRAL HQ.
THE EVERGLADE COMPOUND IS IMPOSSIBLE TO GET TO VIA GROUND TRANSPORT, MEANING YOU'RE GONNA HAVE TO ***HOOF IT.***
THERE ARE EIGHT "SENTRY" STATIONS SURROUNDING TWO LARGE, FENCED IN COMPOUND AREAS, AND JOINING THOSE BY ONLY SMALL BRIDGES IS ***BIG Z'S*** BUNKER.
A HEAVILY ARMORED, HEAVILY GUARDED, VIRTUALLY IMPENETRABLE FORTRESS.
SO NATURALLY, GUESS WHERE EVERYONE'S GONNA BE HIDING?
IF YOU'RE WONDERING WHY WE DON'T JUST BLAST THE PLACE FROM ABOVE, I'VE SOME NEWS FOR YOU. ***FRONT PAGE*** NEWS.

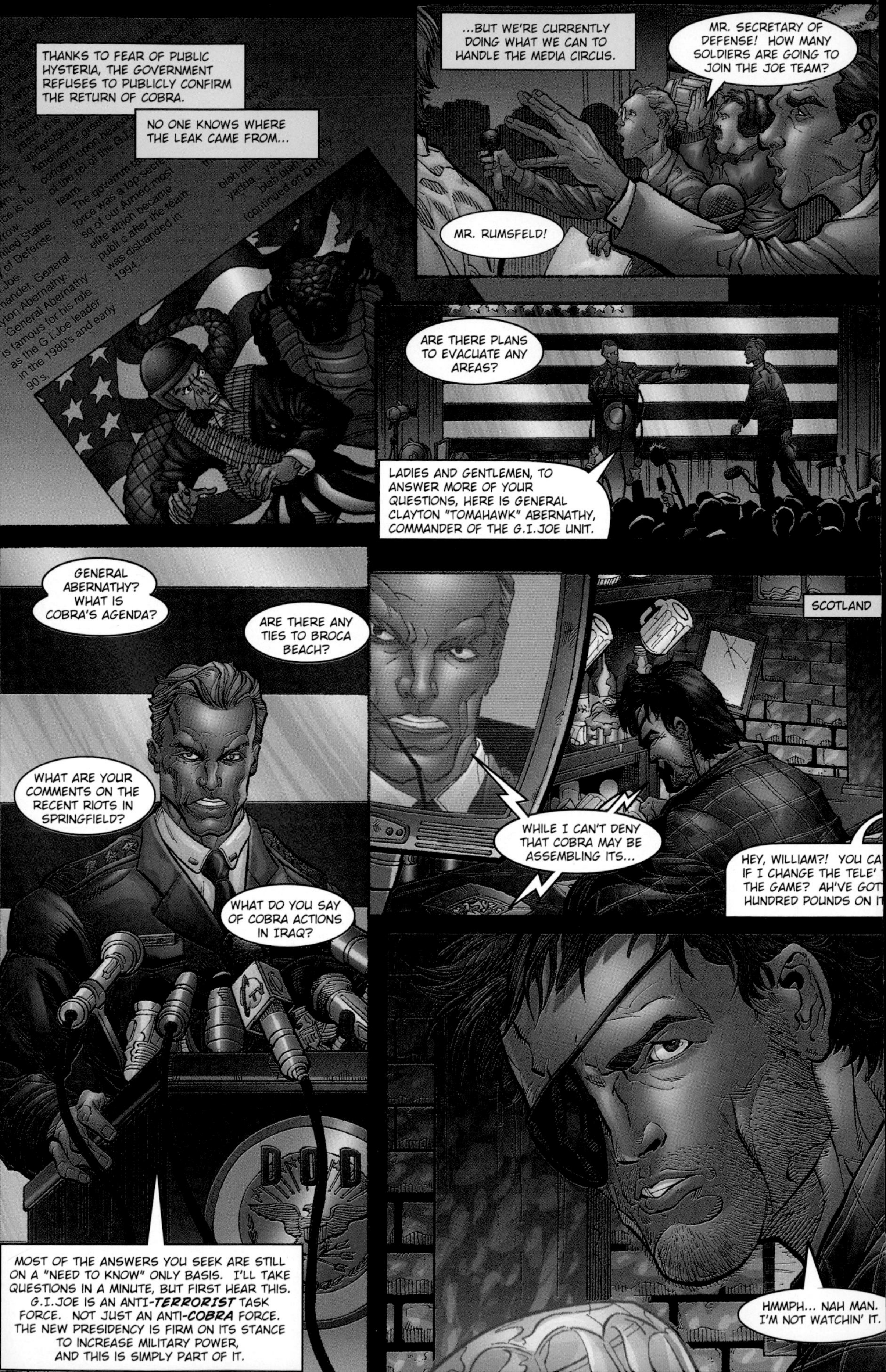

THANKS TO FEAR OF PUBLIC HYSTERIA, THE GOVERNMENT REFUSES TO PUBLICLY CONFIRM THE RETURN OF COBRA.
NO ONE KNOWS WHERE THE LEAK CAME FROM...
...BUT WE'RE CURRENTLY DOING WHAT WE CAN TO HANDLE THE MEDIA CIRCUS.
MR. SECRETARY OF DEFENSE! HOW MANY SOLDIERS ARE GOING TO JOIN THE JOE TEAM?
MR. RUMSFELD!
ARE THERE PLANS TO EVACUATE ANY AREAS?
LADIES AND GENTLEMEN, TO ANSWER MORE OF YOUR QUESTIONS, HERE IS GENERAL CLAYTON "TOMAHAWK" ABERNATHY, COMMANDER OF THE G.I.JOE UNIT.
GENERAL ABERNATHY? WHAT IS COBRA'S AGENDA?
ARE THERE ANY TIES TO BROCA BEACH?
WHAT ARE YOUR COMMENTS ON THE RECENT RIOTS IN SPRINGFIELD?
WHAT DO YOU SAY OF COBRA ACTIONS IN IRAQ?
MOST OF THE ANSWERS YOU SEEK ARE STILL ON A "NEED TO KNOW" ONLY BASIS. I'LL TAKE QUESTIONS IN A MINUTE, BUT FIRST HEAR THIS. G.I.JOE IS AN ANTI-TERRORIST TASK FORCE. NOT JUST AN ANTI-COBRA FORCE. THE NEW PRESIDENCY IS FIRM ON ITS STANCE TO INCREASE MILITARY POWER, AND THIS IS SIMPLY PART OF IT.
SCOTLAND
WHILE I CAN'T DENY THAT COBRA MAY BE ASSEMBLING ITS...
HEY, WILLIAM?! YOU CA IF I CHANGE THE TELE' THE GAME? AH'VE GOT HUNDRED POUNDS ON IT
HMMPH... NAH MAN. I'M NOT WATCHIN' IT.

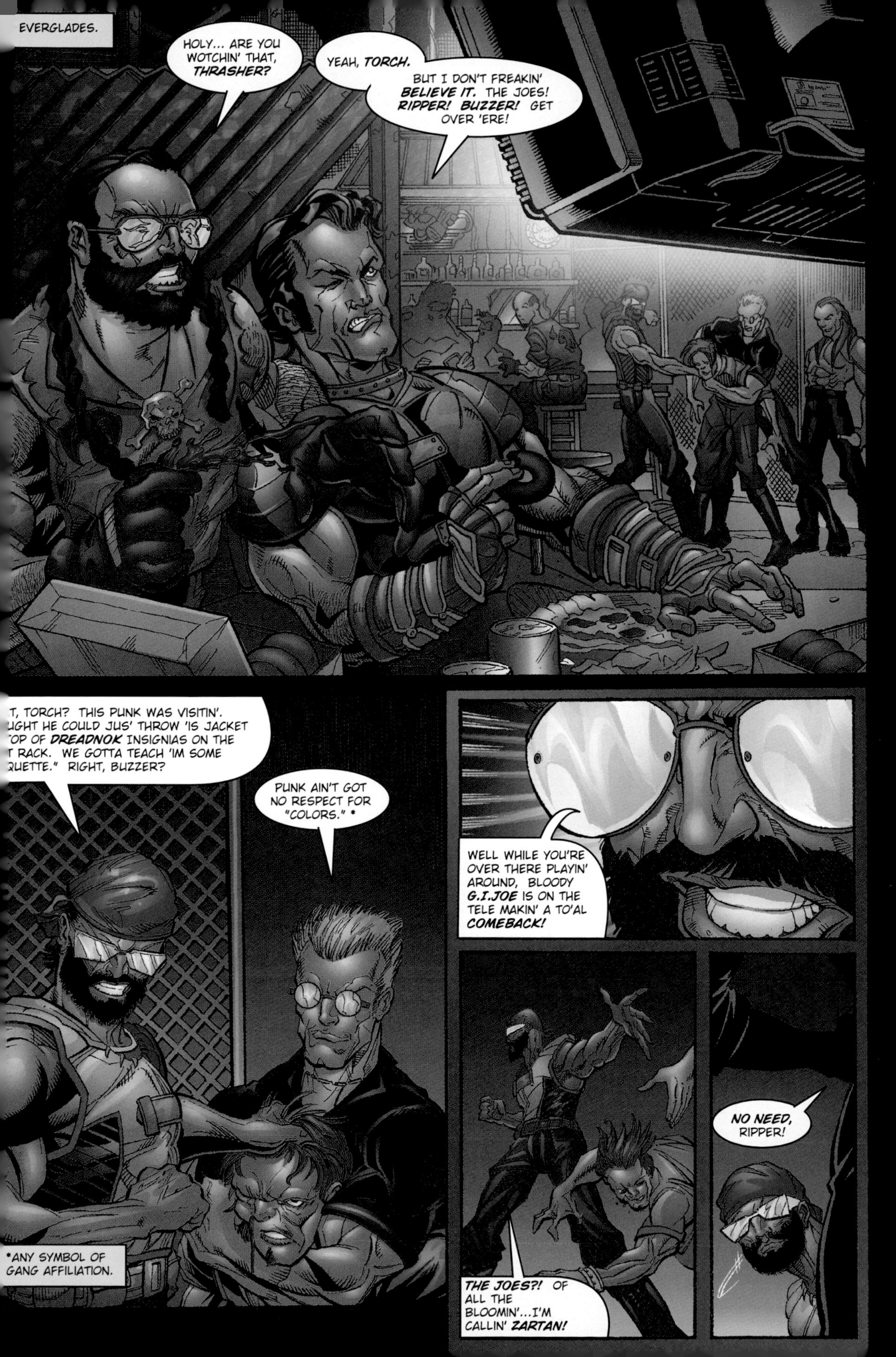
EVERGLADES.
HOLY... ARE YOU WOTCHIN' THAT, THRASHER?
YEAH, TORCH.
BUT I DON'T FREAKIN' BELIEVE IT. THE JOES! RIPPER! BUZZER! GET OVER 'ERE!
T, TORCH? THIS PUNK WAS VISITIN'. UGHT HE COULD JUS' THROW 'IS JACKET OP OF DREADNOK INSIGNIAS ON THE T RACK. WE GOTTA TEACH 'IM SOME QUETTE." RIGHT, BUZZER?
PUNK AIN'T GOT NO RESPECT FOR "COLORS." *
*ANY SYMBOL OF GANG AFFILIATION.
WELL WHILE YOU'RE OVER THERE PLAYIN' AROUND, BLOODY G.I.JOE IS ON THE TELE MAKIN' A TO'AL COMEBACK!
THE JOES?! OF ALL THE BLOOMIN'...I'M CALLIN' ZARTAN!
NO NEED, RIPPER!

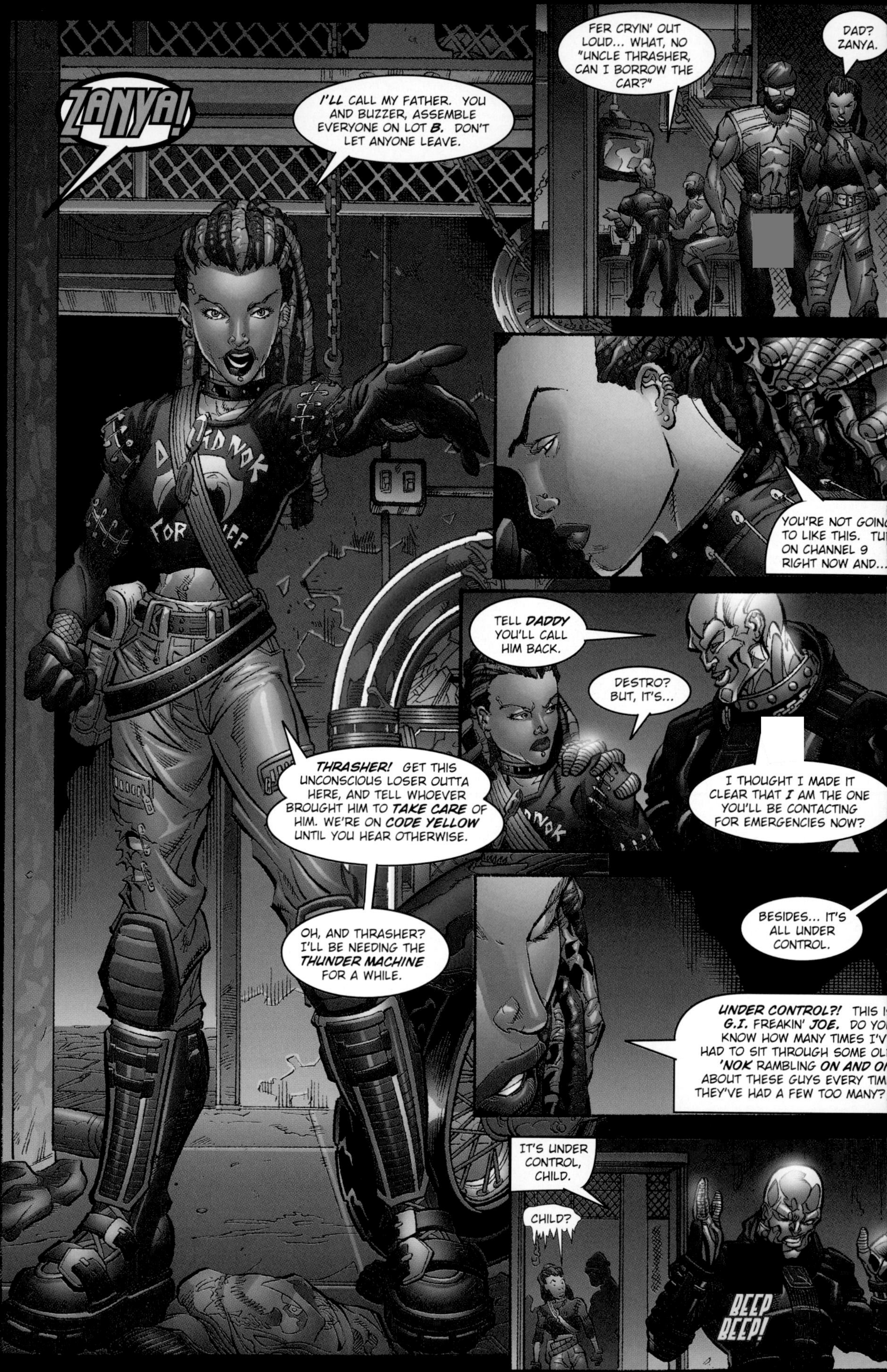
ZANYA!
I'LL CALL MY FATHER. YOU AND BUZZER, ASSEMBLE EVERYONE ON LOT B. DON'T LET ANYONE LEAVE.
THRASHER! GET THIS UNCONSCIOUS LOSER OUTTA HERE, AND TELL WHOEVER BROUGHT HIM TO TAKE CARE OF HIM. WE'RE ON CODE YELLOW UNTIL YOU HEAR OTHERWISE.
OH, AND THRASHER? I'LL BE NEEDING THE THUNDER MACHINE FOR A WHILE.
FER CRYIN' OUT LOUD... WHAT, NO "UNCLE THRASHER, CAN I BORROW THE CAR?"
DAD? ZANYA.
YOU'RE NOT GOING TO LIKE THIS. TU
ON CHANNEL 9
RIGHT NOW AND...
TELL DADDY YOU'LL CALL HIM BACK.
DESTRO? BUT, IT'S...
I THOUGHT I MADE IT CLEAR THAT I AM THE ONE YOU'LL BE CONTACTING FOR EMERGENCIES NOW?
BESIDES... IT'S ALL UNDER CONTROL.
UNDER CONTROL?! THIS IS
G.I. FREAKIN' JOE. DO YO
KNOW HOW MANY TIMES I'V
HAD TO SIT THROUGH SOME OL
'NOK RAMBLING ON AND O
ABOUT THESE GUYS EVERY TIM
THEY'VE HAD A FEW TOO MANY?
IT'S UNDER CONTROL, CHILD.
CHILD?
BEEP BEEP!

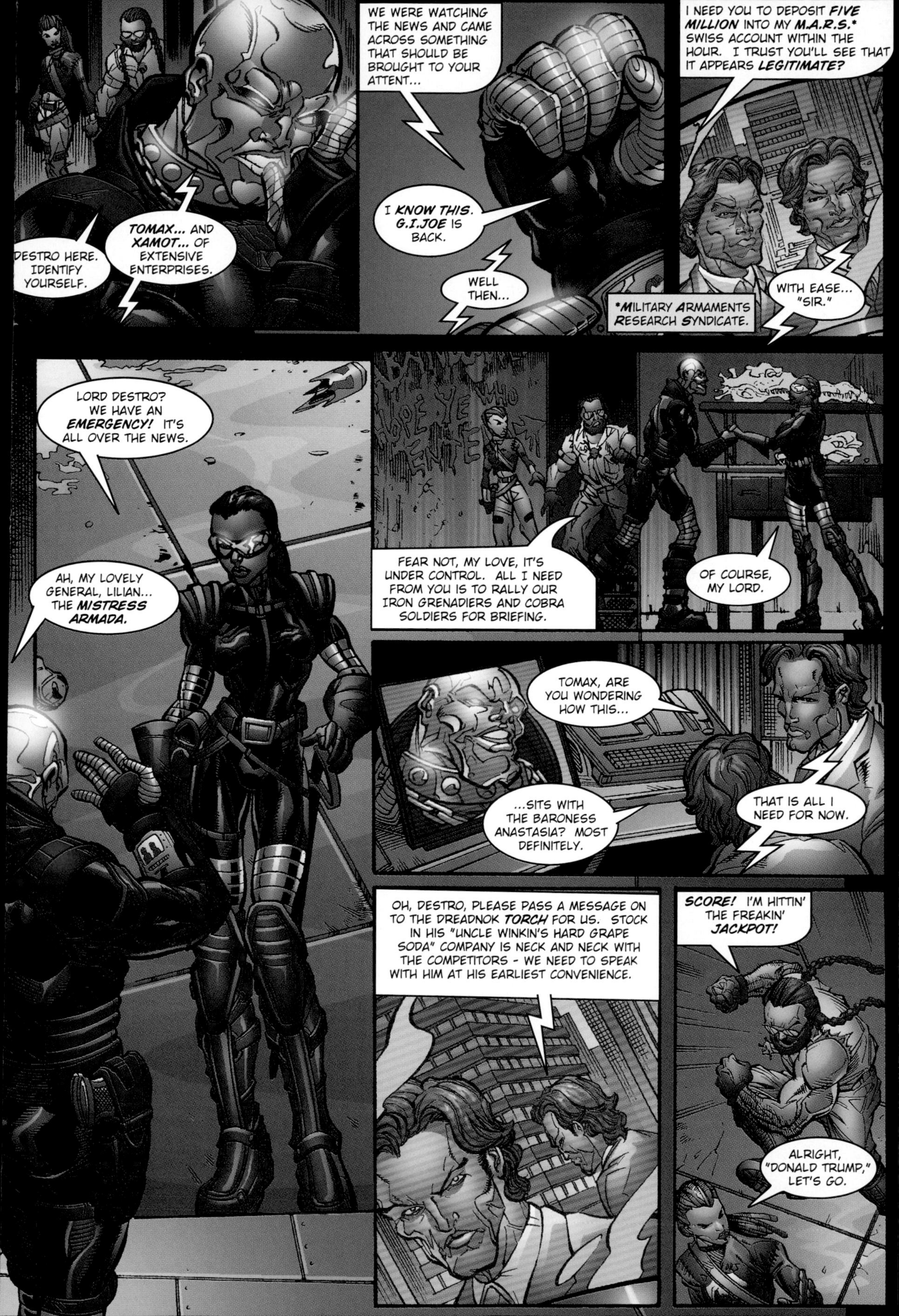

DESTRO HERE. IDENTIFY YOURSELF.
TOMAX... AND XAMOT... OF EXTENSIVE ENTERPRISES.
WE WERE WATCHING THE NEWS AND CAME ACROSS SOMETHING THAT SHOULD BE BROUGHT TO YOUR ATTENT...
I KNOW THIS. G.I.JOE IS BACK.
WELL THEN...
I NEED YOU TO DEPOSIT FIVE MILLION INTO MY M.A.R.S.* SWISS ACCOUNT WITHIN THE HOUR. I TRUST YOU'LL SEE THAT IT APPEARS LEGITIMATE?
WITH EASE... "SIR."
*MILITARY ARMAMENTS RESEARCH SYNDICATE.
LORD DESTRO? WE HAVE AN EMERGENCY! IT'S ALL OVER THE NEWS.
AH, MY LOVELY GENERAL, LILIAN... THE MISTRESS ARMADA.
FEAR NOT, MY LOVE, IT'S UNDER CONTROL. ALL I NEED FROM YOU IS TO RALLY OUR IRON GRENADIERS AND COBRA SOLDIERS FOR BRIEFING.
OF COURSE, MY LORD.
TOMAX, ARE YOU WONDERING HOW THIS...
...SITS WITH THE BARONESS ANASTASIA? MOST DEFINITELY.
THAT IS ALL I NEED FOR NOW.
OH, DESTRO, PLEASE PASS A MESSAGE ON TO THE DREADNOK TORCH FOR US. STOCK IN HIS "UNCLE WINKIN'S HARD GRAPE SODA" COMPANY IS NECK AND NECK WITH THE COMPETITORS - WE NEED TO SPEAK WITH HIM AT HIS EARLIEST CONVENIENCE.
SCORE! I'M HITTIN' THE FREAKIN' JACKPOT!
ALRIGHT, "DONALD TRUMP," LET'S GO.

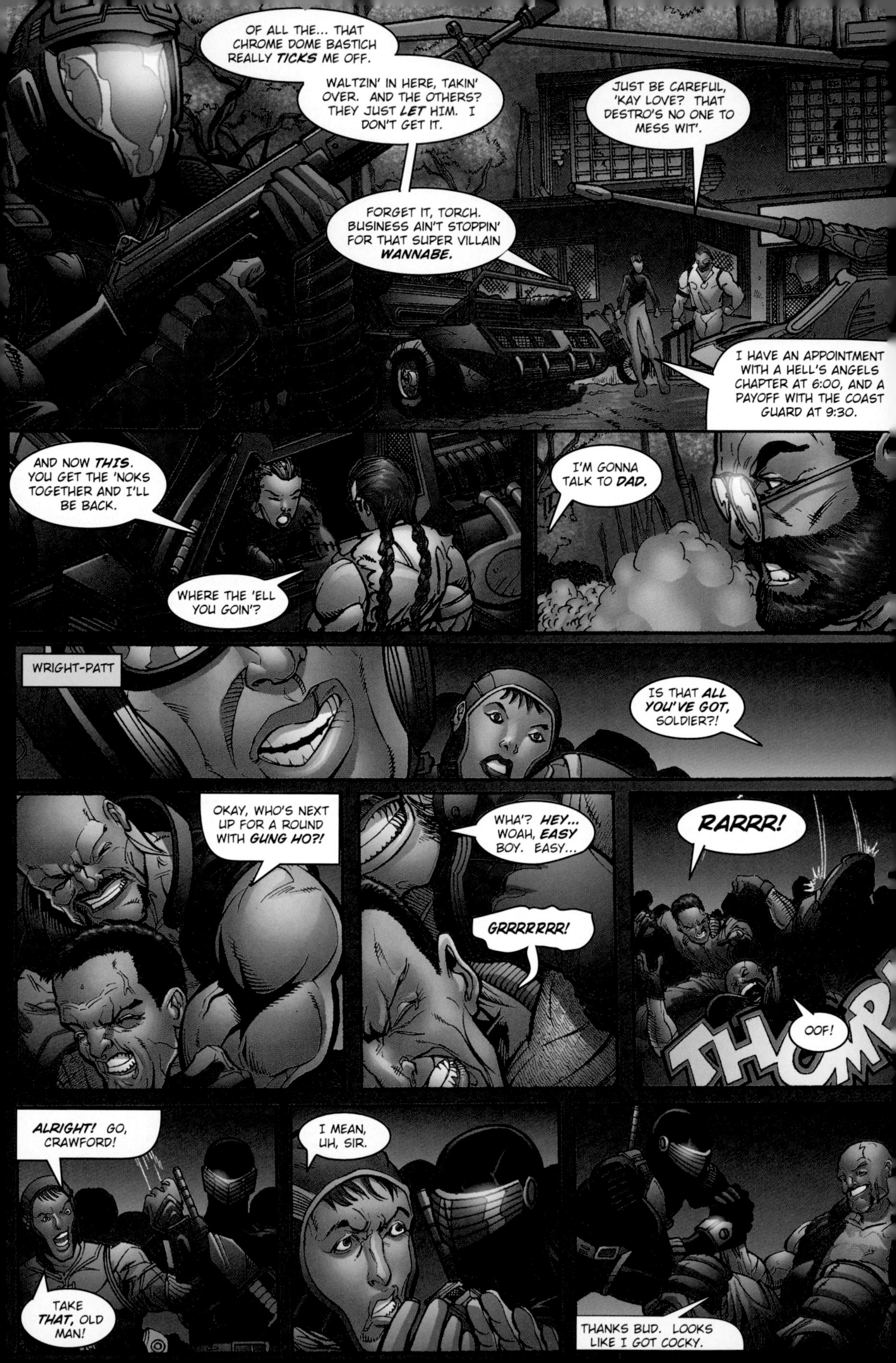
OF ALL THE... THAT CHROME DOME BASTICH REALLY TICKS ME OFF.
WALTZIN' IN HERE, TAKIN' OVER. AND THE OTHERS? THEY JUST LET HIM. I DON'T GET IT.
JUST BE CAREFUL, 'KAY LOVE? THAT DESTRO'S NO ONE TO MESS WIT'.
FORGET IT, TORCH. BUSINESS AIN'T STOPPIN' FOR THAT SUPER VILLAIN WANNABE.
I HAVE AN APPOINTMENT WITH A HELL'S ANGELS CHAPTER AT 6:00, AND A PAYOFF WITH THE COAST GUARD AT 9:30.
AND NOW THIS. YOU GET THE 'NOKS TOGETHER AND I'LL BE BACK.
WHERE THE 'ELL YOU GOIN'?
I'M GONNA TALK TO DAD.
WRIGHT-PATT
IS THAT ALL YOU'VE GOT, SOLDIER?!
OKAY, WHO'S NEXT UP FOR A ROUND WITH GUNG HO?!
WHA'? HEY... WOAH, EASY BOY. EASY...
GRRRRRRR!
RARRR!
OOF!
ALRIGHT! GO, CRAWFORD!
TAKE THAT, OLD MAN!
I MEAN, UH, SIR.
THANKS BUD. LOOKS LIKE I GOT COCKY.

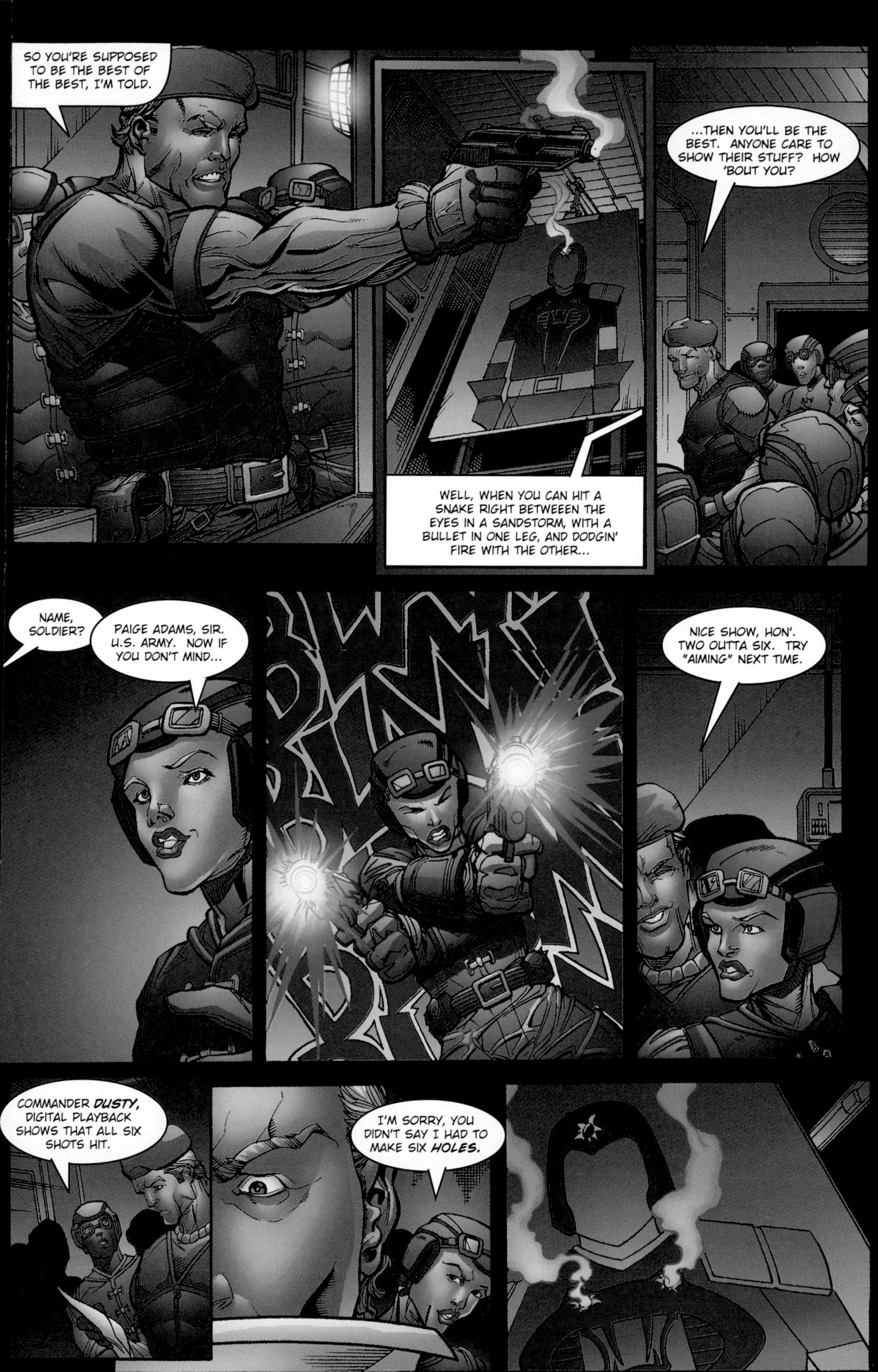
SO YOU'RE SUPPOSED TO BE THE BEST OF THE BEST, I'M TOLD.
WELL, WHEN YOU CAN HIT A SNAKE RIGHT BETWEEEN THE EYES IN A SANDSTORM, WITH A BULLET IN ONE LEG, AND DODGIN' FIRE WITH THE OTHER...
...THEN YOU'LL BE THE BEST. ANYONE CARE TO SHOW THEIR STUFF? HOW 'BOUT YOU?
NAME, SOLDIER?
PAIGE ADAMS, SIR. U.S. ARMY. NOW IF YOU DON'T MIND...
NICE SHOW, HON'. TWO OUTTA SIX. TRY "AIMING" NEXT TIME.
COMMANDER *DUSTY*, DIGITAL PLAYBACK SHOWS THAT ALL SIX SHOTS HIT.
I'M SORRY, YOU DIDN'T SAY I HAD TO MAKE SIX *HOLES.*

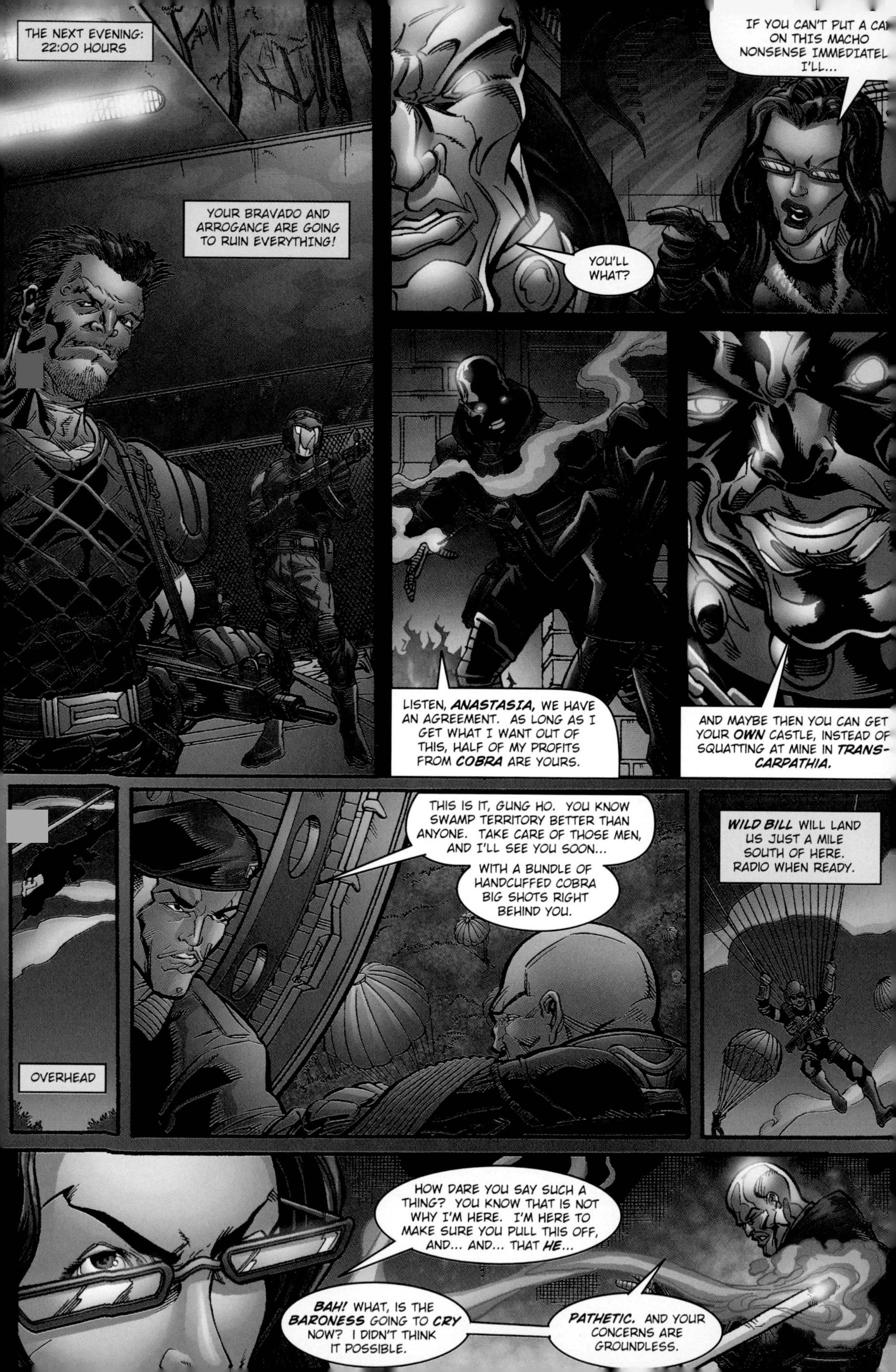
THE NEXT EVENING: 22:00 HOURS
YOUR BRAVADO AND ARROGANCE ARE GOING TO RUIN EVERYTHING!
IF YOU CAN'T PUT A CA ON THIS MACHO NONSENSE IMMEDIATEL I'LL...
YOU'LL WHAT?
LISTEN, ANASTASIA, WE HAVE AN AGREEMENT. AS LONG AS I GET WHAT I WANT OUT OF THIS, HALF OF MY PROFITS FROM COBRA ARE YOURS.
AND MAYBE THEN YOU CAN GET YOUR OWN CASTLE, INSTEAD OF SQUATTING AT MINE IN TRANS-CARPATHIA.
OVERHEAD
THIS IS IT, GUNG HO. YOU KNOW SWAMP TERRITORY BETTER THAN ANYONE. TAKE CARE OF THOSE MEN, AND I'LL SEE YOU SOON...
WITH A BUNDLE OF HANDCUFFED COBRA BIG SHOTS RIGHT BEHIND YOU.
WILD BILL WILL LAND US JUST A MILE SOUTH OF HERE. RADIO WHEN READY.
HOW DARE YOU SAY SUCH A THING? YOU KNOW THAT IS NOT WHY I'M HERE. I'M HERE TO MAKE SURE YOU PULL THIS OFF, AND... AND... THAT HE...
BAH! WHAT, IS THE BARONESS GOING TO CRY NOW? I DIDN'T THINK IT POSSIBLE.
PATHETIC. AND YOUR CONCERNS ARE GROUNDLESS.

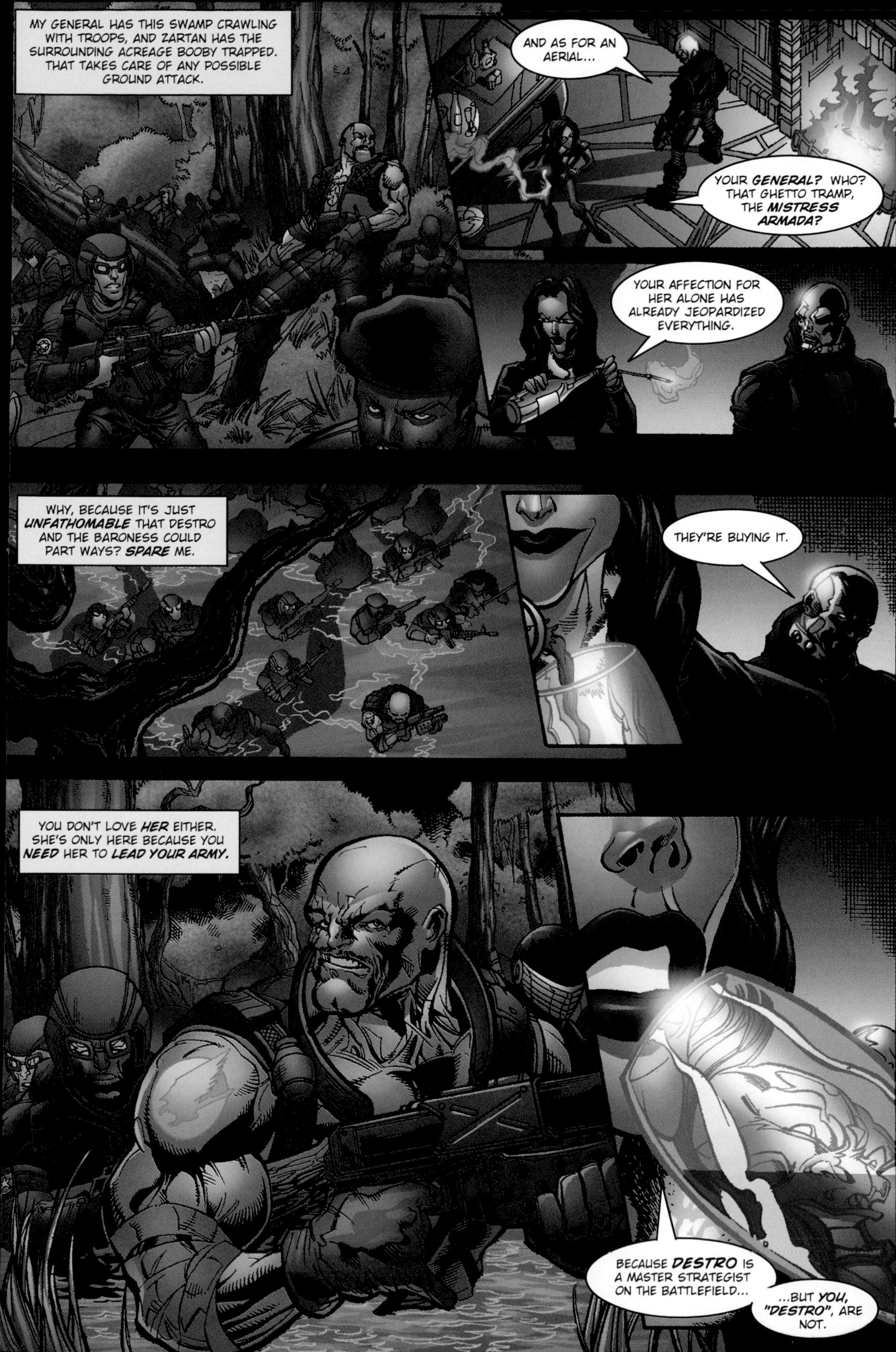
MY GENERAL HAS THIS SWAMP CRAWLING WITH TROOPS, AND ZARTAN HAS THE SURROUNDING ACREAGE BOOBY TRAPPED. THAT TAKES CARE OF ANY POSSIBLE GROUND ATTACK.
AND AS FOR AN AERIAL...
YOUR GENERAL? WHO? THAT GHETTO TRAMP, THE MISTRESS ARMADA?
YOUR AFFECTION FOR HER ALONE HAS ALREADY JEOPARDIZED EVERYTHING.
WHY, BECAUSE IT'S JUST UNFATHOMABLE THAT DESTRO AND THE BARONESS COULD PART WAYS? SPARE ME.
THEY'RE BUYING IT.
YOU DON'T LOVE HER EITHER. SHE'S ONLY HERE BECAUSE YOU NEED HER TO LEAD YOUR ARMY.
BECAUSE DESTRO IS A MASTER STRATEGIST ON THE BATTLEFIELD...
...BUT YOU, "DESTRO", ARE NOT.

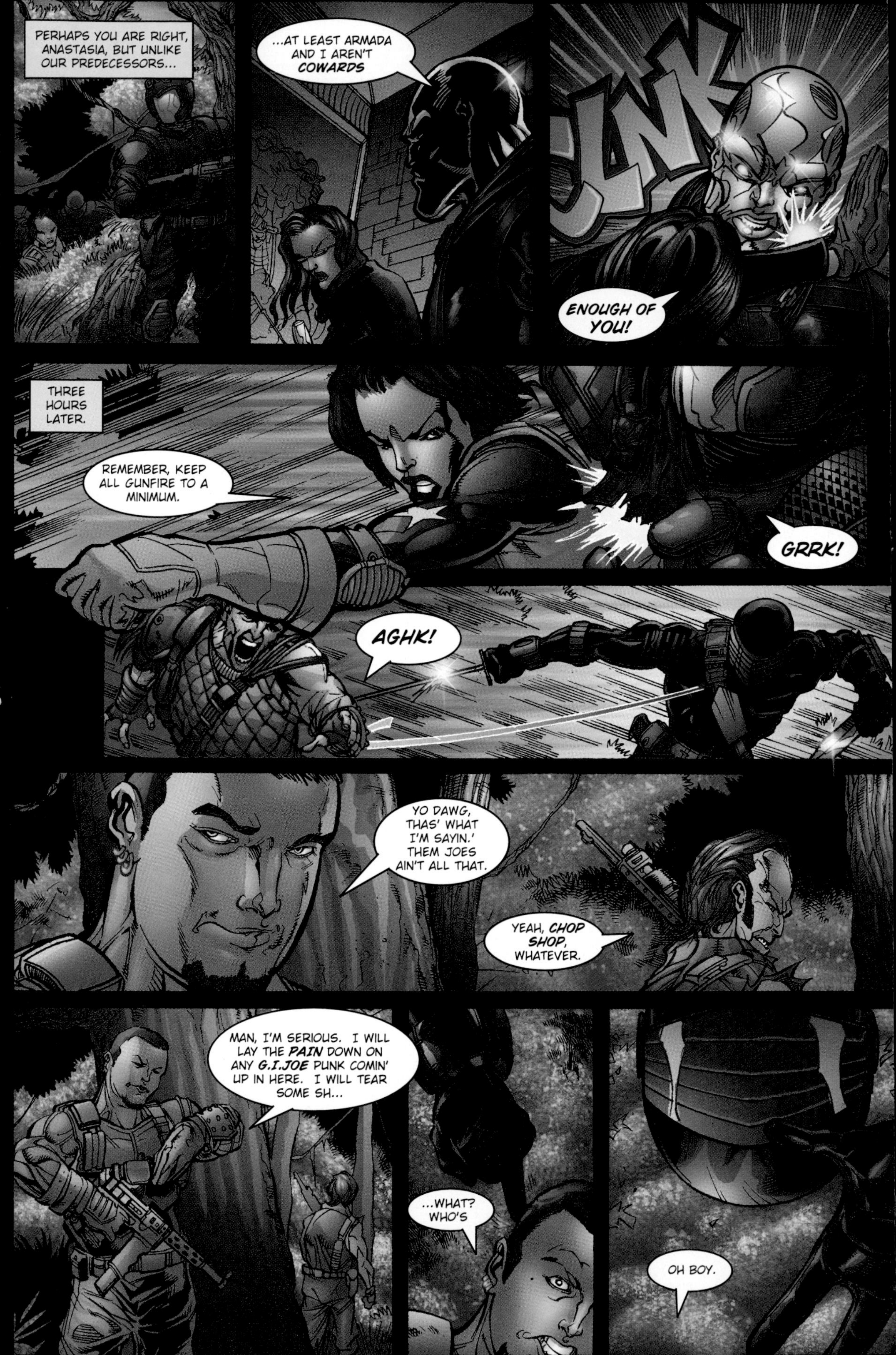
PERHAPS YOU ARE RIGHT, ANASTASIA, BUT UNLIKE OUR PREDECESSORS...
...AT LEAST ARMADA AND I AREN'T COWARDS
ENOUGH OF YOU!
THREE HOURS LATER.
REMEMBER, KEEP ALL GUNFIRE TO A MINIMUM.
GRRK!
AGHK!
YO DAWG, THAS' WHAT I'M SAYIN.' THEM JOES AIN'T ALL THAT.
YEAH, CHOP SHOP, WHATEVER.
MAN, I'M SERIOUS. I WILL LAY THE PAIN DOWN ON ANY G.I.JOE PUNK COMIN' UP IN HERE. I WILL TEAR SOME SH...
...WHAT? WHO'S
OH BOY.

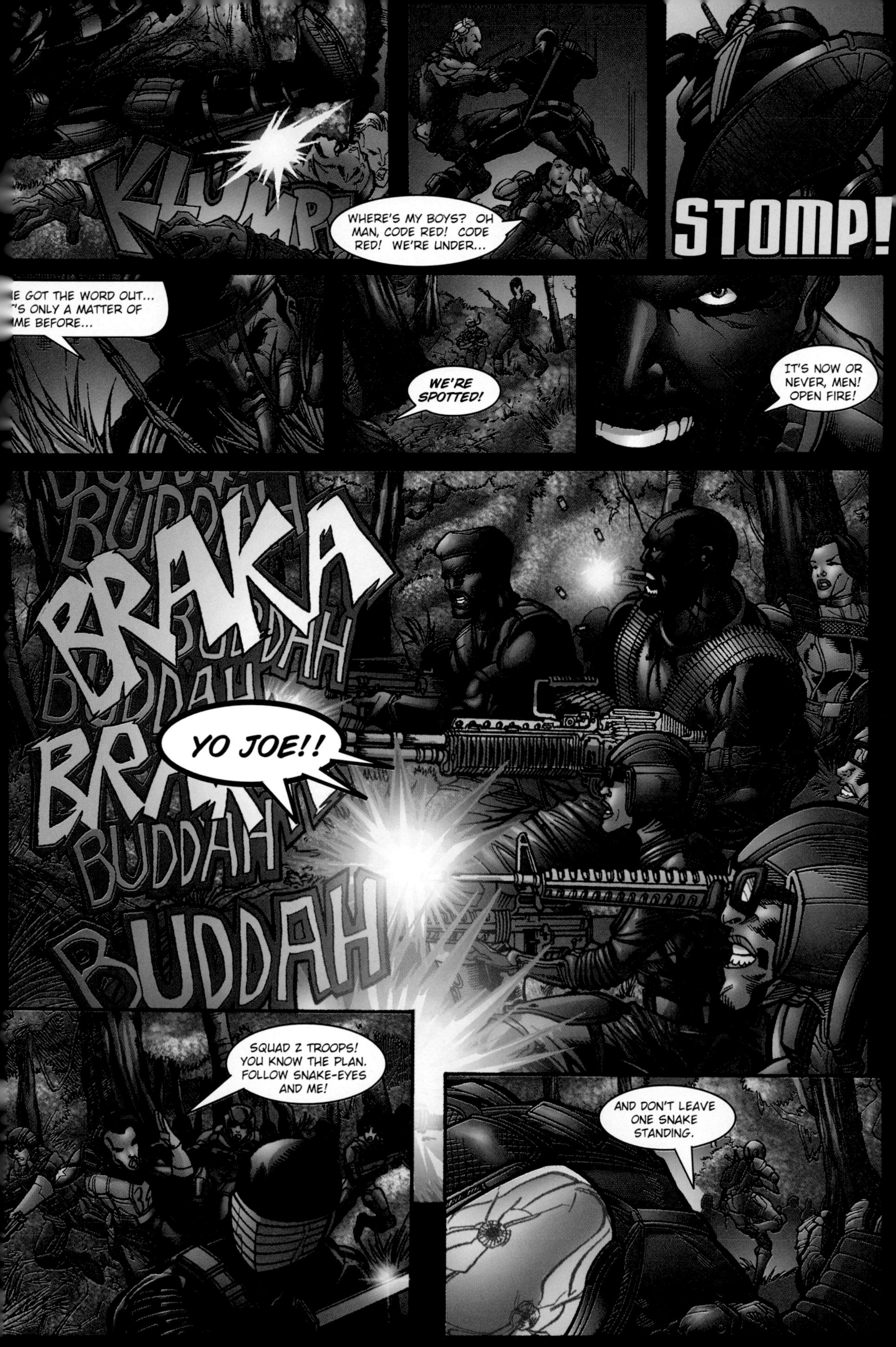
KLUMP!
WHERE'S MY BOYS? OH MAN, CODE RED! CODE RED! WE'RE UNDER...
STOMP!
E GOT THE WORD OUT... 'S ONLY A MATTER OF ME BEFORE...
WE'RE SPOTTED!
IT'S NOW OR NEVER, MEN! OPEN FIRE!
BUDDAH BUDDAH
BRAKA
BUDDAH BUDDAH
YO JOE!!
BUDDAH
BUDDAH
SQUAD Z TROOPS! YOU KNOW THE PLAN. FOLLOW SNAKE-EYES AND ME!
AND DON'T LEAVE ONE SNAKE STANDING.

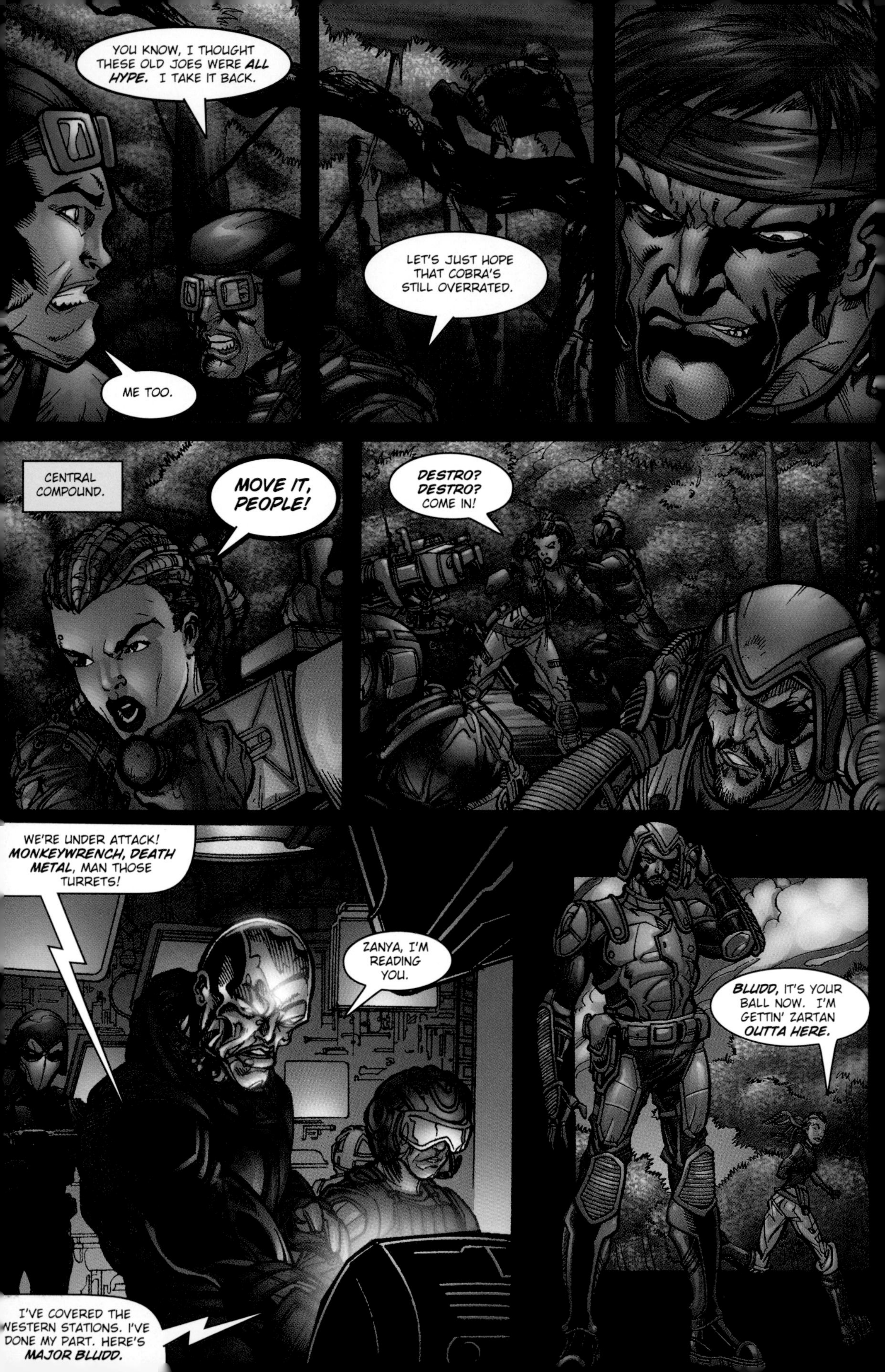
YOU KNOW, I THOUGHT THESE OLD JOES WERE ALL HYPE. I TAKE IT BACK.
ME TOO.
LET'S JUST HOPE THAT COBRA'S STILL OVERRATED.
CENTRAL COMPOUND.
MOVE IT, PEOPLE!
DESTRO? DESTRO? COME IN!
WE'RE UNDER ATTACK! MONKEYWRENCH, DEATH METAL, MAN THOSE TURRETS!
ZANYA, I'M READING YOU.
I'VE COVERED THE WESTERN STATIONS. I'VE DONE MY PART. HERE'S MAJOR BLUDD.
BLUDD, IT'S YOUR BALL NOW. I'M GETTIN' ZARTAN OUTTA HERE.

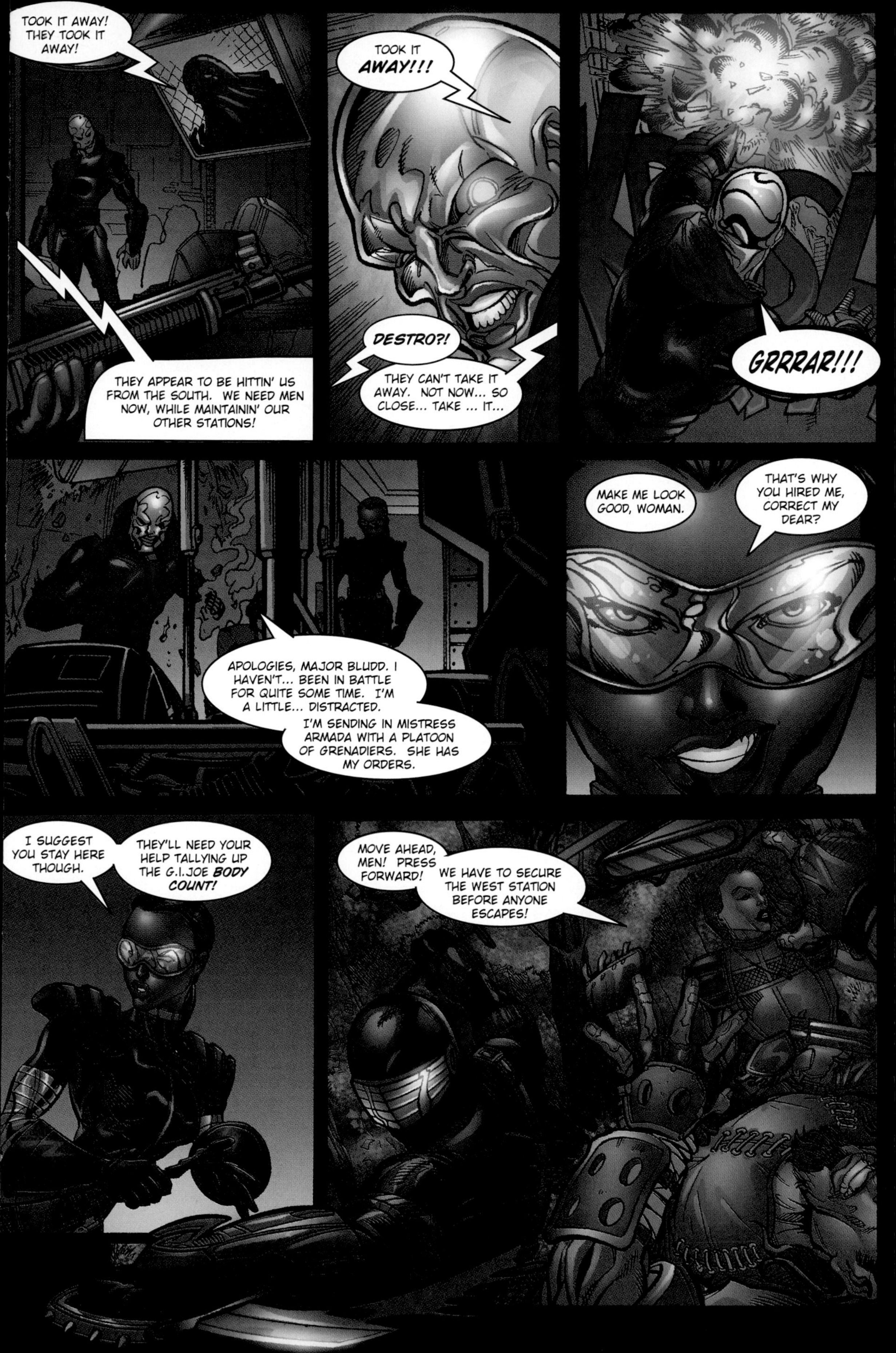
TOOK IT AWAY! THEY TOOK IT AWAY!
THEY APPEAR TO BE HITTIN' US FROM THE SOUTH. WE NEED MEN NOW, WHILE MAINTAININ' OUR OTHER STATIONS!
TOOK IT AWAY!!!
DESTRO?!
THEY CAN'T TAKE IT AWAY. NOT NOW... SO CLOSE... TAKE ... IT...
GRRRAR!!!
APOLOGIES, MAJOR BLUDD. I HAVEN'T... BEEN IN BATTLE FOR QUITE SOME TIME. I'M A LITTLE... DISTRACTED.
I'M SENDING IN MISTRESS ARMADA WITH A PLATOON OF GRENADIERS. SHE HAS MY ORDERS.
MAKE ME LOOK GOOD, WOMAN.
THAT'S WHY YOU HIRED ME, CORRECT MY DEAR?
I SUGGEST YOU STAY HERE THOUGH.
THEY'LL NEED YOUR HELP TALLYING UP THE G.I.JOE BODY COUNT!
MOVE AHEAD, MEN! PRESS FORWARD!
WE HAVE TO SECURE THE WEST STATION BEFORE ANYONE ESCAPES!

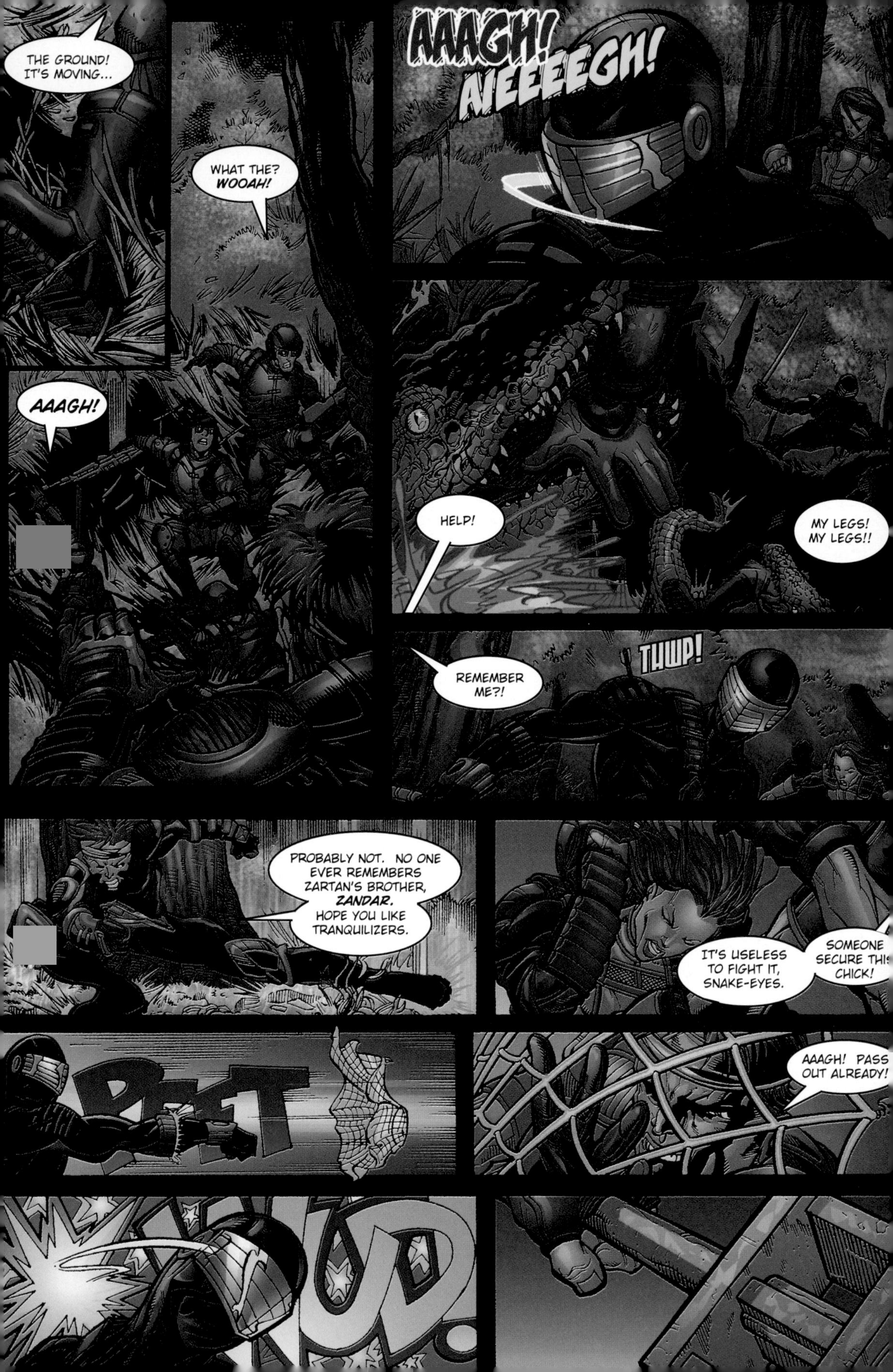
THE GROUND! IT'S MOVING...
WHAT THE? WOOAH!
AAAGH! AIEEEEGH!
AAAGH!
HELP!
MY LEGS! MY LEGS!!
REMEMBER ME?!
THWP!
PROBABLY NOT. NO ONE EVER REMEMBERS ZARTAN'S BROTHER, ZANDAR. HOPE YOU LIKE TRANQUILIZERS.
IT'S USELESS TO FIGHT IT, SNAKE-EYES.
SOMEONE SECURE THIS CHICK!
AAAGH! PASS OUT ALREADY!

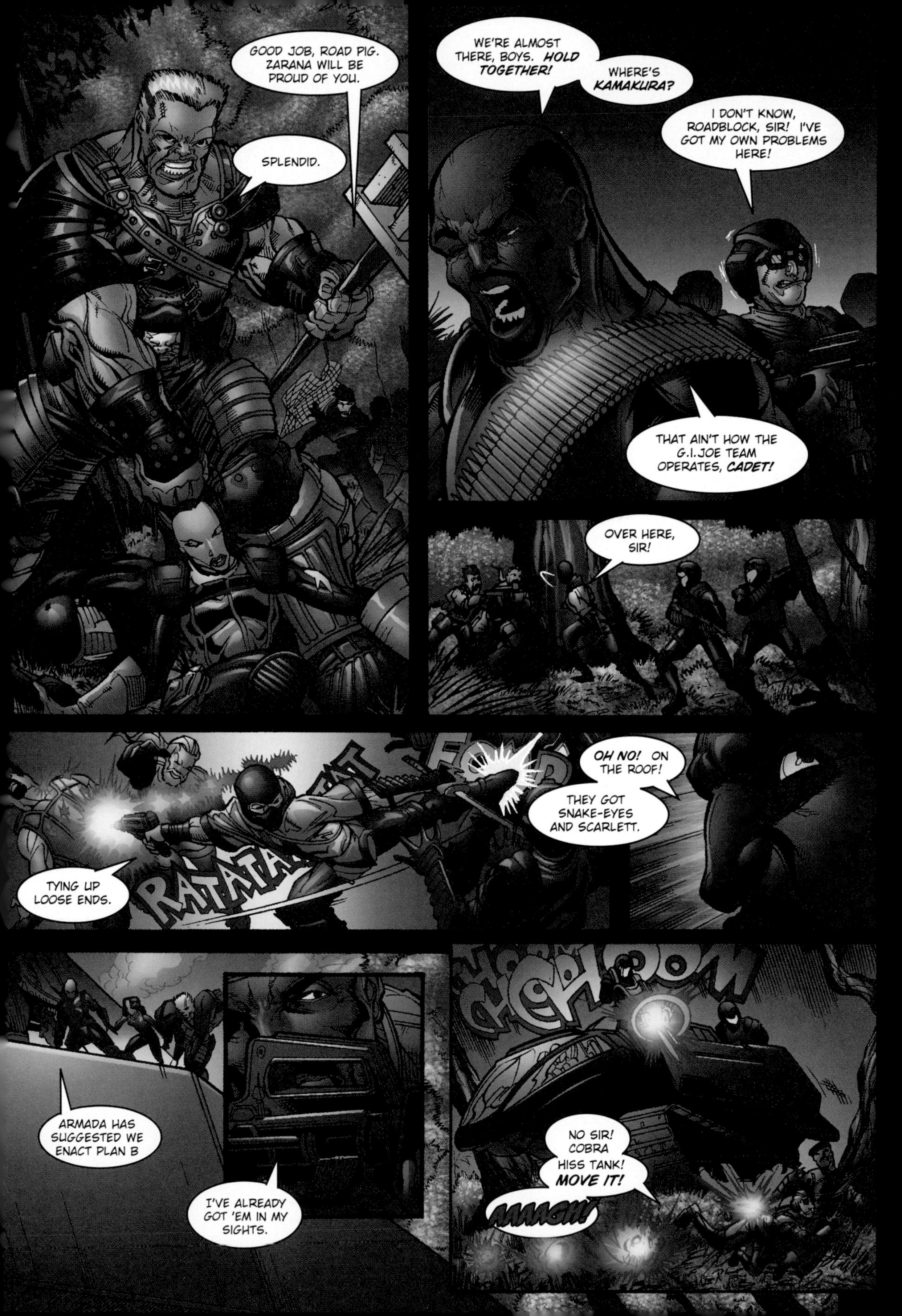
GOOD JOB, ROAD PIG. ZARANA WILL BE PROUD OF YOU.
SPLENDID.
WE'RE ALMOST THERE, BOYS. **HOLD TOGETHER!**
WHERE'S **KAMAKURA?**
I DON'T KNOW, ROADBLOCK, SIR! I'VE GOT MY OWN PROBLEMS HERE!
THAT AIN'T HOW THE G.I.JOE TEAM OPERATES, **CADET!**
OVER HERE, SIR!
TYING UP LOOSE ENDS.
RATATAT
OH NO! ON THE ROOF!
THEY GOT SNAKE-EYES AND SCARLETT.
ARMADA HAS SUGGESTED WE ENACT PLAN B
I'VE ALREADY GOT 'EM IN MY SIGHTS.
NO SIR! COBRA HISS TANK! **MOVE IT!**
AAAAGH!

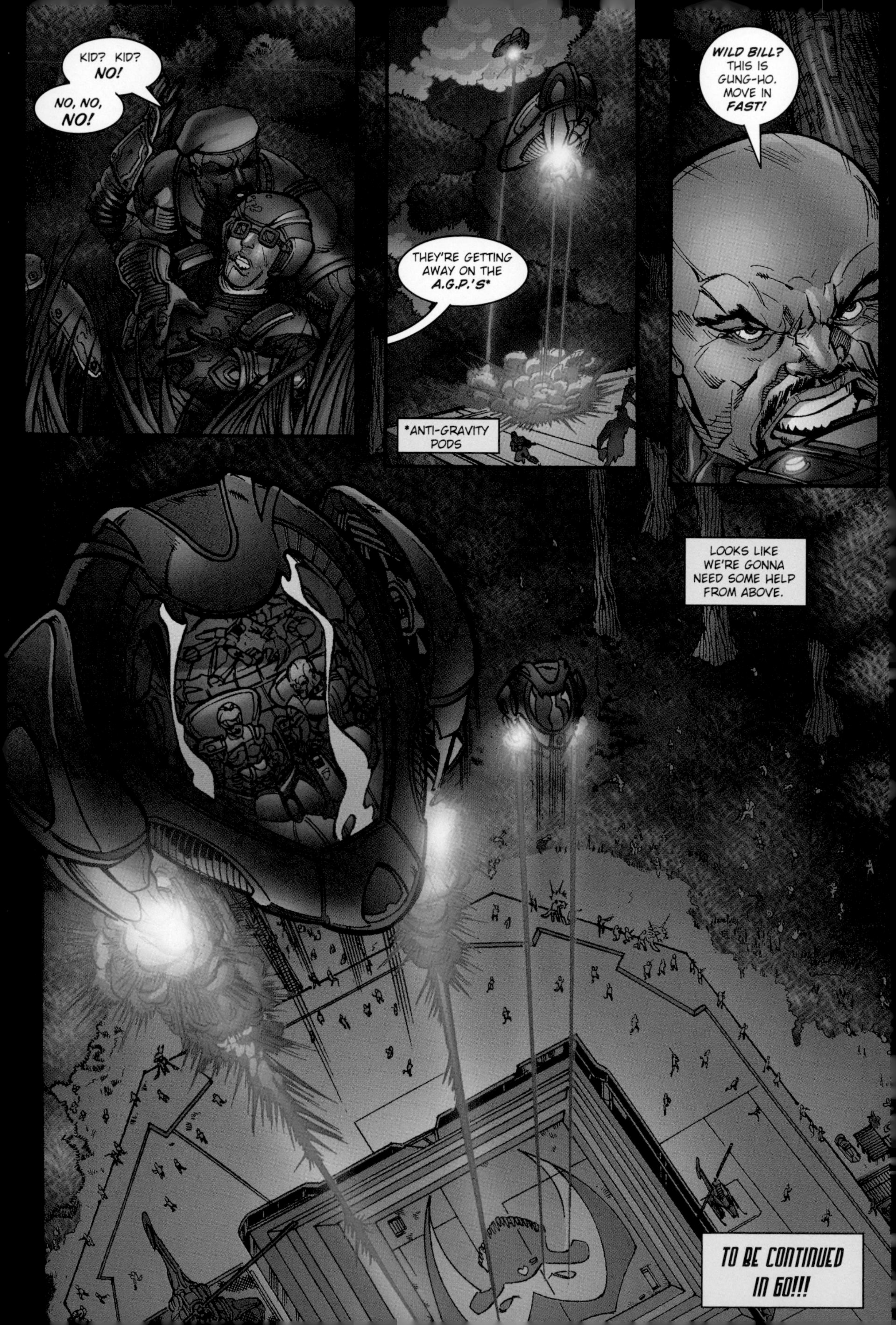
KID? KID? NO!
NO, NO, NO!
THEY'RE GETTING AWAY ON THE A.G.P.'S*
*ANTI-GRAVITY PODS
WILD BILL? THIS IS GUNG-HO. MOVE IN FAST!
LOOKS LIKE WE'RE GONNA NEED SOME HELP FROM ABOVE.
TO BE CONTINUED IN 60!!!

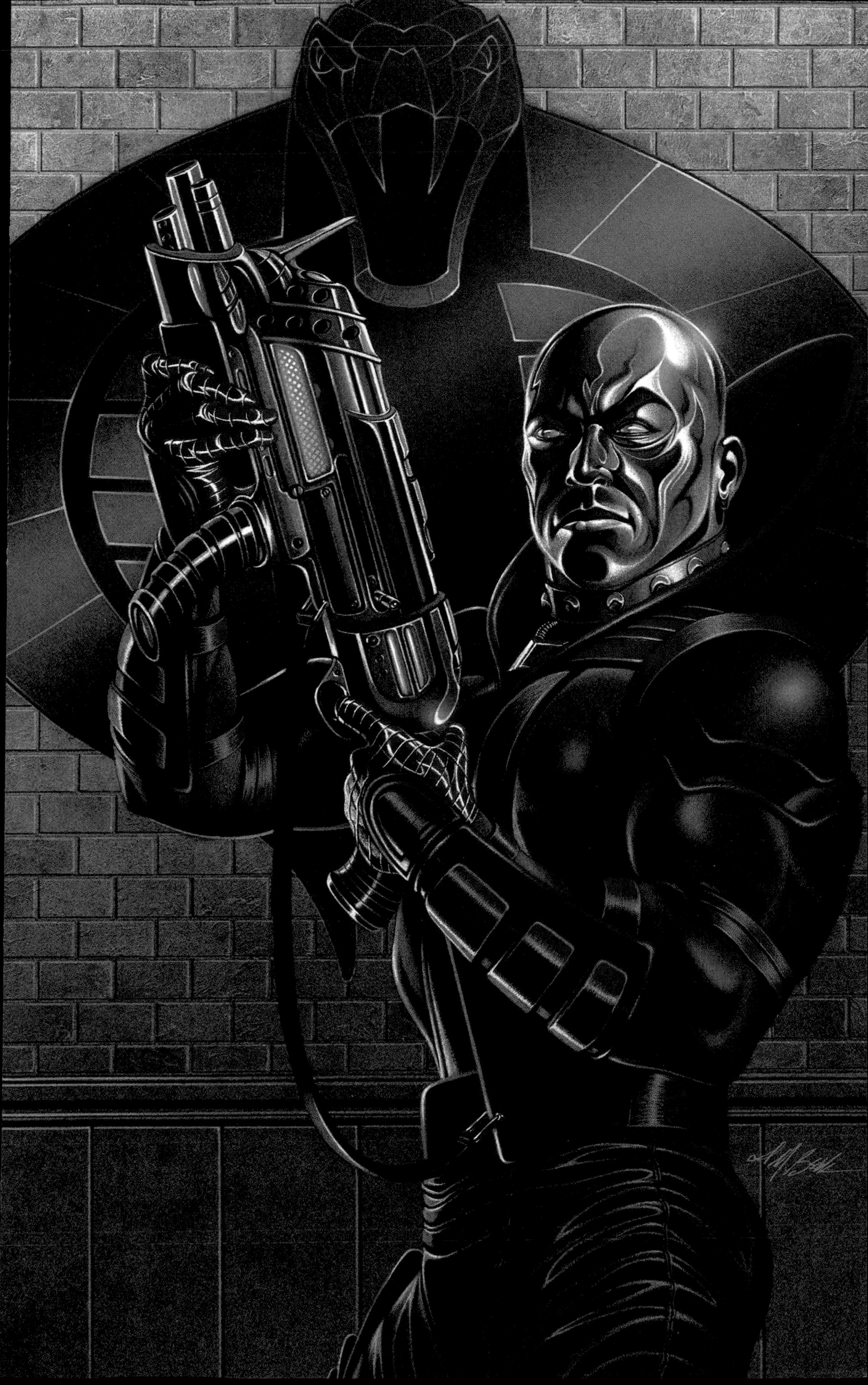

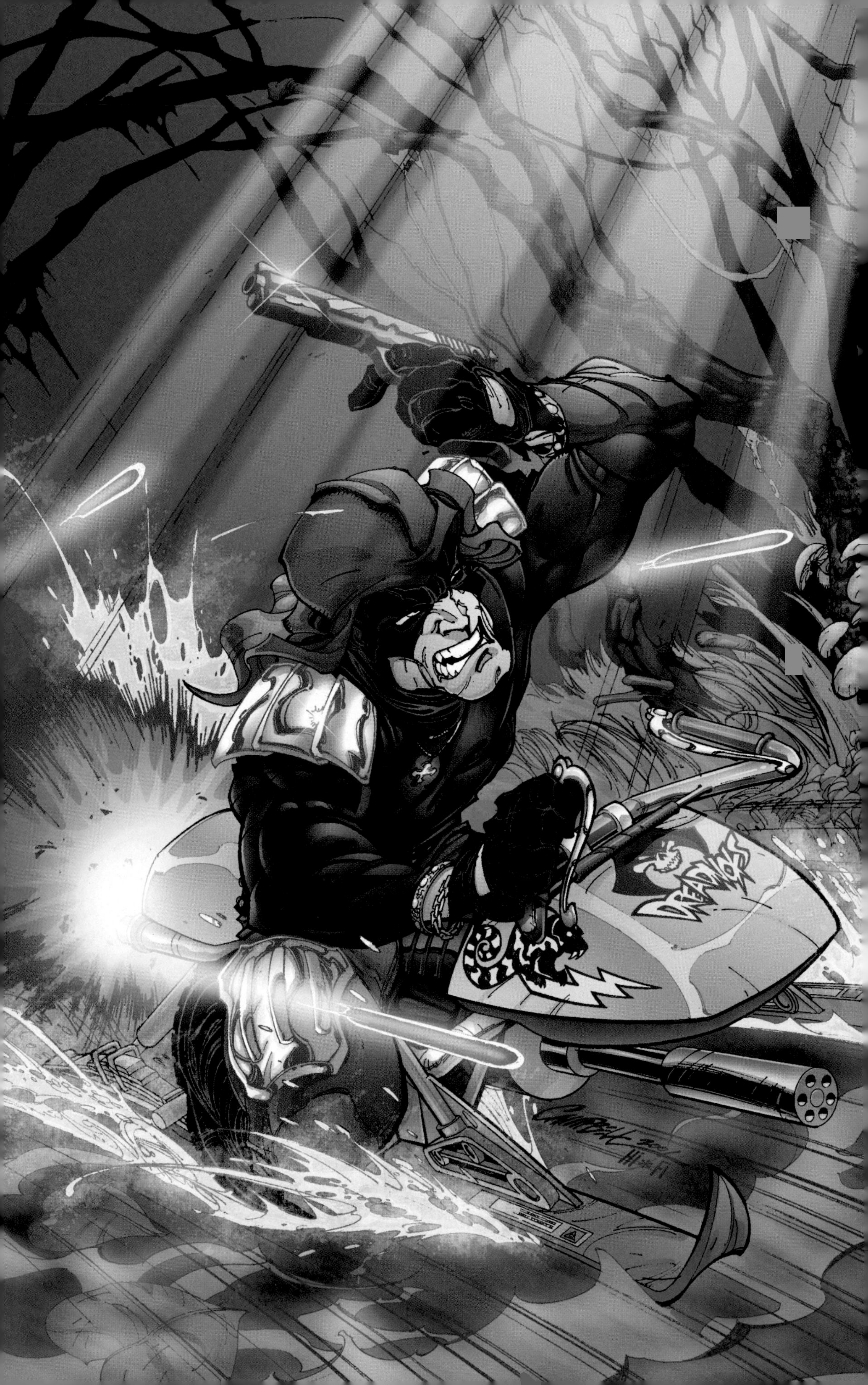

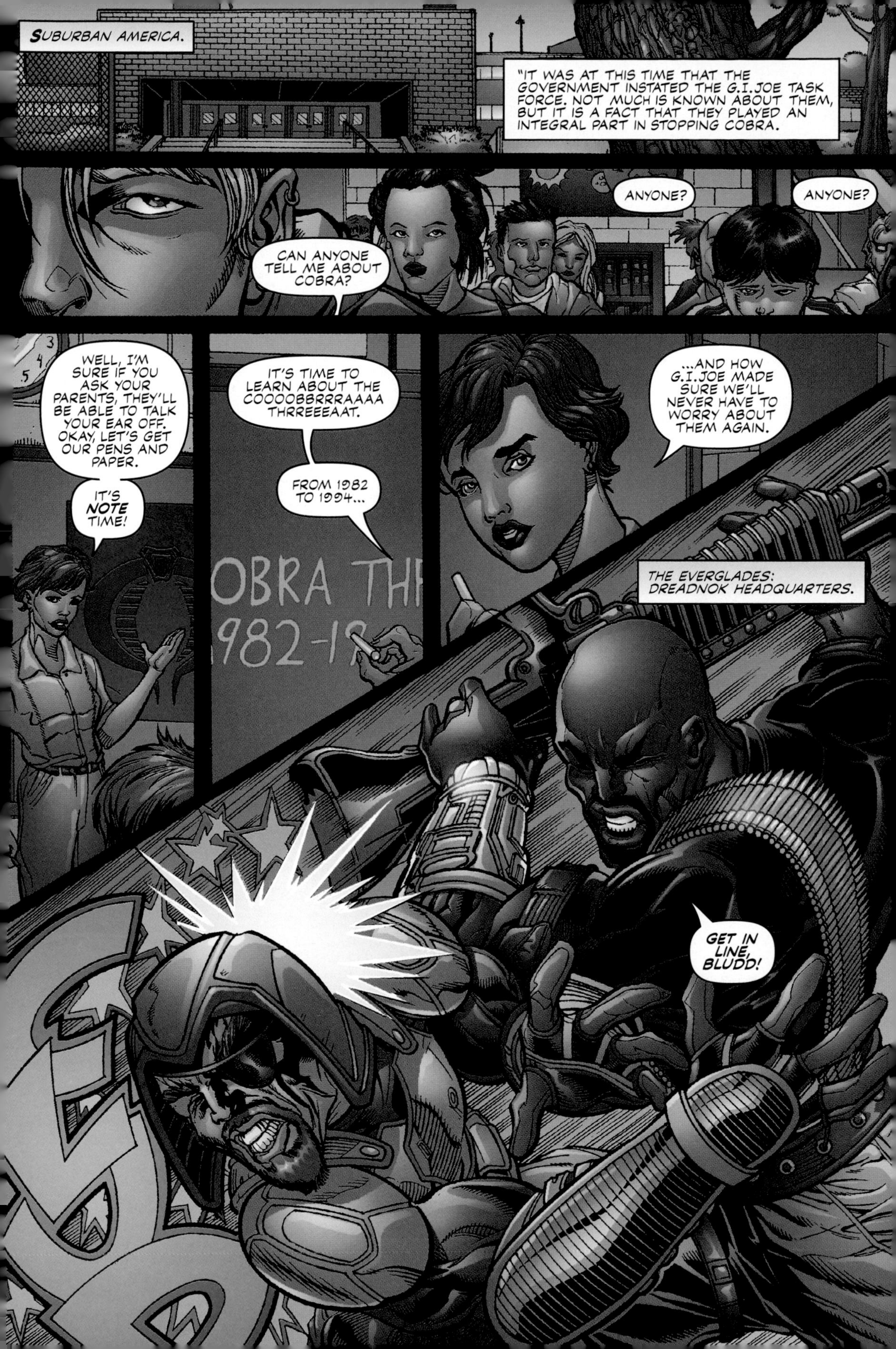
SUBURBAN AMERICA.
"IT WAS AT THIS TIME THAT THE GOVERNMENT INSTATED THE G.I.JOE TASK FORCE. NOT MUCH IS KNOWN ABOUT THEM, BUT IT IS A FACT THAT THEY PLAYED AN INTEGRAL PART IN STOPPING COBRA.
CAN ANYONE TELL ME ABOUT COBRA?
ANYONE?
ANYONE?
WELL, I'M SURE IF YOU ASK YOUR PARENTS, THEY'LL BE ABLE TO TALK YOUR EAR OFF. OKAY, LET'S GET OUR PENS AND PAPER.
IT'S NOTE TIME!
IT'S TIME TO LEARN ABOUT THE COOOOBBRRRAAAA THRREEEAAT.
FROM 1982 TO 1994...
OBRA THR
982-19
...AND HOW G.I.JOE MADE SURE WE'LL NEVER HAVE TO WORRY ABOUT THEM AGAIN.
THE EVERGLADES: DREADNOK HEADQUARTERS.
GET IN LINE, BLUDD!

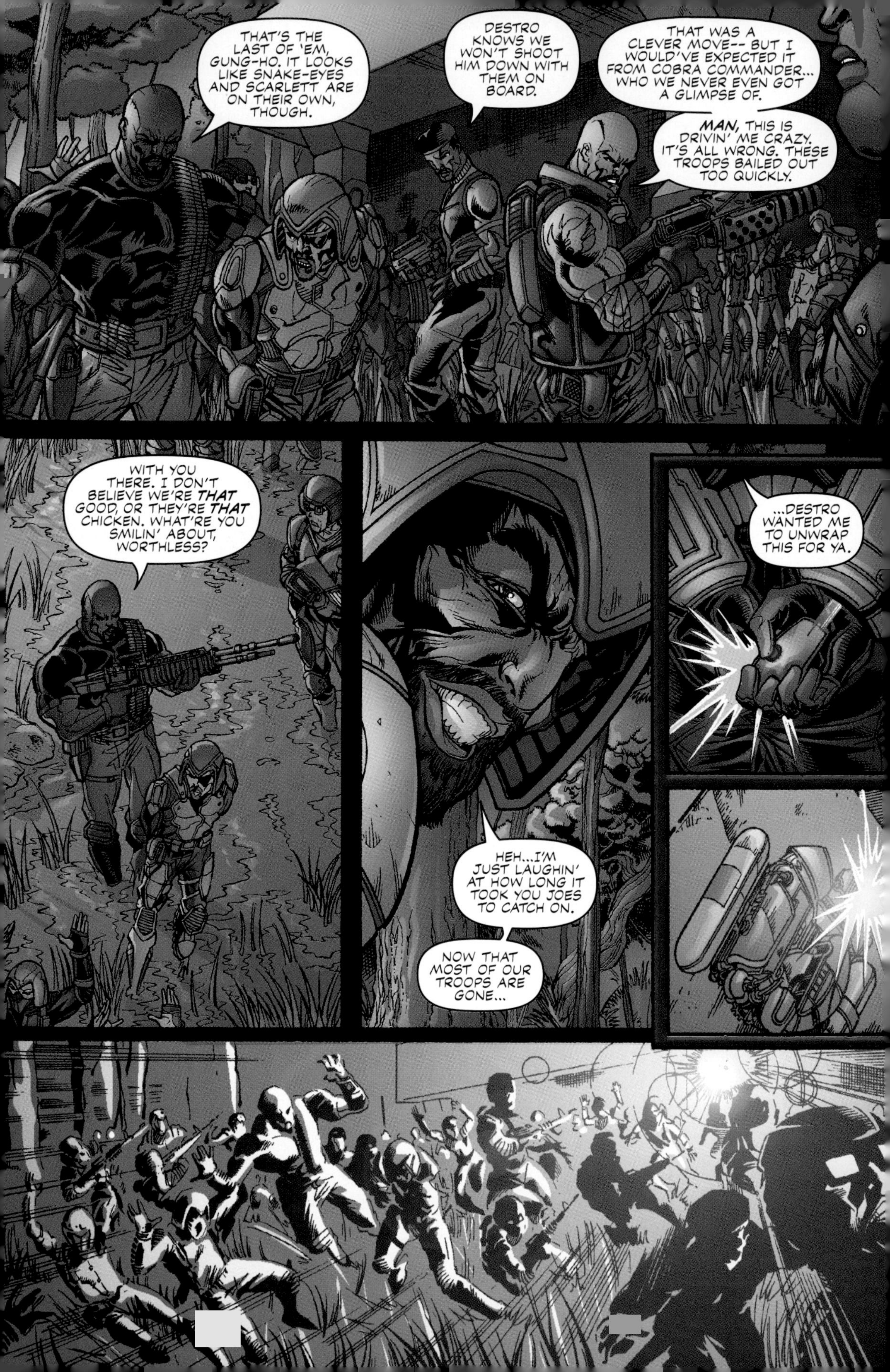
THAT'S THE LAST OF 'EM, GUNG-HO. IT LOOKS LIKE SNAKE-EYES AND SCARLETT ARE ON THEIR OWN, THOUGH.
DESTRO KNOWS WE WON'T SHOOT HIM DOWN WITH THEM ON BOARD.
THAT WAS A CLEVER MOVE-- BUT I WOULD'VE EXPECTED IT FROM COBRA COMMANDER... WHO WE NEVER EVEN GOT A GLIMPSE OF.
MAN, THIS IS DRIVIN' ME CRAZY. IT'S ALL WRONG. THESE TROOPS BAILED OUT TOO QUICKLY.
WITH YOU THERE. I DON'T BELIEVE WE'RE THAT GOOD, OR THEY'RE THAT CHICKEN. WHAT'RE YOU SMILIN' ABOUT, WORTHLESS?
HEH...I'M JUST LAUGHIN' AT HOW LONG IT TOOK YOU JOES TO CATCH ON.
NOW THAT MOST OF OUR TROOPS ARE GONE...
...DESTRO WANTED ME TO UNWRAP THIS FOR YA.

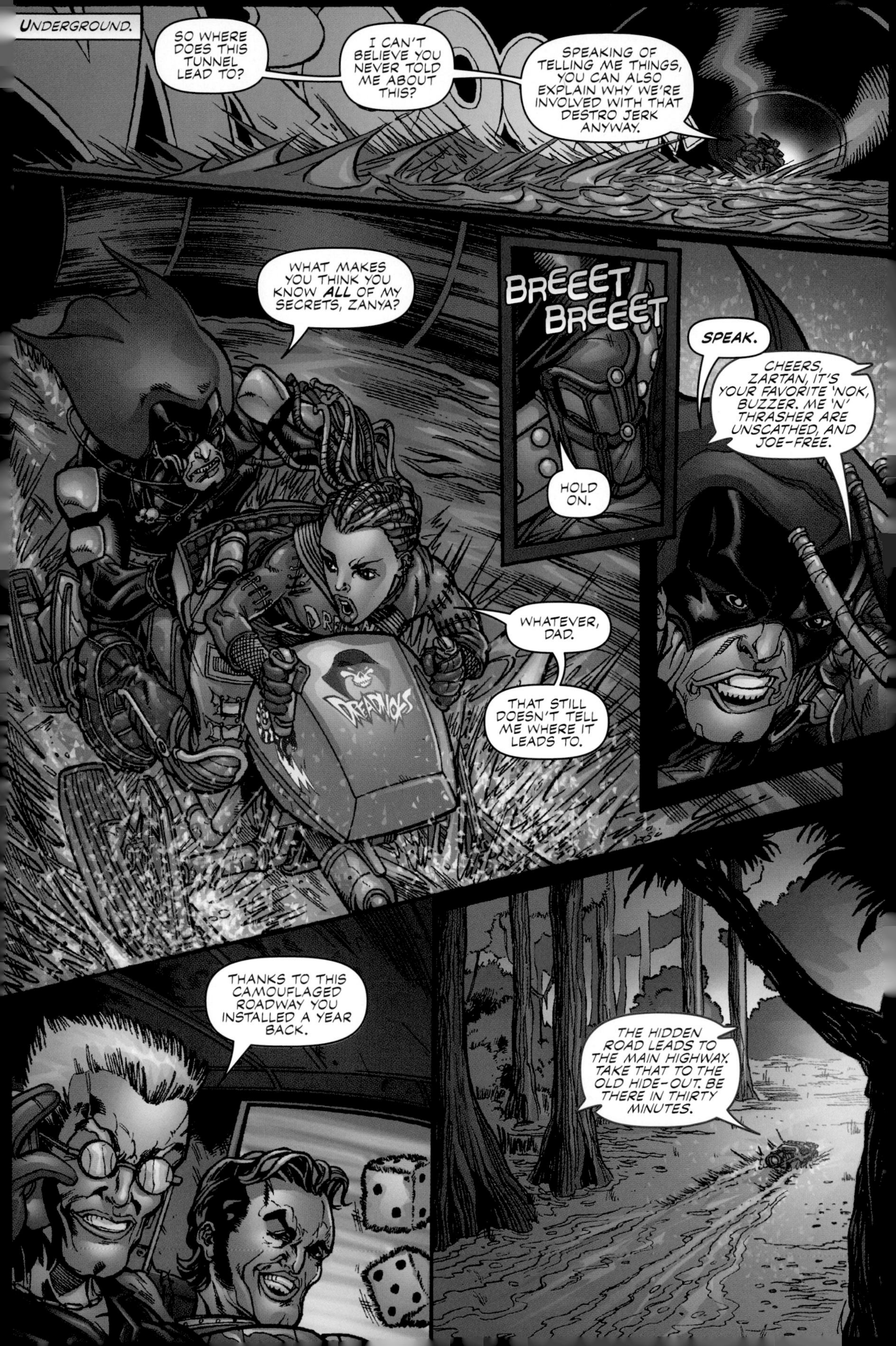
UNDERGROUND.
SO WHERE DOES THIS TUNNEL LEAD TO?
I CAN'T BELIEVE YOU NEVER TOLD ME ABOUT THIS?
SPEAKING OF TELLING ME THINGS, YOU CAN ALSO EXPLAIN WHY WE'RE INVOLVED WITH THAT DESTRO JERK ANYWAY.
WHAT MAKES YOU THINK YOU KNOW ALL OF MY SECRETS, ZANYA?
WHATEVER, DAD.
THAT STILL DOESN'T TELL ME WHERE IT LEADS TO.
BREEET BREEET
HOLD ON.
SPEAK.
CHEERS, ZARTAN, IT'S YOUR FAVORITE 'NOK, BUZZER. ME 'N' THRASHER ARE UNSCATHED, AND JOE-FREE.
THANKS TO THIS CAMOUFLAGED ROADWAY YOU INSTALLED A YEAR BACK.
THE HIDDEN ROAD LEADS TO THE MAIN HIGHWAY. TAKE THAT TO THE OLD HIDE-OUT. BE THERE IN THIRTY MINUTES.

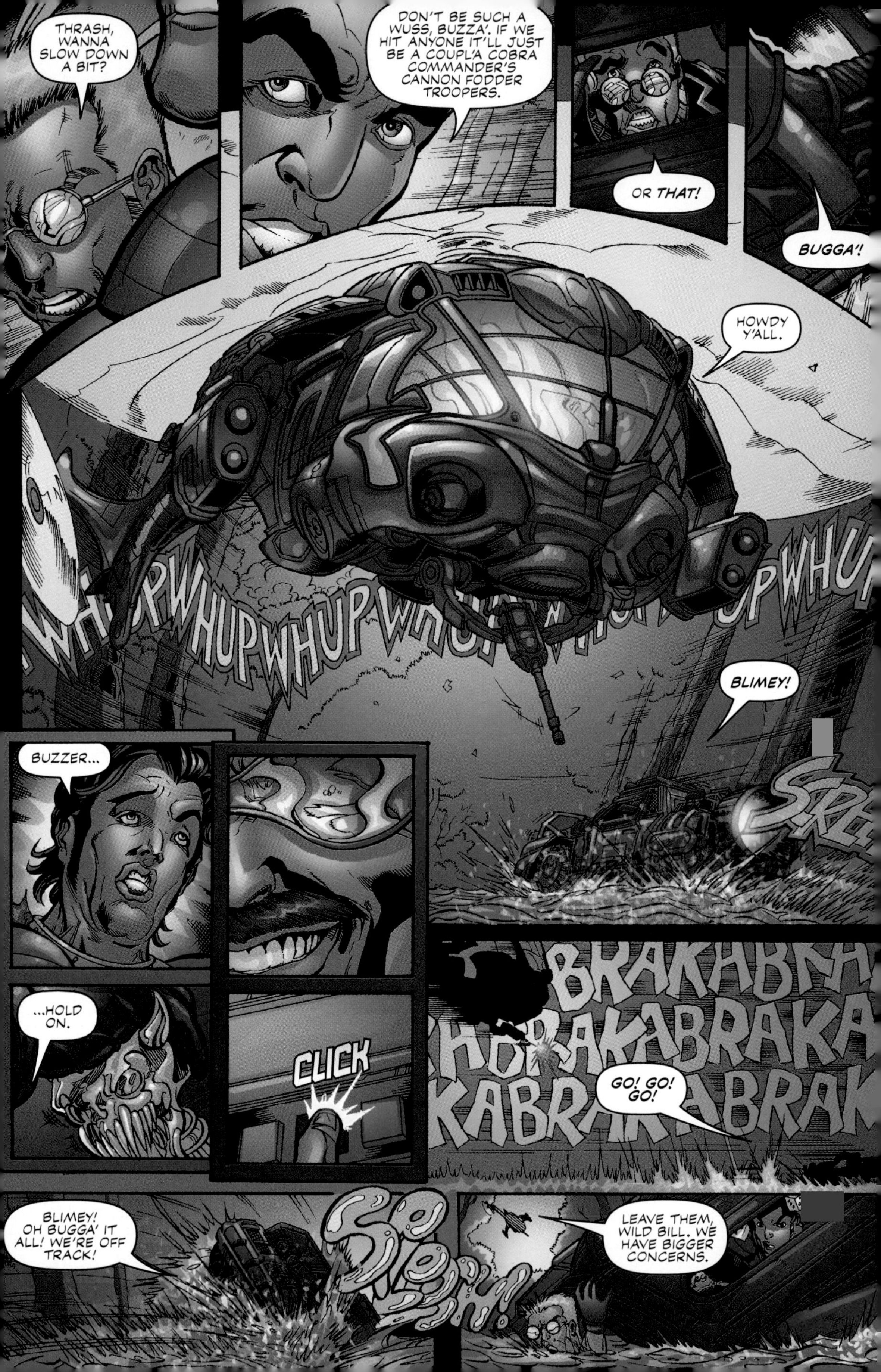
THRASH, WANNA SLOW DOWN A BIT?
DON'T BE SUCH A WUSS, BUZZA'. IF WE HIT ANYONE IT'LL JUST BE A COUPL'A COBRA COMMANDER'S CANNON FODDER TROOPERS.
OR THAT!
BUGGA'!
HOWDY Y'ALL.
WHUPWHUP
BLIMEY!
BUZZER...
...HOLD ON.
CLICK
GO! GO! GO!
BLIMEY! OH BUGGA' IT ALL! WE'RE OFF TRACK!
LEAVE THEM, WILD BILL. WE HAVE BIGGER CONCERNS.

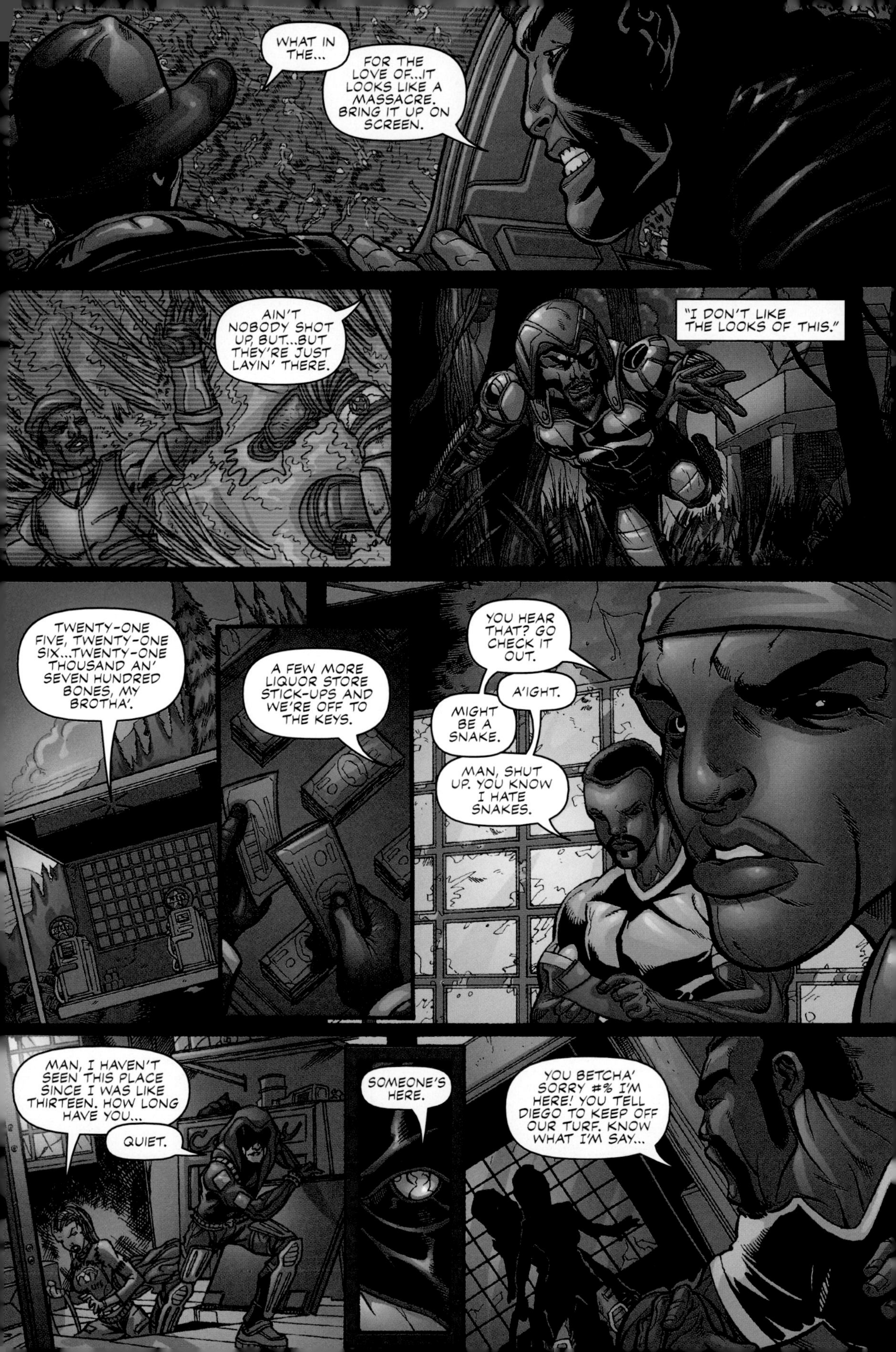
WHAT IN THE...
FOR THE LOVE OF...IT LOOKS LIKE A MASSACRE. BRING IT UP ON SCREEN.
AIN'T NOBODY SHOT UP, BUT...BUT THEY'RE JUST LAYIN' THERE.
"I DON'T LIKE THE LOOKS OF THIS."
TWENTY-ONE FIVE, TWENTY-ONE SIX...TWENTY-ONE THOUSAND AN' SEVEN HUNDRED BONES, MY BROTHA'.
A FEW MORE LIQUOR STORE STICK-UPS AND WE'RE OFF TO THE KEYS.
YOU HEAR THAT? GO CHECK IT OUT.
A'IGHT.
MIGHT BE A SNAKE.
MAN, SHUT UP. YOU KNOW I HATE SNAKES.
MAN, I HAVEN'T SEEN THIS PLACE SINCE I WAS LIKE THIRTEEN. HOW LONG HAVE YOU...
QUIET.
SOMEONE'S HERE.
YOU BETCHA' SORRY #% I'M HERE! YOU TELL DIEGO TO KEEP OFF OUR TURF. KNOW WHAT I'M SAY...

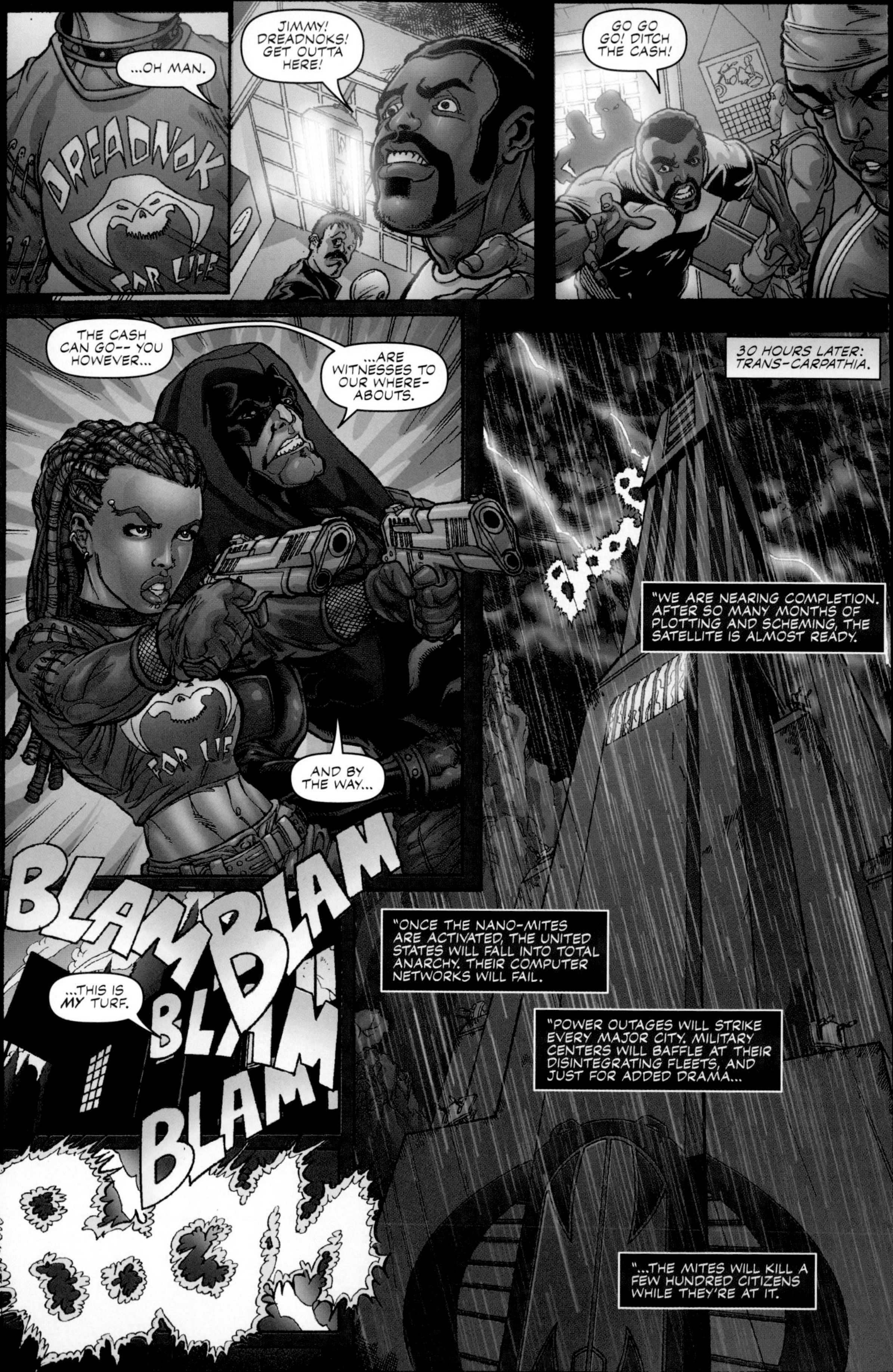
DREADNOK
FOR LIFE
...OH MAN.
JIMMY! DREADNOKS! GET OUTTA HERE!
GO GO GO! DITCH THE CASH!
THE CASH CAN GO-- YOU HOWEVER...
...ARE WITNESSES TO OUR WHERE-ABOUTS.
FOR LIFE
AND BY THE WAY...
BLAM BLAM
...THIS IS MY TURF.
BLAM BLAM BLAM!
30 HOURS LATER: TRANS-CARPATHIA.
"WE ARE NEARING COMPLETION. AFTER SO MANY MONTHS OF PLOTTING AND SCHEMING, THE SATELLITE IS ALMOST READY.
"ONCE THE NANO-MITES ARE ACTIVATED, THE UNITED STATES WILL FALL INTO TOTAL ANARCHY. THEIR COMPUTER NETWORKS WILL FAIL.
"POWER OUTAGES WILL STRIKE EVERY MAJOR CITY. MILITARY CENTERS WILL BAFFLE AT THEIR DISINTEGRATING FLEETS, AND JUST FOR ADDED DRAMA...
"...THE MITES WILL KILL A FEW HUNDRED CITIZENS WHILE THEY'RE AT IT.

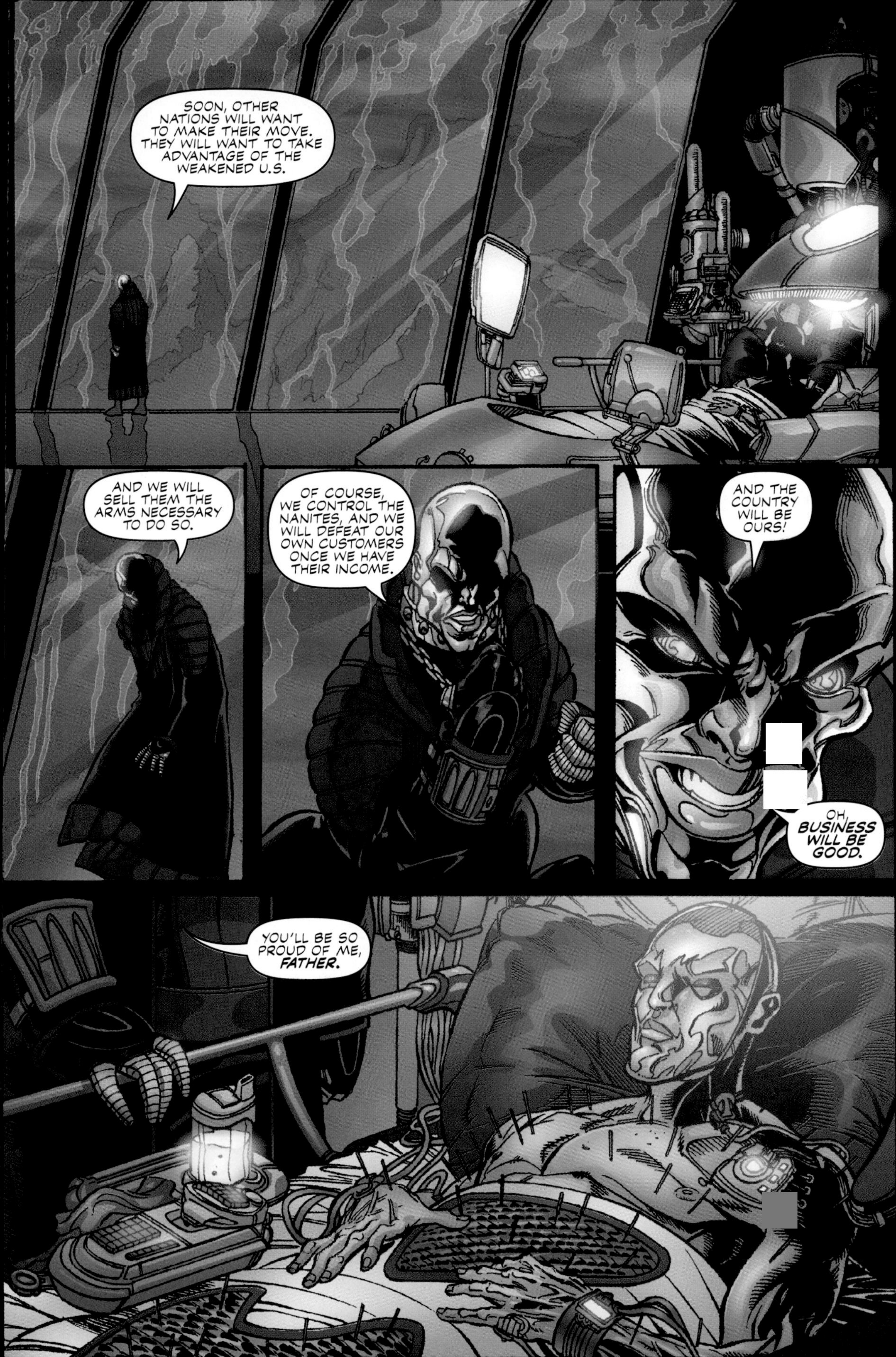
SOON, OTHER NATIONS WILL WANT TO MAKE THEIR MOVE. THEY WILL WANT TO TAKE ADVANTAGE OF THE WEAKENED U.S.
AND WE WILL SELL THEM THE ARMS NECESSARY TO DO SO.
OF COURSE, WE CONTROL THE NANITES, AND WE WILL DEFEAT OUR OWN CUSTOMERS ONCE WE HAVE THEIR INCOME.
AND THE COUNTRY WILL BE OURS!
OH, BUSINESS WILL BE GOOD.
YOU'LL BE SO PROUD OF ME, FATHER.

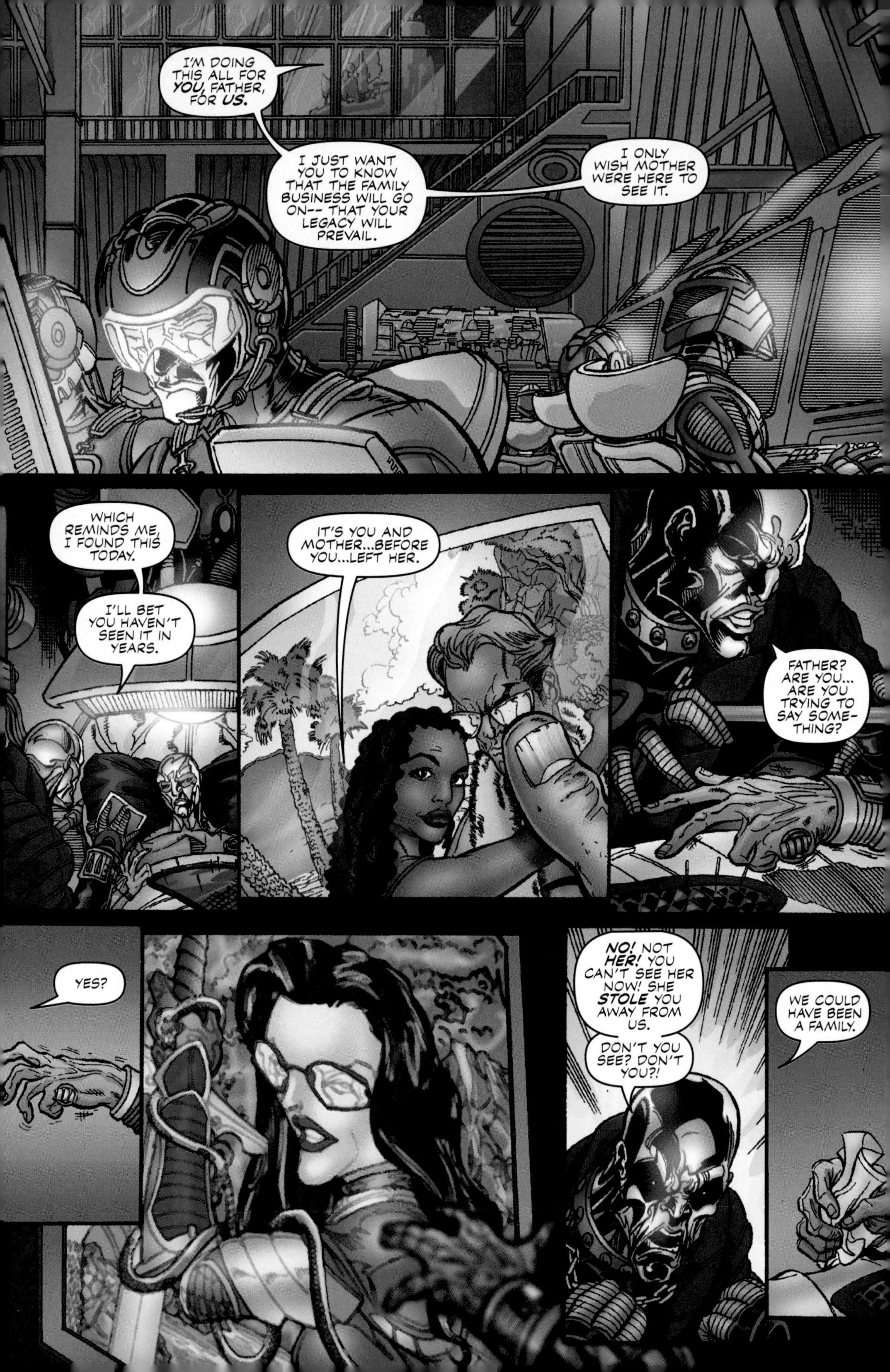
I'M DOING THIS ALL FOR *YOU*, FATHER, FOR *US*.
I JUST WANT YOU TO KNOW THAT THE FAMILY BUSINESS WILL GO ON-- THAT YOUR LEGACY WILL PREVAIL.
I ONLY WISH MOTHER WERE HERE TO SEE IT.
WHICH REMINDS ME, I FOUND THIS TODAY.
I'LL BET YOU HAVEN'T SEEN IT IN YEARS.
IT'S YOU AND MOTHER...BEFORE YOU...LEFT HER.
FATHER? ARE YOU... ARE YOU TRYING TO SAY SOME-THING?
YES?
NO! NOT *HER!* YOU CAN'T SEE HER NOW! SHE *STOLE* YOU AWAY FROM US.
DON'T YOU SEE? DON'T YOU?!
WE COULD HAVE BEEN A FAMILY.

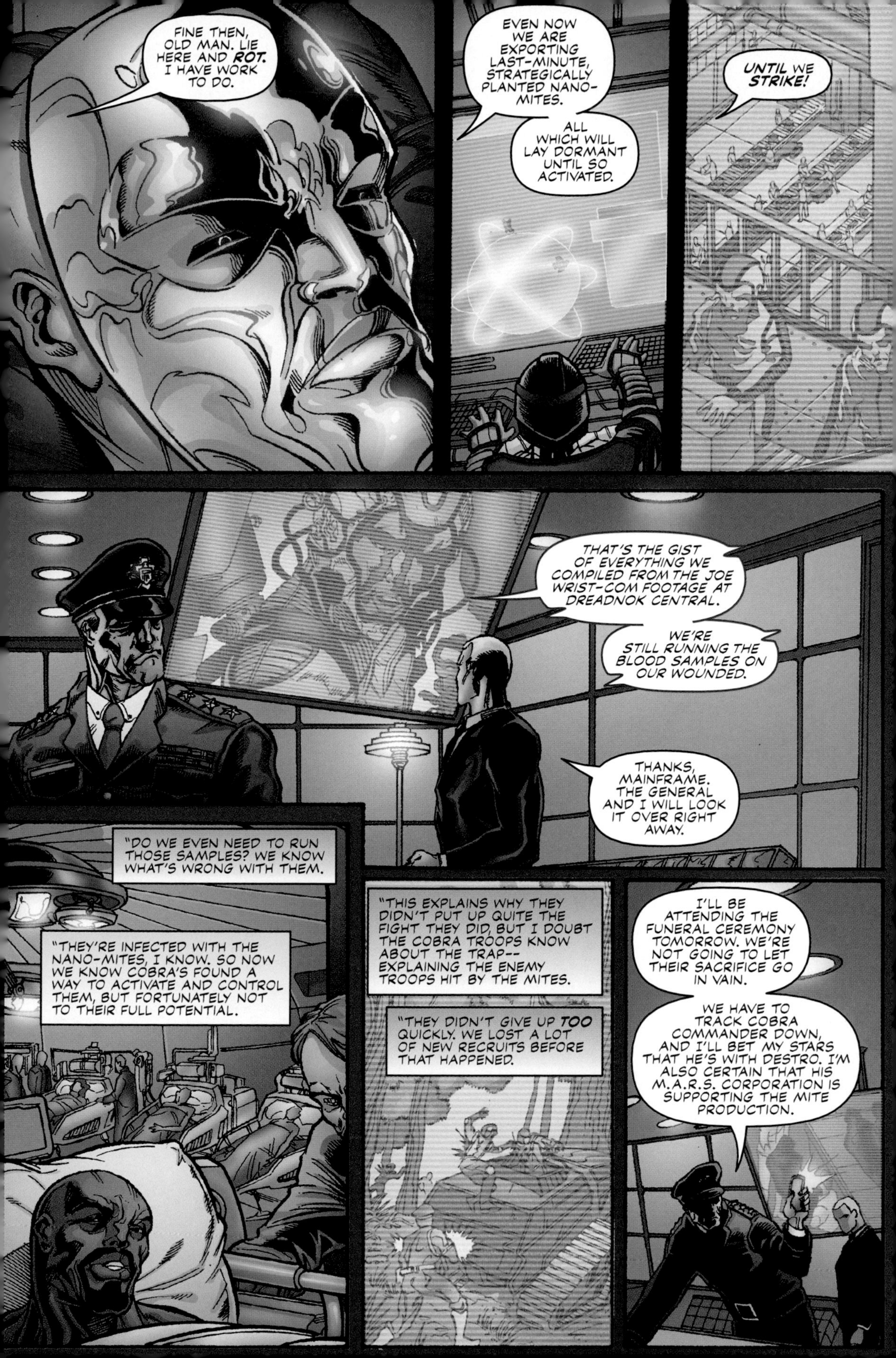

FINE THEN, OLD MAN. LIE HERE AND *ROT.* I HAVE WORK TO DO.
EVEN NOW WE ARE EXPORTING LAST-MINUTE, STRATEGICALLY PLANTED NANO-MITES.
ALL WHICH WILL LAY DORMANT UNTIL SO ACTIVATED.
UNTIL WE *STRIKE!*
THAT'S THE GIST OF EVERYTHING WE COMPILED FROM THE JOE WRIST-COM FOOTAGE AT DREADNOK CENTRAL.
WE'RE STILL RUNNING THE BLOOD SAMPLES ON OUR WOUNDED.
THANKS, MAINFRAME. THE GENERAL AND I WILL LOOK IT OVER RIGHT AWAY.
"DO WE EVEN NEED TO RUN THOSE SAMPLES? WE KNOW WHAT'S WRONG WITH THEM.
"THEY'RE INFECTED WITH THE NANO-MITES, I KNOW. SO NOW WE KNOW COBRA'S FOUND A WAY TO ACTIVATE AND CONTROL THEM, BUT FORTUNATELY NOT TO THEIR FULL POTENTIAL.
"THIS EXPLAINS WHY THEY DIDN'T PUT UP QUITE THE FIGHT THEY DID, BUT I DOUBT THE COBRA TROOPS KNOW ABOUT THE TRAP-- EXPLAINING THE ENEMY TROOPS HIT BY THE MITES.
"THEY DIDN'T GIVE UP *TOO* QUICKLY. WE LOST A LOT OF NEW RECRUITS BEFORE THAT HAPPENED.
I'LL BE ATTENDING THE FUNERAL CEREMONY TOMORROW. WE'RE NOT GOING TO LET THEIR SACRIFICE GO IN VAIN.
WE HAVE TO TRACK COBRA COMMANDER DOWN, AND I'LL BET MY STARS THAT HE'S WITH DESTRO. I'M ALSO CERTAIN THAT HIS M.A.R.S. CORPORATION IS SUPPORTING THE MITE PRODUCTION.

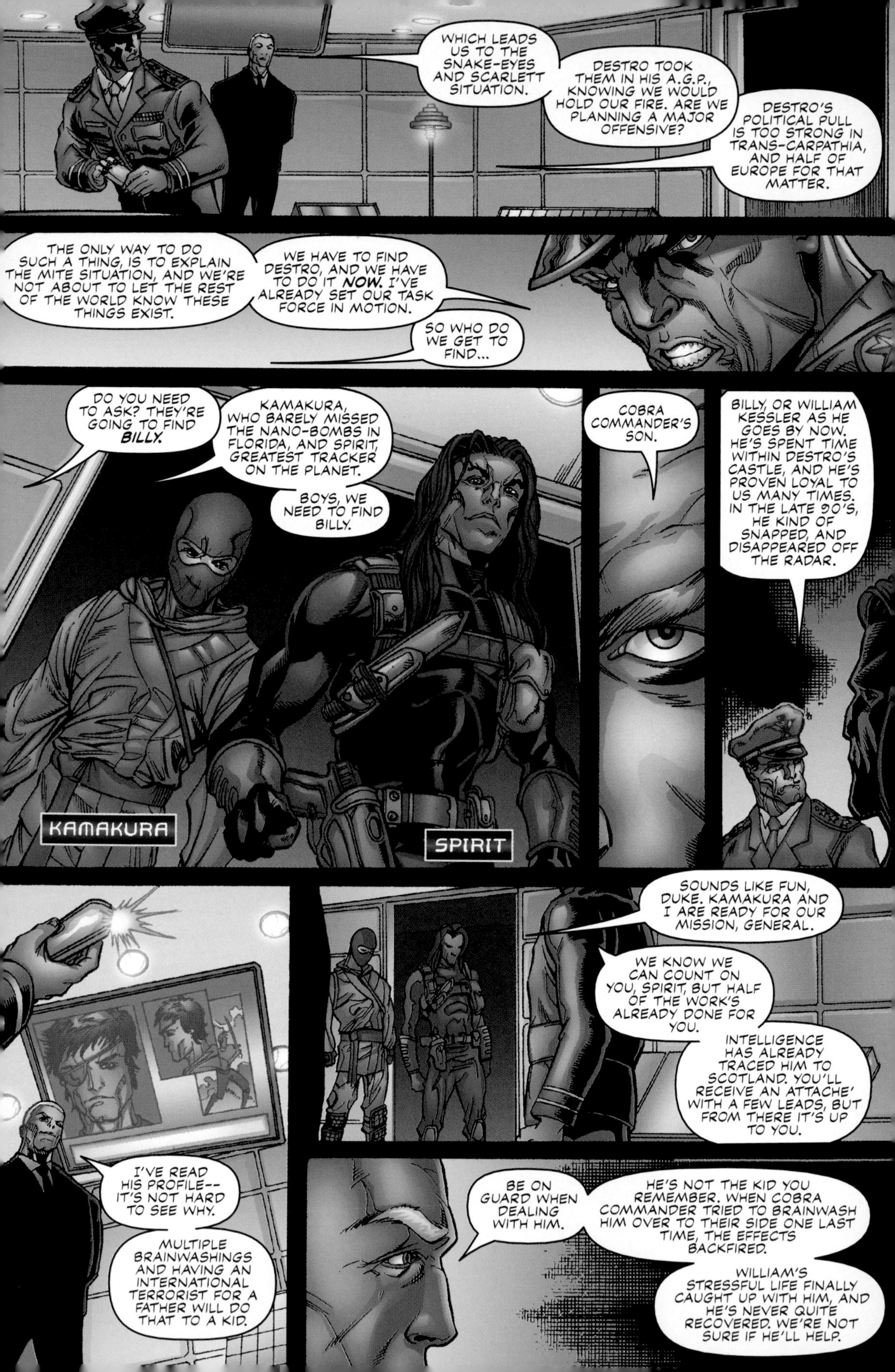
WHICH LEADS US TO THE SNAKE-EYES AND SCARLETT SITUATION.
DESTRO TOOK THEM IN HIS A.G.P., KNOWING WE WOULD HOLD OUR FIRE. ARE WE PLANNING A MAJOR OFFENSIVE?
DESTRO'S POLITICAL PULL IS TOO STRONG IN TRANS-CARPATHIA, AND HALF OF EUROPE FOR THAT MATTER.
THE ONLY WAY TO DO SUCH A THING, IS TO EXPLAIN THE MITE SITUATION, AND WE'RE NOT ABOUT TO LET THE REST OF THE WORLD KNOW THESE THINGS EXIST.
WE HAVE TO FIND DESTRO, AND WE HAVE TO DO IT NOW. I'VE ALREADY SET OUR TASK FORCE IN MOTION.
SO WHO DO WE GET TO FIND...
DO YOU NEED TO ASK? THEY'RE GOING TO FIND BILLY.
KAMAKURA, WHO BARELY MISSED THE NANO-BOMBS IN FLORIDA, AND SPIRIT, GREATEST TRACKER ON THE PLANET.
BOYS, WE NEED TO FIND BILLY.
KAMAKURA
SPIRIT
COBRA COMMANDER'S SON.
BILLY, OR WILLIAM KESSLER AS HE GOES BY NOW. HE'S SPENT TIME WITHIN DESTRO'S CASTLE, AND HE'S PROVEN LOYAL TO US MANY TIMES. IN THE LATE 90'S, HE KIND OF SNAPPED, AND DISAPPEARED OFF THE RADAR.
SOUNDS LIKE FUN, DUKE. KAMAKURA AND I ARE READY FOR OUR MISSION, GENERAL.
WE KNOW WE CAN COUNT ON YOU, SPIRIT, BUT HALF OF THE WORK'S ALREADY DONE FOR YOU.
INTELLIGENCE HAS ALREADY TRACED HIM TO SCOTLAND. YOU'LL RECEIVE AN ATTACHE' WITH A FEW LEADS, BUT FROM THERE IT'S UP TO YOU.
I'VE READ HIS PROFILE-- IT'S NOT HARD TO SEE WHY.
MULTIPLE BRAINWASHINGS AND HAVING AN INTERNATIONAL TERRORIST FOR A FATHER WILL DO THAT TO A KID.
BE ON GUARD WHEN DEALING WITH HIM.
HE'S NOT THE KID YOU REMEMBER. WHEN COBRA COMMANDER TRIED TO BRAINWASH HIM OVER TO THEIR SIDE ONE LAST TIME, THE EFFECTS BACKFIRED.
WILLIAM'S STRESSFUL LIFE FINALLY CAUGHT UP WITH HIM, AND HE'S NEVER QUITE RECOVERED. WE'RE NOT SURE IF HE'LL HELP.

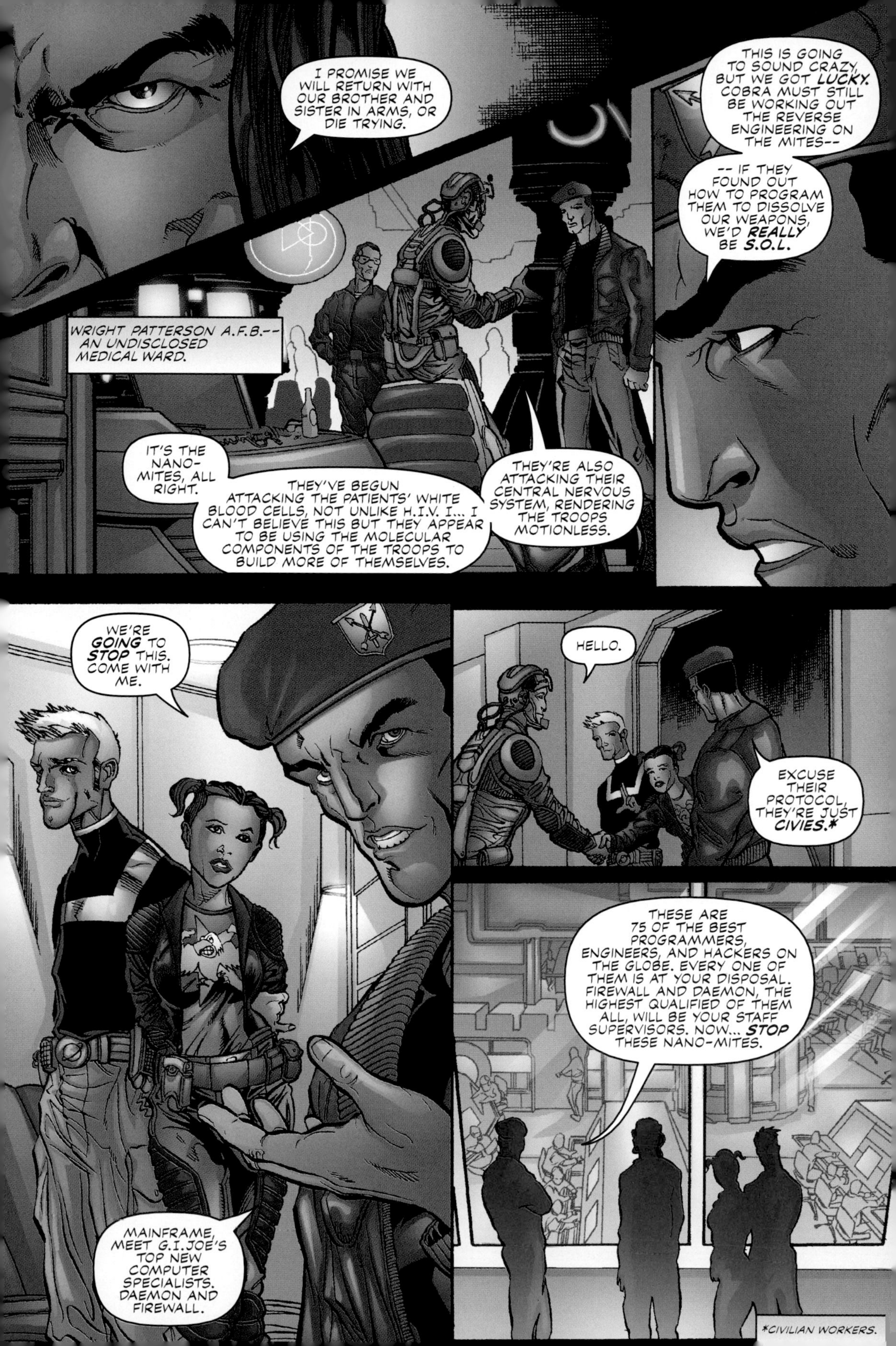
I PROMISE WE WILL RETURN WITH OUR BROTHER AND SISTER IN ARMS, OR DIE TRYING.
WRIGHT PATTERSON A.F.B.-- AN UNDISCLOSED MEDICAL WARD.
IT'S THE NANO-MITES, ALL RIGHT.
THEY'VE BEGUN ATTACKING THE PATIENTS' WHITE BLOOD CELLS, NOT UNLIKE H.I.V. I... I CAN'T BELIEVE THIS BUT THEY APPEAR TO BE USING THE MOLECULAR COMPONENTS OF THE TROOPS TO BUILD MORE OF THEMSELVES.
THEY'RE ALSO ATTACKING THEIR CENTRAL NERVOUS SYSTEM, RENDERING THE TROOPS MOTIONLESS.
THIS IS GOING TO SOUND CRAZY, BUT WE GOT LUCKY. COBRA MUST STILL BE WORKING OUT THE REVERSE ENGINEERING ON THE MITES--
-- IF THEY FOUND OUT HOW TO PROGRAM THEM TO DISSOLVE OUR WEAPONS, WE'D REALLY BE S.O.L.
WE'RE GOING TO STOP THIS. COME WITH ME.
MAINFRAME, MEET G.I.JOE'S TOP NEW COMPUTER SPECIALISTS. DAEMON AND FIREWALL.
HELLO.
EXCUSE THEIR PROTOCOL, THEY'RE JUST CIVIES.*
THESE ARE 75 OF THE BEST PROGRAMMERS, ENGINEERS, AND HACKERS ON THE GLOBE. EVERY ONE OF THEM IS AT YOUR DISPOSAL. FIREWALL AND DAEMON, THE HIGHEST QUALIFIED OF THEM ALL, WILL BE YOUR STAFF SUPERVISORS. NOW... STOP THESE NANO-MITES.
*CIVILIAN WORKERS.

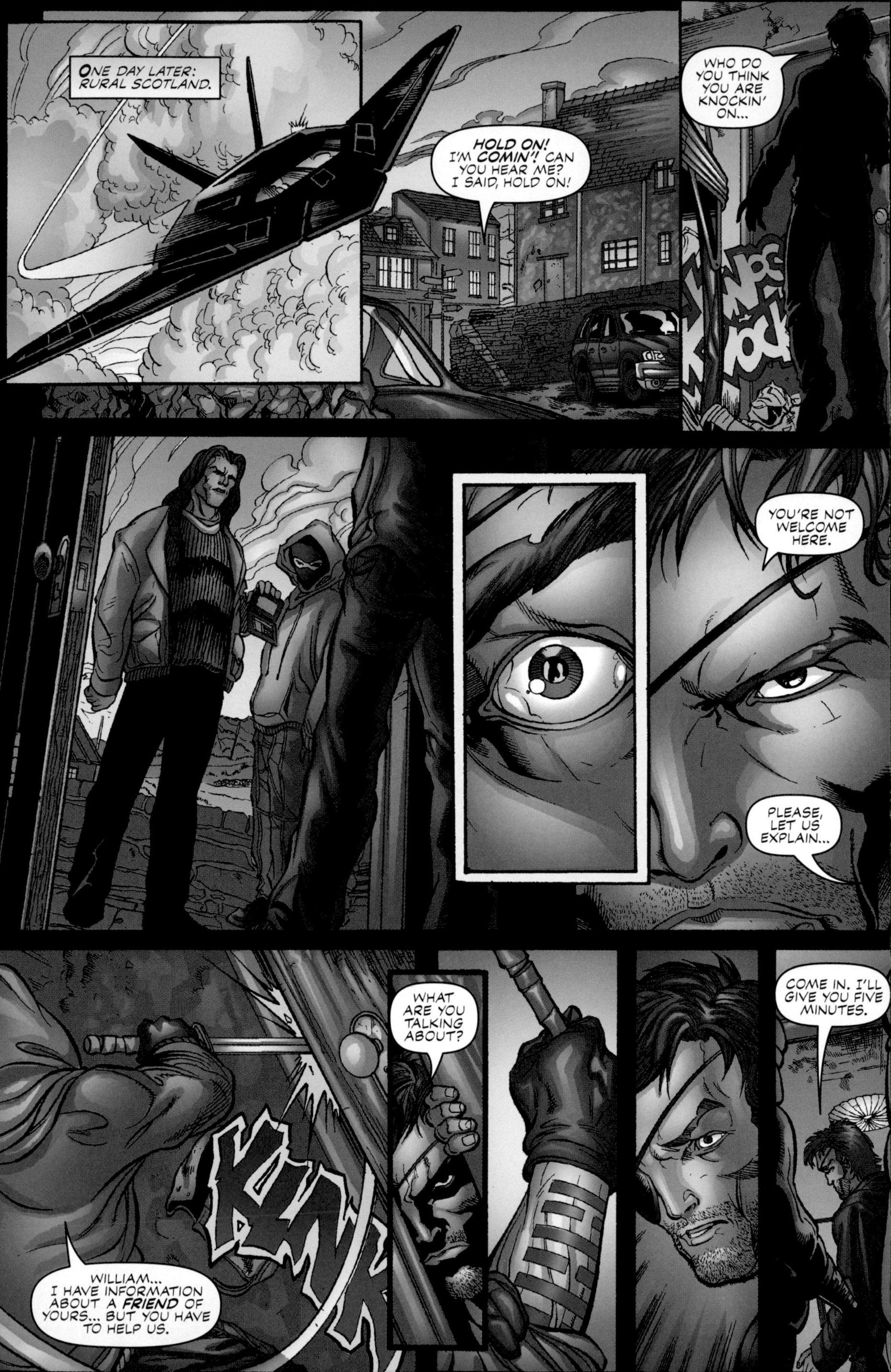

ONE DAY LATER: RURAL SCOTLAND.
HOLD ON! I'M COMIN'! CAN YOU HEAR ME? I SAID, HOLD ON!
WHO DO YOU THINK YOU ARE KNOCKIN' ON...
YOU'RE NOT WELCOME HERE.
PLEASE, LET US EXPLAIN...
WILLIAM... I HAVE INFORMATION ABOUT A FRIEND OF YOURS... BUT YOU HAVE TO HELP US.
WHAT ARE YOU TALKING ABOUT?
COME IN. I'LL GIVE YOU FIVE MINUTES.

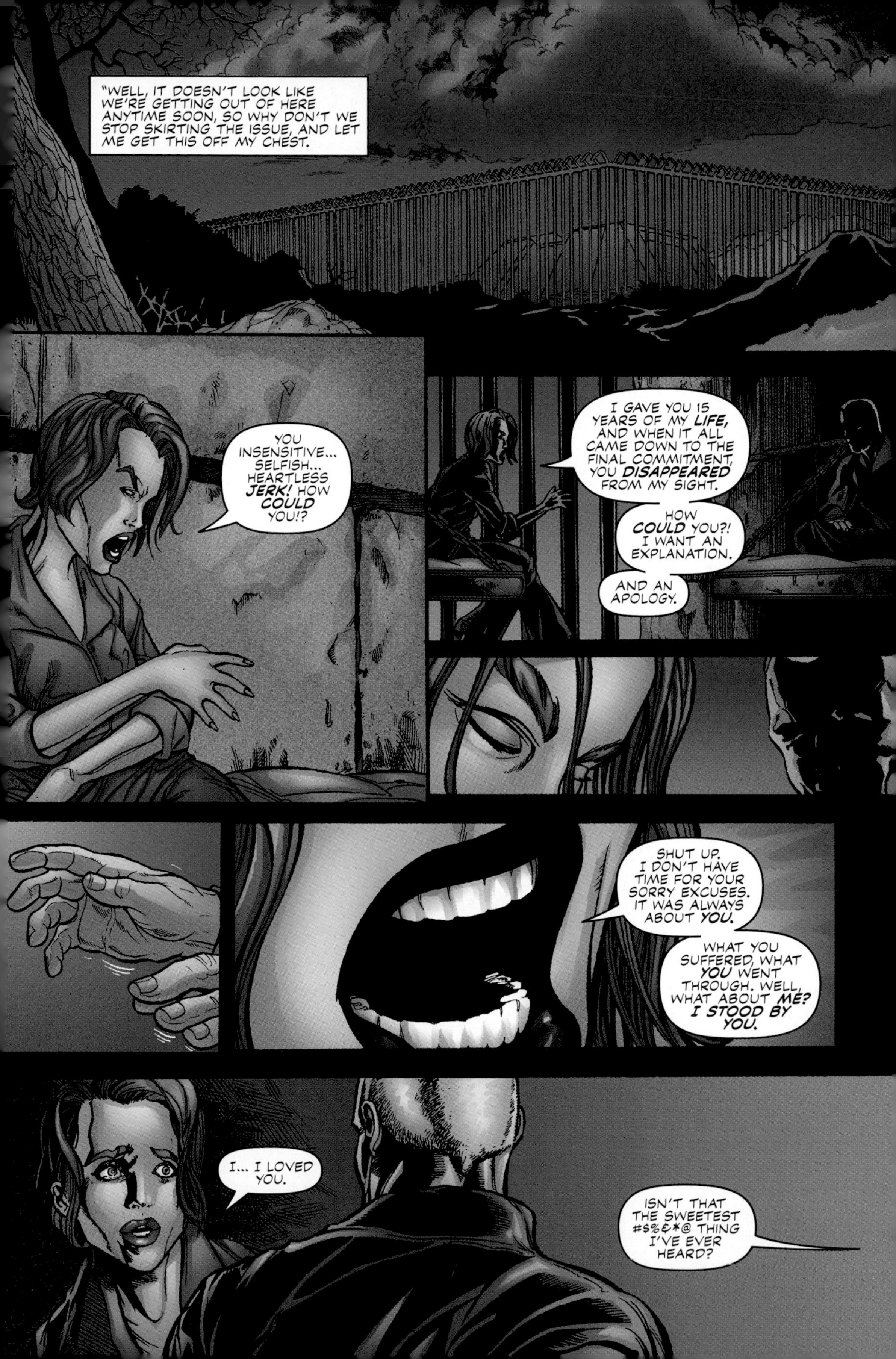
"WELL, IT DOESN'T LOOK LIKE WE'RE GETTING OUT OF HERE ANYTIME SOON, SO WHY DON'T WE STOP SKIRTING THE ISSUE, AND LET ME GET THIS OFF MY CHEST.
YOU INSENSITIVE... SELFISH... HEARTLESS JERK! HOW COULD YOU!?
I GAVE YOU 15 YEARS OF MY LIFE, AND WHEN IT ALL CAME DOWN TO THE FINAL COMMITMENT, YOU DISAPPEARED FROM MY SIGHT.
HOW COULD YOU?! I WANT AN EXPLANATION.
AND AN APOLOGY.
SHUT UP. I DON'T HAVE TIME FOR YOUR SORRY EXCUSES. IT WAS ALWAYS ABOUT YOU.
WHAT YOU SUFFERED, WHAT YOU WENT THROUGH. WELL, WHAT ABOUT ME? I STOOD BY YOU.
I... I LOVED YOU.
ISN'T THAT THE SWEETEST #$%&*@ THING I'VE EVER HEARD?

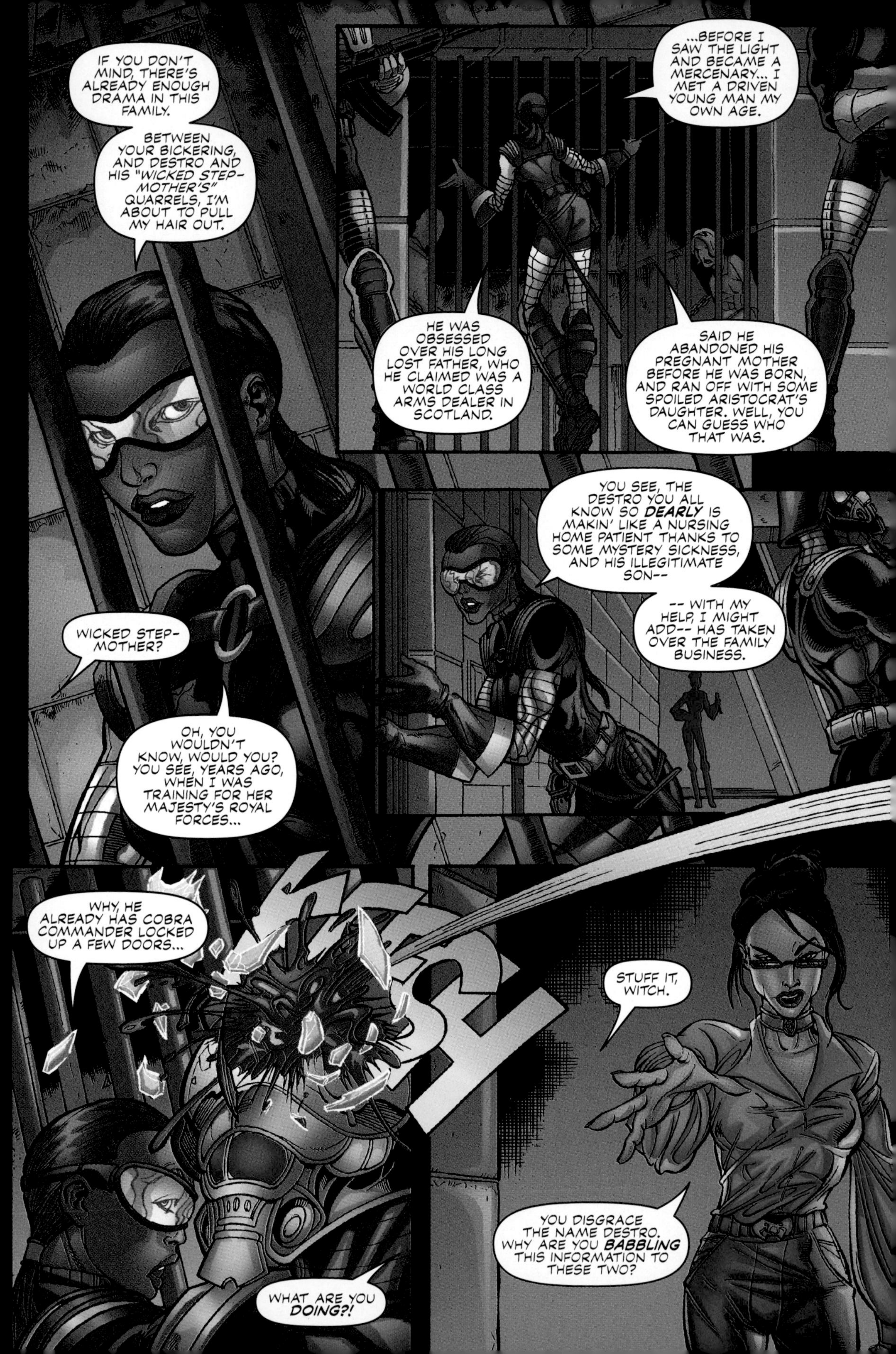
IF YOU DON'T MIND, THERE'S ALREADY ENOUGH DRAMA IN THIS FAMILY.
BETWEEN YOUR BICKERING, AND DESTRO AND HIS "WICKED STEP-MOTHER'S" QUARRELS, I'M ABOUT TO PULL MY HAIR OUT.
WICKED STEP-MOTHER?
OH, YOU WOULDN'T KNOW, WOULD YOU? YOU SEE, YEARS AGO, WHEN I WAS TRAINING FOR HER MAJESTY'S ROYAL FORCES...
...BEFORE I SAW THE LIGHT AND BECAME A MERCENARY... I MET A DRIVEN YOUNG MAN MY OWN AGE.
HE WAS OBSESSED OVER HIS LONG LOST FATHER, WHO HE CLAIMED WAS A WORLD CLASS ARMS DEALER IN SCOTLAND.
SAID HE ABANDONED HIS PREGNANT MOTHER BEFORE HE WAS BORN, AND RAN OFF WITH SOME SPOILED ARISTOCRAT'S DAUGHTER. WELL, YOU CAN GUESS WHO THAT WAS.
YOU SEE, THE DESTRO YOU ALL KNOW SO DEARLY IS MAKIN' LIKE A NURSING HOME PATIENT THANKS TO SOME MYSTERY SICKNESS, AND HIS ILLEGITIMATE SON--
-- WITH MY HELP, I MIGHT ADD-- HAS TAKEN OVER THE FAMILY BUSINESS.
WHY, HE ALREADY HAS COBRA COMMANDER LOCKED UP A FEW DOORS...
WHAT ARE YOU DOING?!
STUFF IT, WITCH.
YOU DISGRACE THE NAME DESTRO. WHY ARE YOU BABBLING THIS INFORMATION TO THESE TWO?

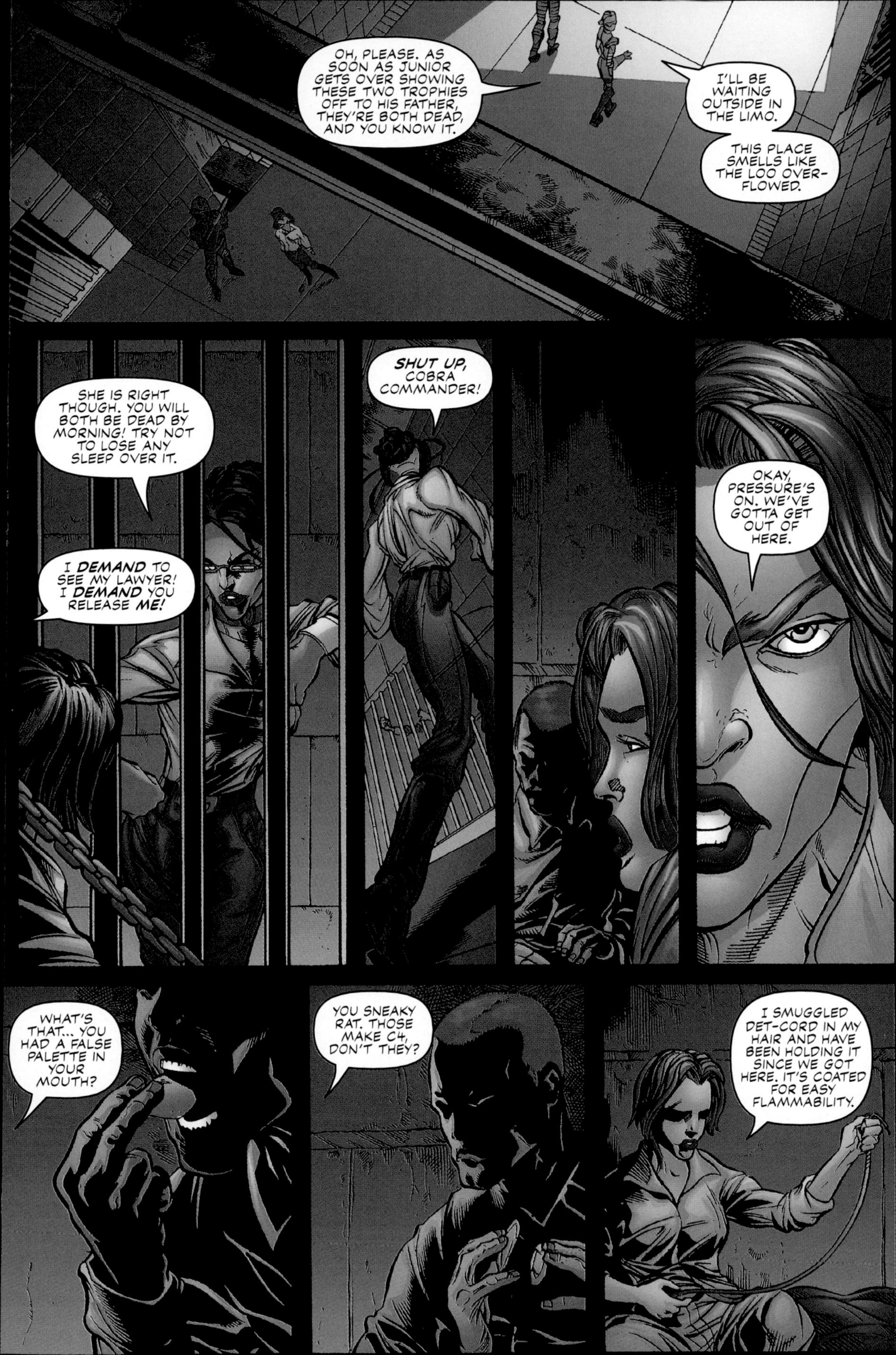

OH, PLEASE. AS SOON AS JUNIOR GETS OVER SHOWING THESE TWO TROPHIES OFF TO HIS FATHER, THEY'RE BOTH DEAD, AND YOU KNOW IT.
I'LL BE WAITING OUTSIDE IN THE LIMO.
THIS PLACE SMELLS LIKE THE LOO OVER-FLOWED.
SHE IS RIGHT THOUGH. YOU WILL BOTH BE DEAD BY MORNING! TRY NOT TO LOSE ANY SLEEP OVER IT.
I **DEMAND** TO SEE MY LAWYER! I **DEMAND** YOU RELEASE **ME!**
SHUT UP, COBRA COMMANDER!
OKAY, PRESSURE'S ON. WE'VE GOTTA GET OUT OF HERE.
WHAT'S THAT... YOU HAD A FALSE PALETTE IN YOUR MOUTH?
YOU SNEAKY RAT. THOSE MAKE C4, DON'T THEY?
I SMUGGLED DET-CORD IN MY HAIR AND HAVE BEEN HOLDING IT SINCE WE GOT HERE. IT'S COATED FOR EASY FLAMMABILITY.

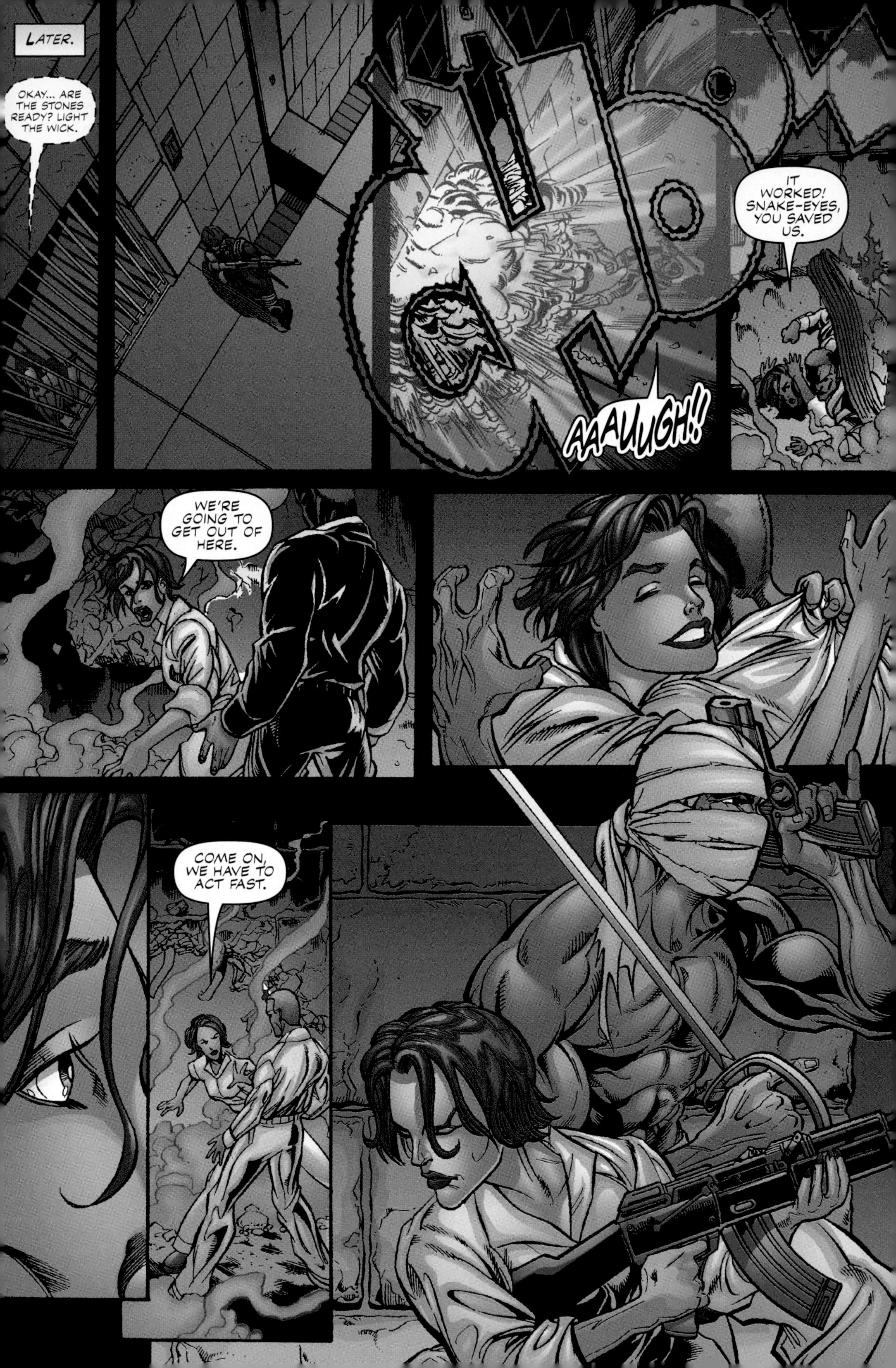
LATER.
OKAY... ARE THE STONES READY? LIGHT THE WICK.
KA-BOOM
AAAUUGH!!
IT WORKED! SNAKE-EYES, YOU SAVED US.
WE'RE GOING TO GET OUT OF HERE.
COME ON, WE HAVE TO ACT FAST.

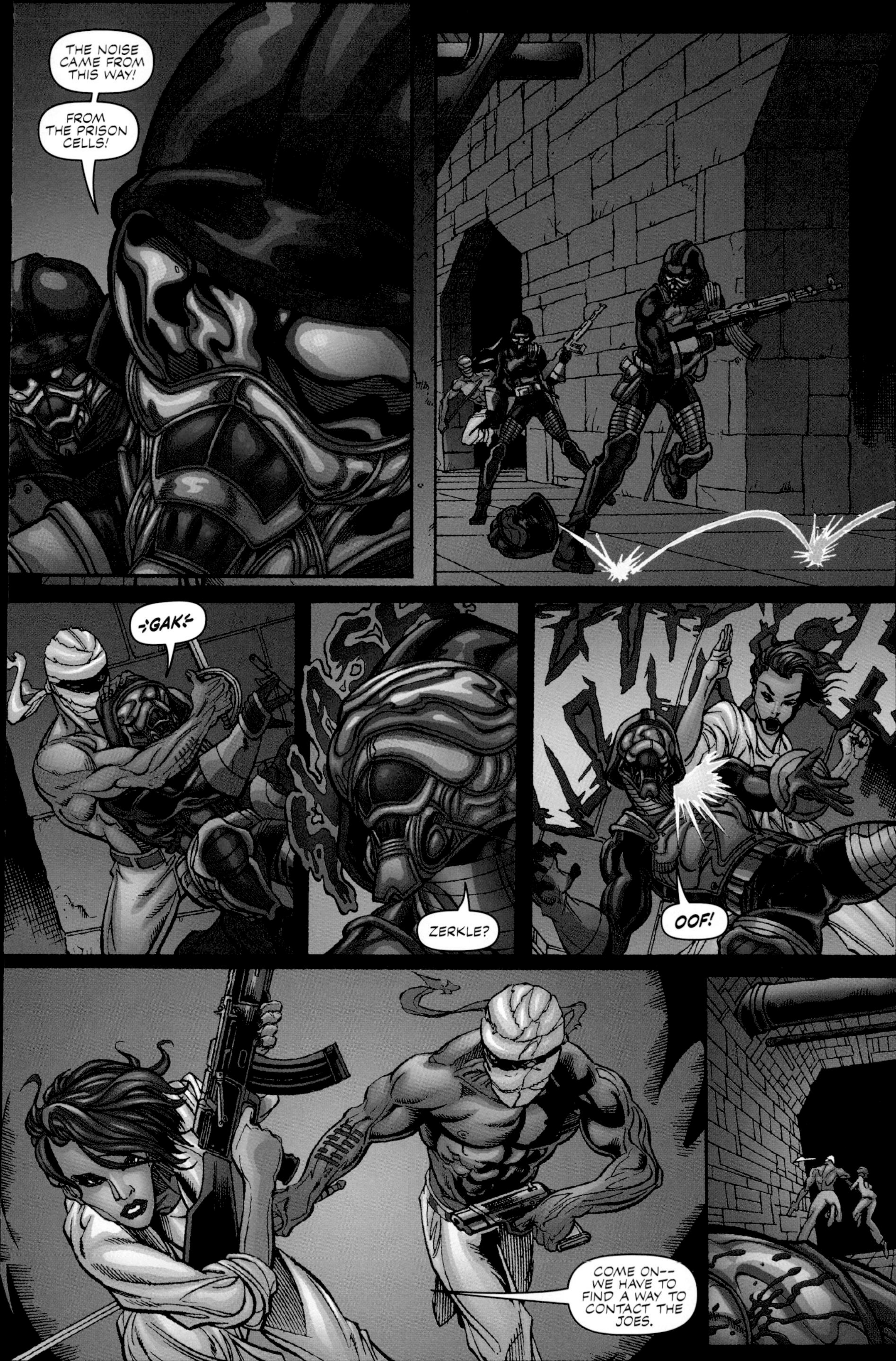
THE NOISE CAME FROM THIS WAY!
FROM THE PRISON CELLS!
-GAK-
ZERKLE?
OOF!
COME ON-- WE HAVE TO FIND A WAY TO CONTACT THE JOES.

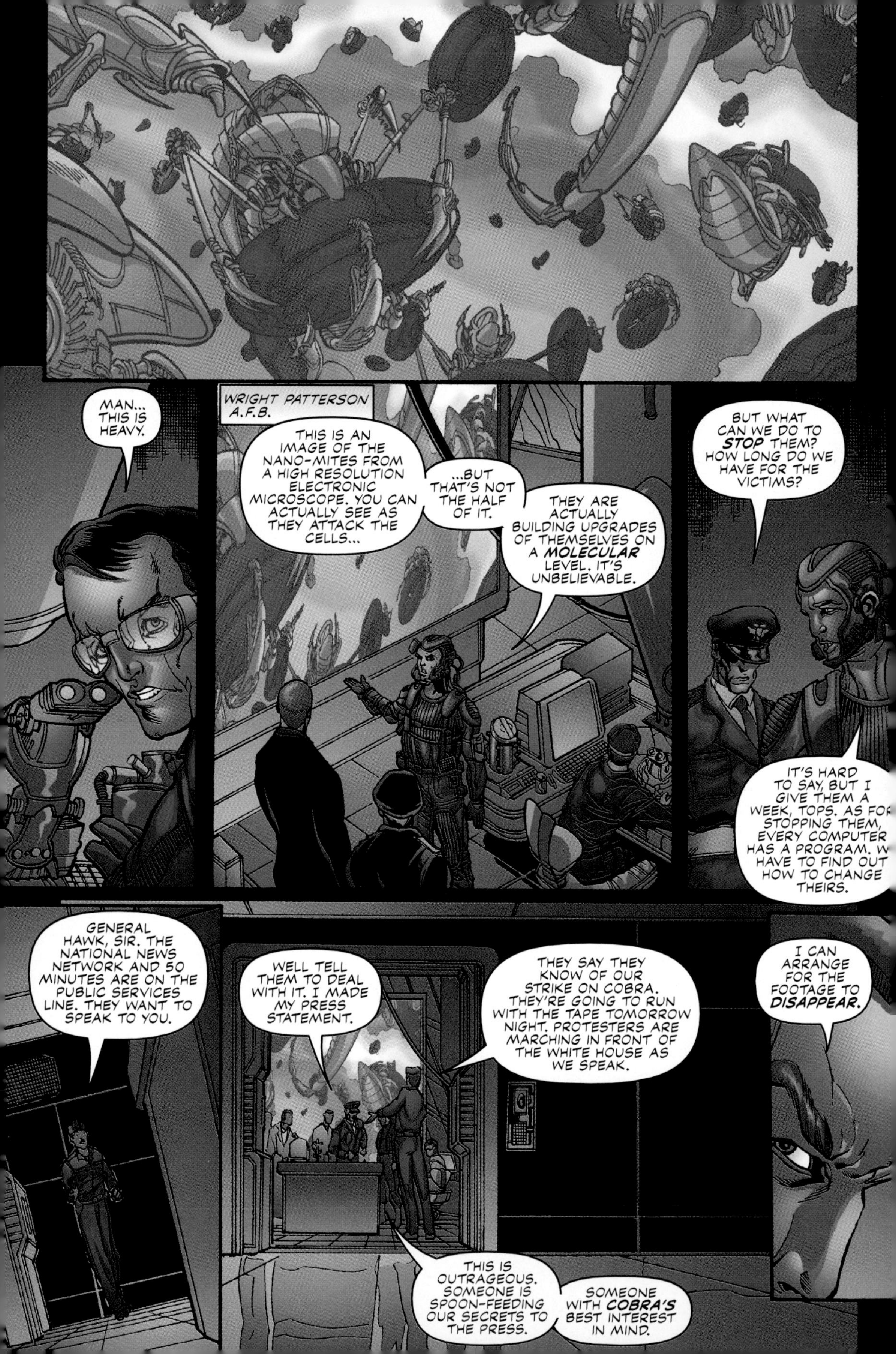
MAN... THIS IS HEAVY.
WRIGHT PATTERSON A.F.B.
THIS IS AN IMAGE OF THE NANO-MITES FROM A HIGH RESOLUTION ELECTRONIC MICROSCOPE. YOU CAN ACTUALLY SEE AS THEY ATTACK THE CELLS...
...BUT THAT'S NOT THE HALF OF IT.
THEY ARE ACTUALLY BUILDING UPGRADES OF THEMSELVES ON A MOLECULAR LEVEL. IT'S UNBELIEVABLE.
BUT WHAT CAN WE DO TO STOP THEM? HOW LONG DO WE HAVE FOR THE VICTIMS?
IT'S HARD TO SAY, BUT I GIVE THEM A WEEK, TOPS. AS FOR STOPPING THEM, EVERY COMPUTER HAS A PROGRAM. WE HAVE TO FIND OUT HOW TO CHANGE THEIRS.
GENERAL HAWK, SIR. THE NATIONAL NEWS NETWORK AND 50 MINUTES ARE ON THE PUBLIC SERVICES LINE. THEY WANT TO SPEAK TO YOU.
WELL TELL THEM TO DEAL WITH IT. I MADE MY PRESS STATEMENT.
THEY SAY THEY KNOW OF OUR STRIKE ON COBRA. THEY'RE GOING TO RUN WITH THE TAPE TOMORROW NIGHT. PROTESTERS ARE MARCHING IN FRONT OF THE WHITE HOUSE AS WE SPEAK.
I CAN ARRANGE FOR THE FOOTAGE TO DISAPPEAR.
THIS IS OUTRAGEOUS. SOMEONE IS SPOON-FEEDING OUR SECRETS TO THE PRESS.
SOMEONE WITH COBRA'S BEST INTEREST IN MIND.

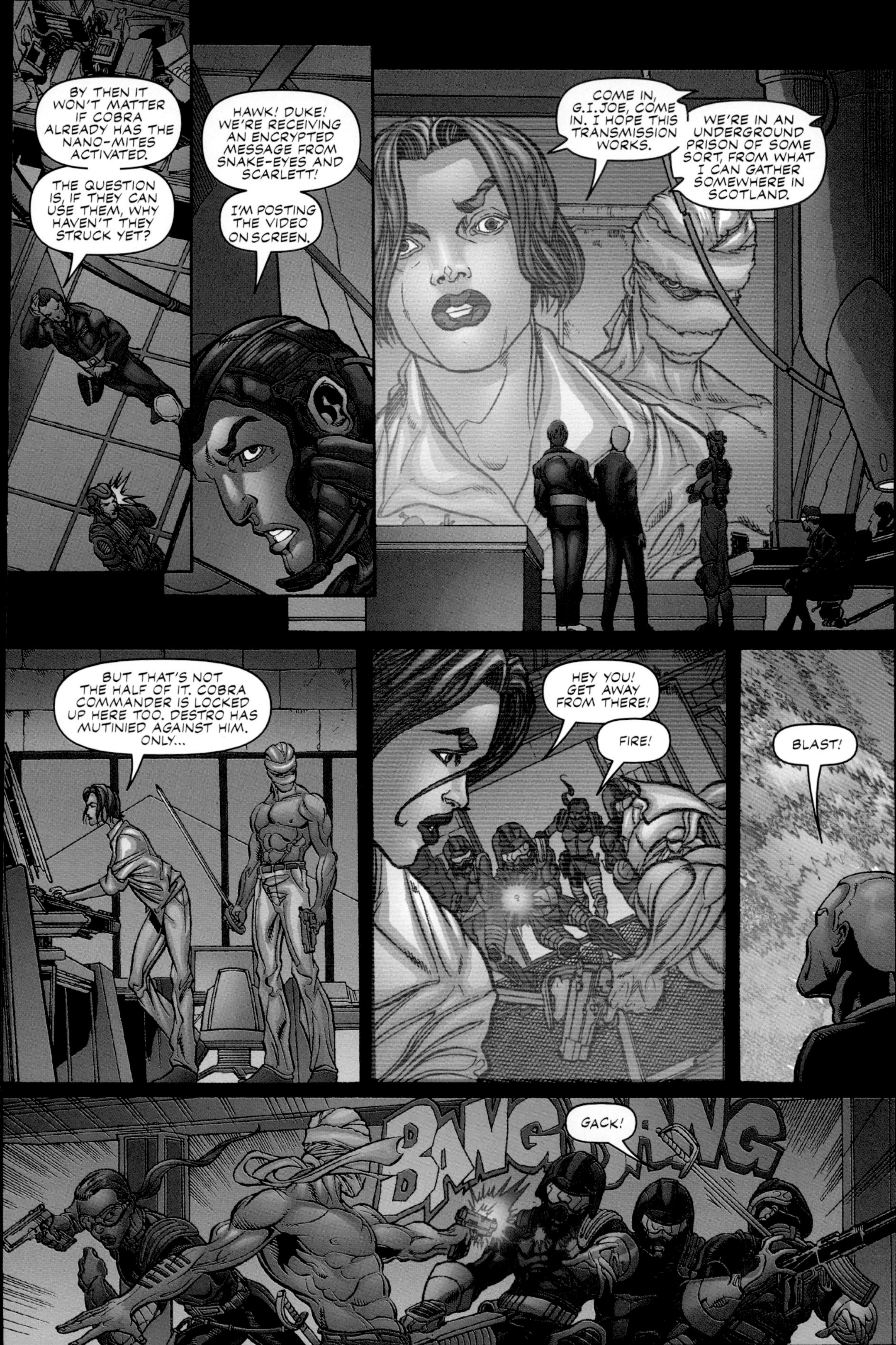
BY THEN IT WON'T MATTER IF COBRA ALREADY HAS THE NANO-MITES ACTIVATED.
THE QUESTION IS, IF THEY CAN USE THEM, WHY HAVEN'T THEY STRUCK YET?
HAWK! DUKE! WE'RE RECEIVING AN ENCRYPTED MESSAGE FROM SNAKE-EYES AND SCARLETT!
I'M POSTING THE VIDEO ON SCREEN.
COME IN, G.I.JOE, COME IN. I HOPE THIS TRANSMISSION WORKS.
WE'RE IN AN UNDERGROUND PRISON OF SOME SORT, FROM WHAT I CAN GATHER SOMEWHERE IN SCOTLAND.
BUT THAT'S NOT THE HALF OF IT. COBRA COMMANDER IS LOCKED UP HERE TOO. DESTRO HAS MUTINIED AGAINST HIM. ONLY...
HEY YOU! GET AWAY FROM THERE!
FIRE!
BLAST!
GACK!
BANG BANG

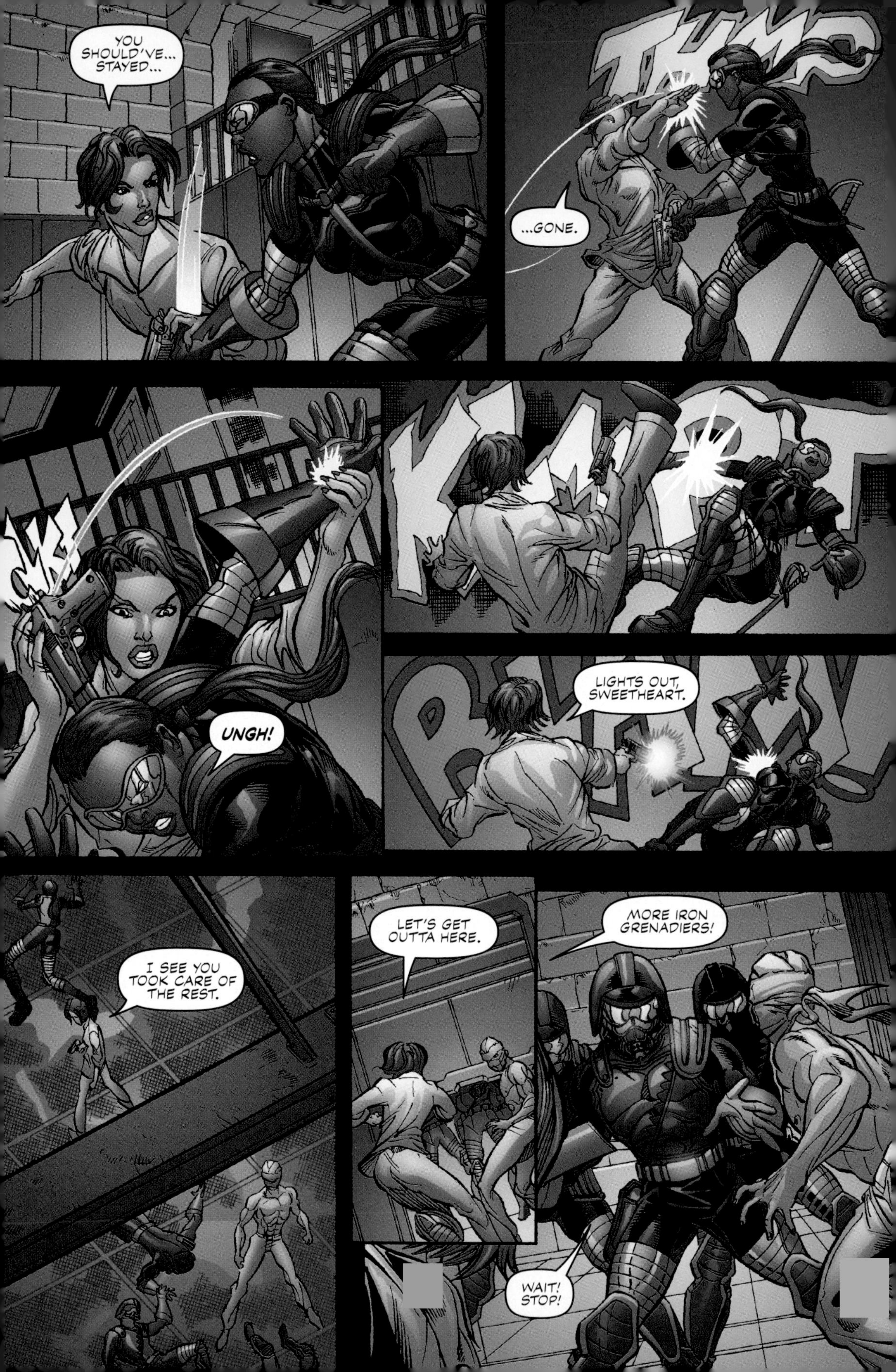
YOU SHOULD'VE... STAYED...
...GONE.
UNGH!
LIGHTS OUT, SWEETHEART.
I SEE YOU TOOK CARE OF THE REST.
LET'S GET OUTTA HERE.
MORE IRON GRENADIERS!
WAIT! STOP!

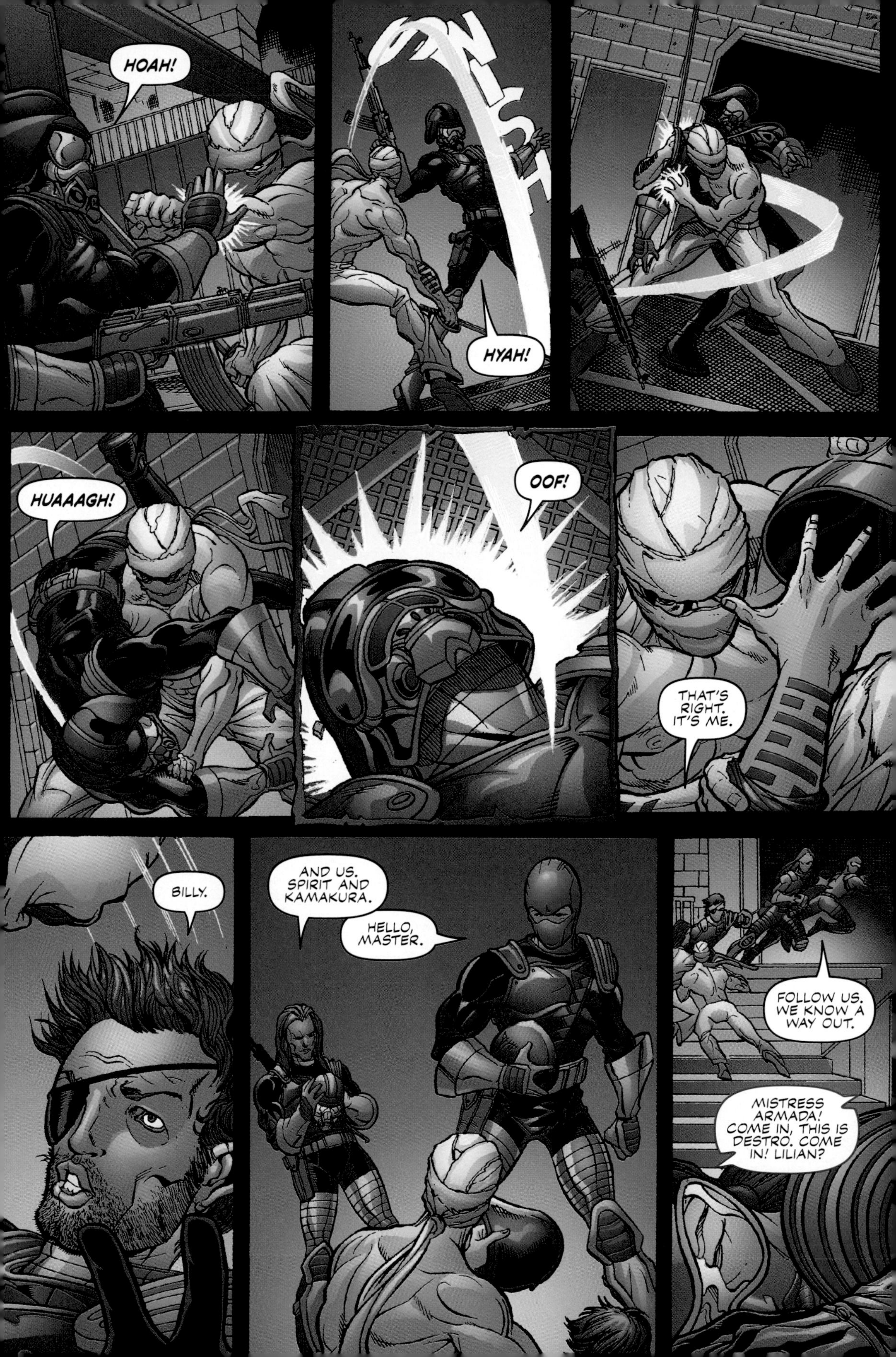
HOAH!
HYAH!
HUAAAGH!
OOF!
THAT'S RIGHT. IT'S ME.
BILLY.
AND US. SPIRIT AND KAMAKURA.
HELLO, MASTER.
FOLLOW US. WE KNOW A WAY OUT.
MISTRESS ARMADA! COME IN, THIS IS DESTRO. COME IN! LILIAN?

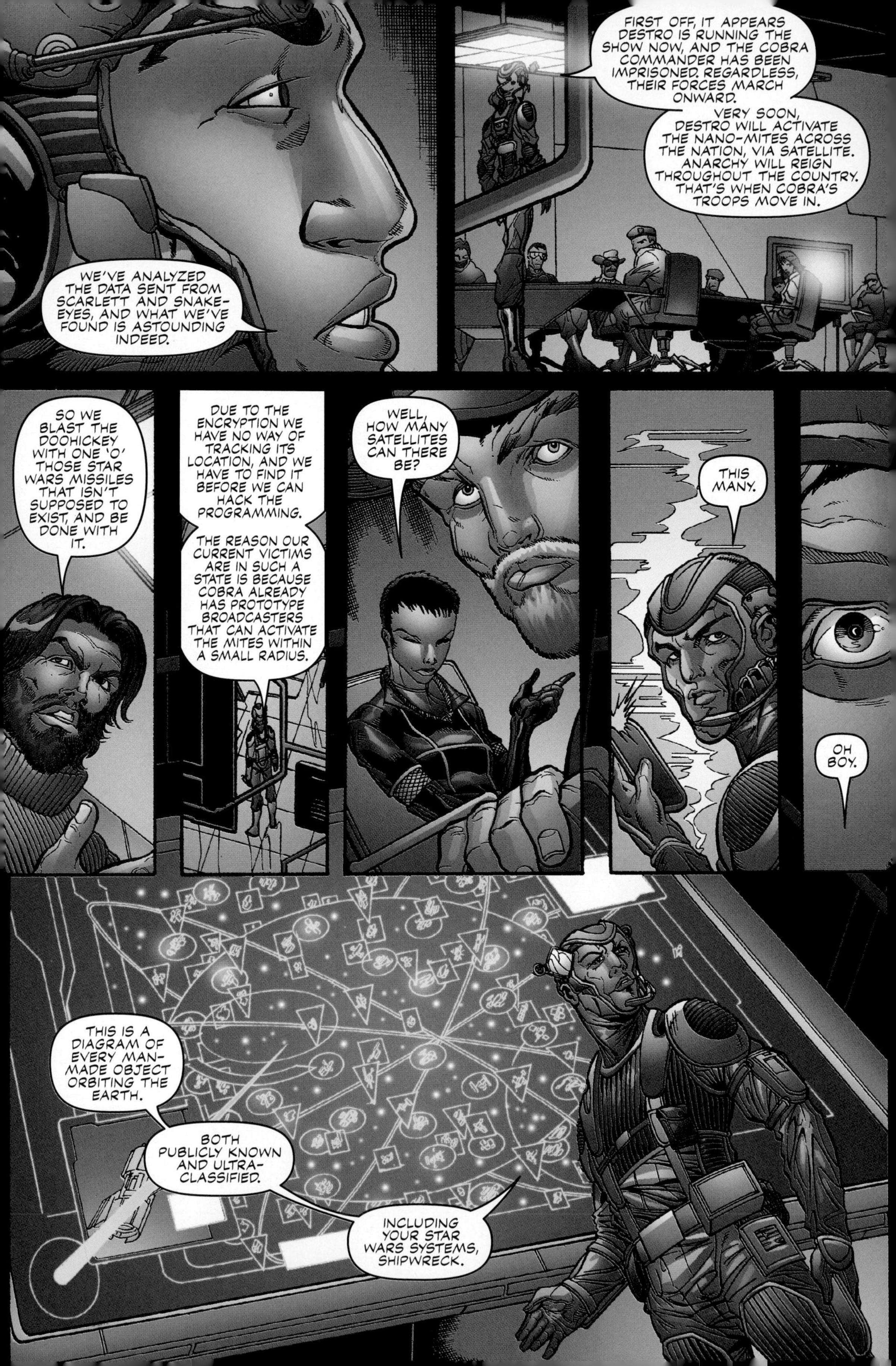

WE'VE ANALYZED THE DATA SENT FROM SCARLETT AND SNAKE-EYES, AND WHAT WE'VE FOUND IS ASTOUNDING INDEED.
FIRST OFF, IT APPEARS DESTRO IS RUNNING THE SHOW NOW, AND THE COBRA COMMANDER HAS BEEN IMPRISONED. REGARDLESS, THEIR FORCES MARCH ONWARD.
VERY SOON, DESTRO WILL ACTIVATE THE NANO-MITES ACROSS THE NATION, VIA SATELLITE. ANARCHY WILL REIGN THROUGHOUT THE COUNTRY. THAT'S WHEN COBRA'S TROOPS MOVE IN.
SO WE BLAST THE DOOHICKEY WITH ONE 'O' THOSE STAR WARS MISSILES THAT ISN'T SUPPOSED TO EXIST, AND BE DONE WITH IT.
DUE TO THE ENCRYPTION WE HAVE NO WAY OF TRACKING ITS LOCATION, AND WE HAVE TO FIND IT BEFORE WE CAN HACK THE PROGRAMMING.
THE REASON OUR CURRENT VICTIMS ARE IN SUCH A STATE IS BECAUSE COBRA ALREADY HAS PROTOTYPE BROADCASTERS THAT CAN ACTIVATE THE MITES WITHIN A SMALL RADIUS.
WELL, HOW MANY SATELLITES CAN THERE BE?
THIS MANY.
OH BOY.
THIS IS A DIAGRAM OF EVERY MAN-MADE OBJECT ORBITING THE EARTH.
BOTH PUBLICLY KNOWN AND ULTRA-CLASSIFIED.
INCLUDING YOUR STAR WARS SYSTEMS, SHIPWRECK.

SO WHAT ARE WE SUPPOSED TO DO?

WHAT YOU DO BEST.

WHEN THE MITES HIT, COBRA WILL MOVE IN THE GROUND FORCES.

"NO PRESSURE."

YOU'LL BE THERE TO STOP THEM. OUR MEN WILL HANDLE THE SATELLITE-- YOU JUST KEEP THE WORLD SAFE UNTIL THEN.

SO FATHER, THE TIME HAS COME.

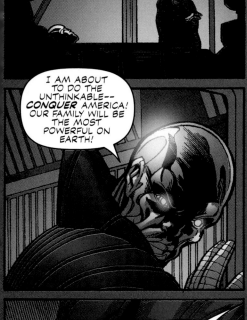

I AM ABOUT TO DO THE UNTHINKABLE-- *CONQUER* AMERICA! OUR FAMILY WILL BE THE MOST POWERFUL ON EARTH!

NO ONE CAN STOP US! DON'T YOU SEE?

YOU ARE GOING TO BE SO *PROUD!*

ACTIVATE THE *GAIJIN* SATELLITE!

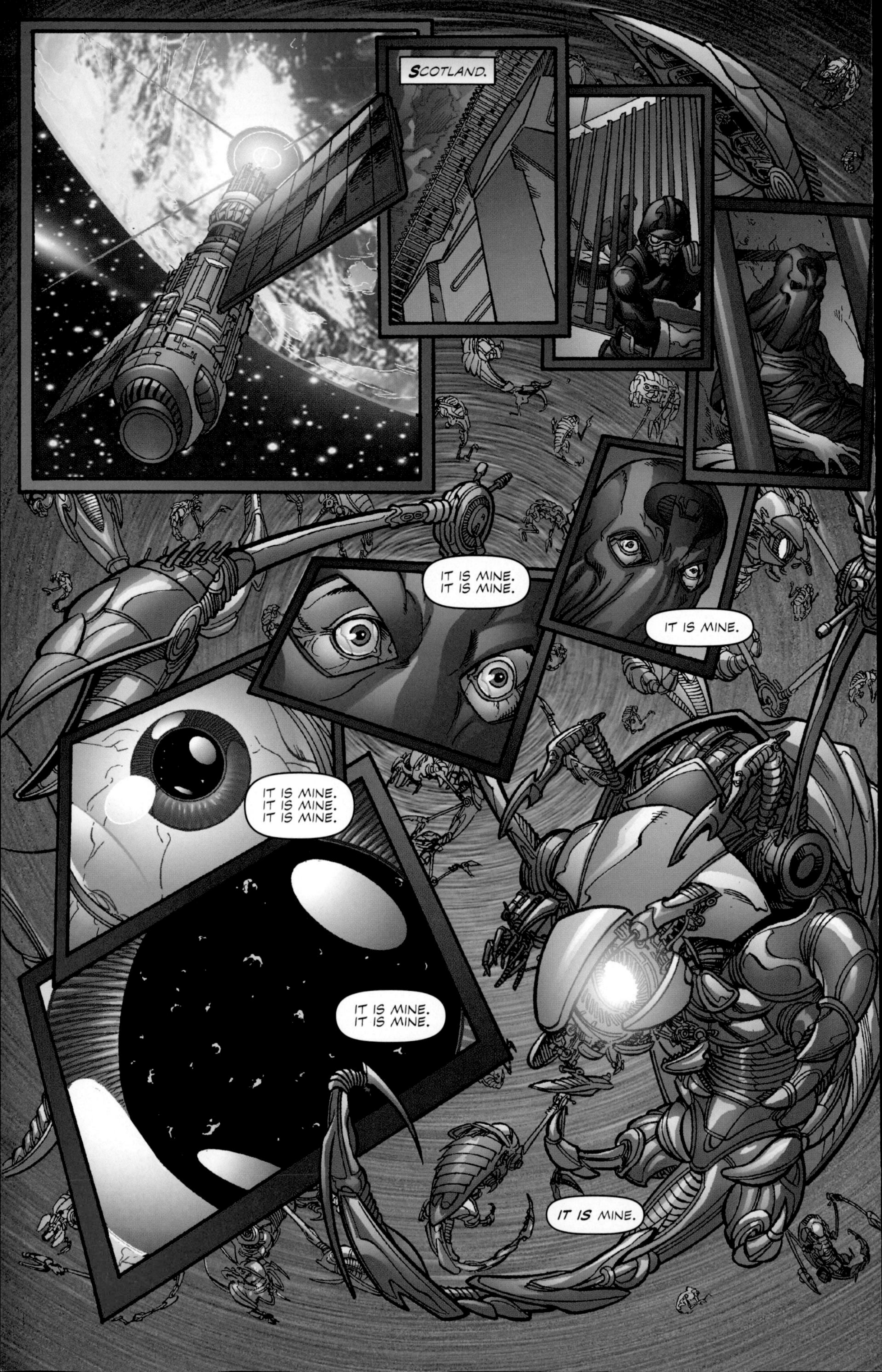
SCOTLAND.
IT IS MINE. IT IS MINE.
IT IS MINE.
IT IS MINE. IT IS MINE. IT IS MINE.
IT IS MINE. IT IS MINE.
IT IS MINE.

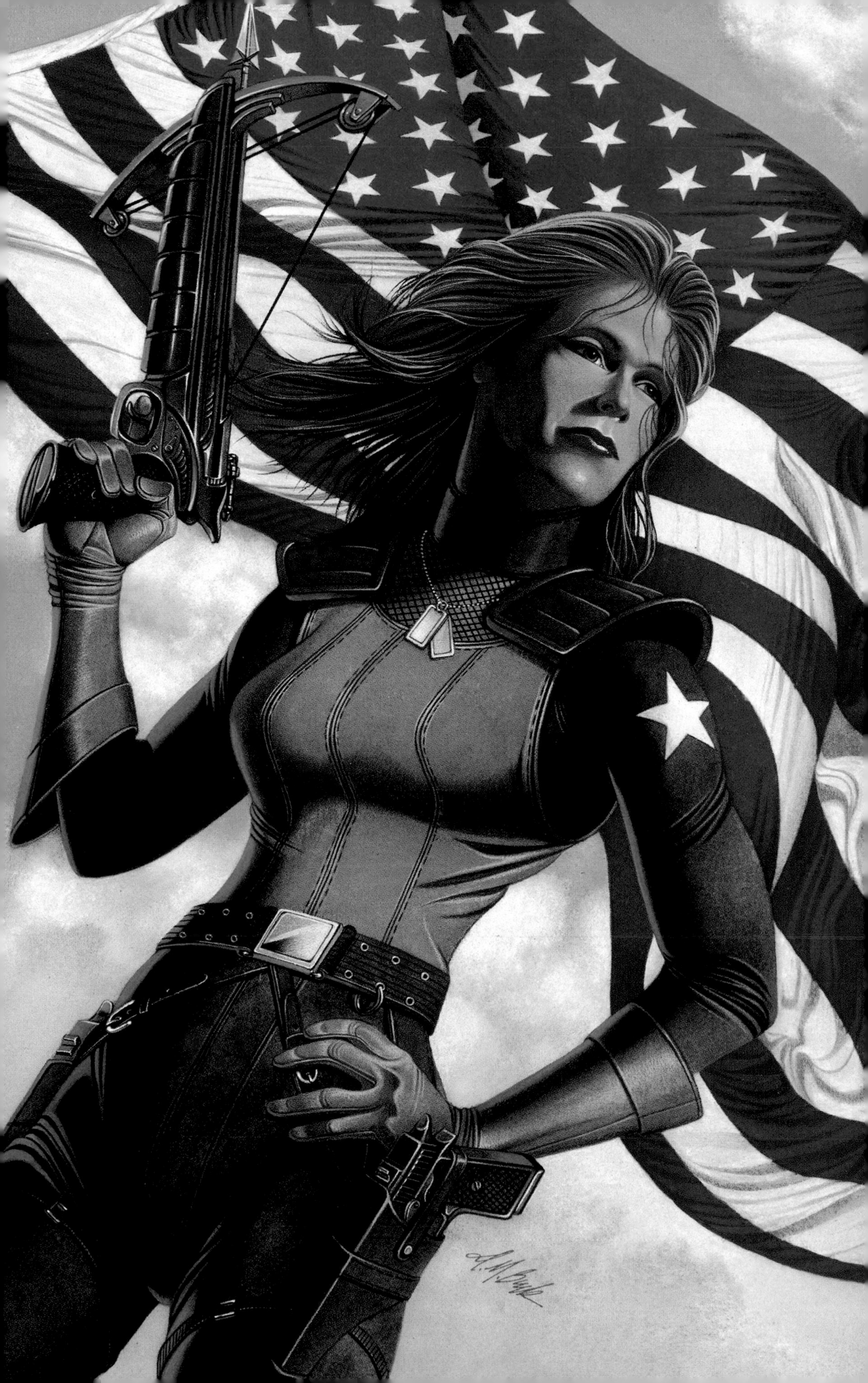

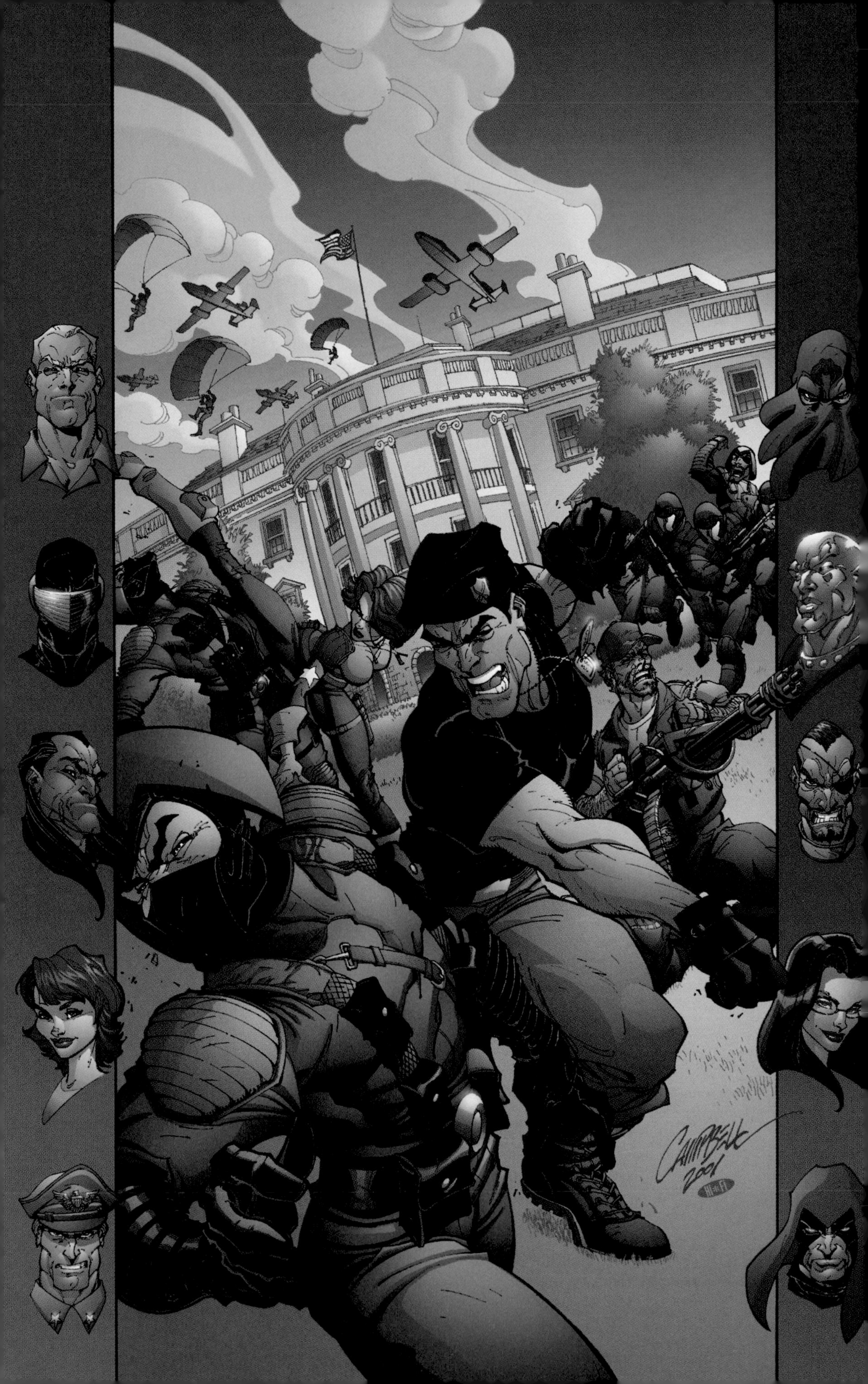

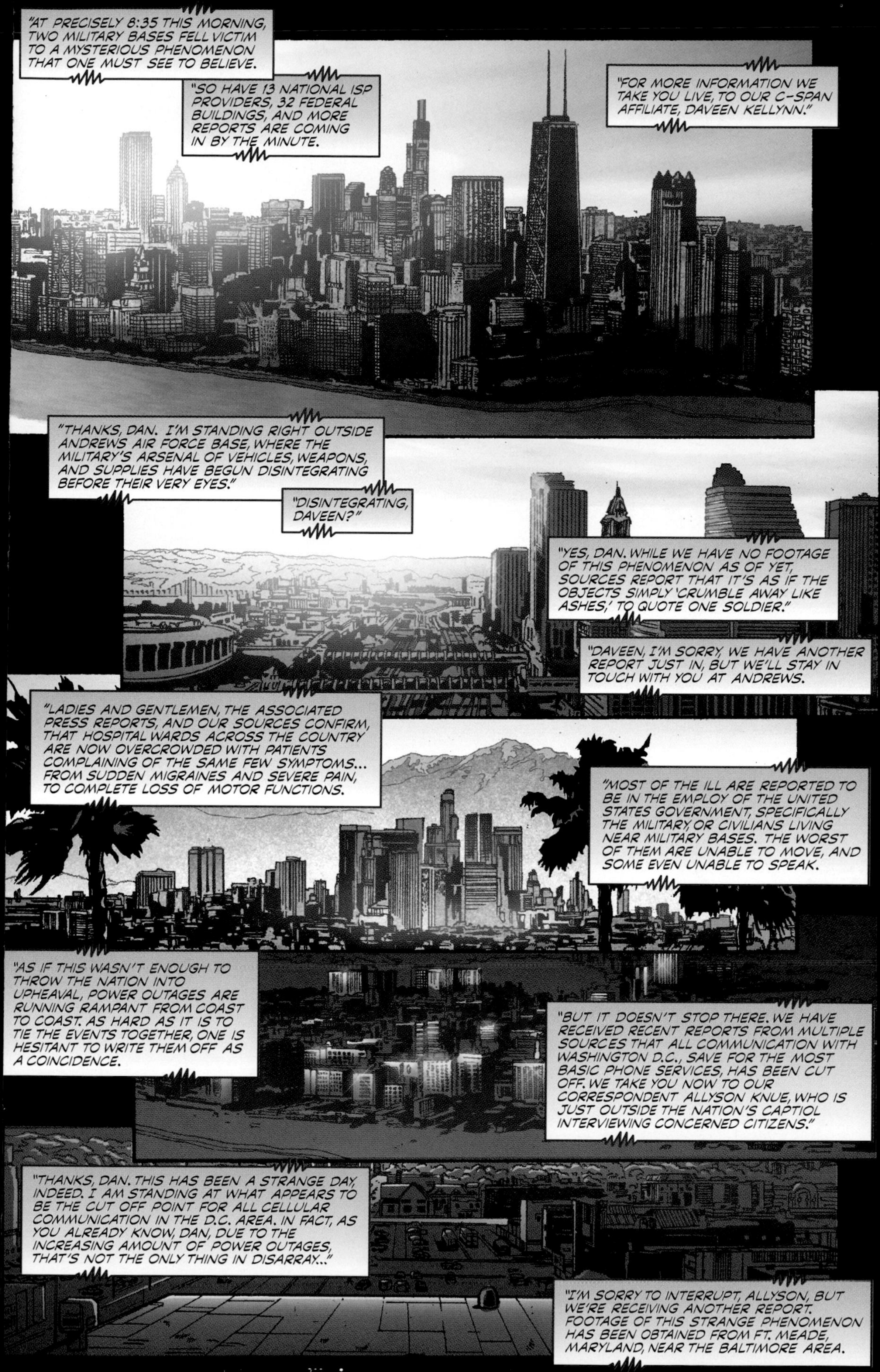
"AT PRECISELY 8:35 THIS MORNING, TWO MILITARY BASES FELL VICTIM TO A MYSTERIOUS PHENOMENON THAT ONE MUST SEE TO BELIEVE.
"SO HAVE 13 NATIONAL ISP PROVIDERS, 32 FEDERAL BUILDINGS, AND MORE REPORTS ARE COMING IN BY THE MINUTE.
"FOR MORE INFORMATION WE TAKE YOU LIVE, TO OUR C-SPAN AFFILIATE, DAVEEN KELLYNN."
"THANKS, DAN. I'M STANDING RIGHT OUTSIDE ANDREWS AIR FORCE BASE, WHERE THE MILITARY'S ARSENAL OF VEHICLES, WEAPONS, AND SUPPLIES HAVE BEGUN DISINTEGRATING BEFORE THEIR VERY EYES."
"DISINTEGRATING, DAVEEN?"
"YES, DAN. WHILE WE HAVE NO FOOTAGE OF THIS PHENOMENON AS OF YET, SOURCES REPORT THAT IT'S AS IF THE OBJECTS SIMPLY 'CRUMBLE AWAY LIKE ASHES,' TO QUOTE ONE SOLDIER."
"DAVEEN, I'M SORRY, WE HAVE ANOTHER REPORT JUST IN, BUT WE'LL STAY IN TOUCH WITH YOU AT ANDREWS.
"LADIES AND GENTLEMEN, THE ASSOCIATED PRESS REPORTS, AND OUR SOURCES CONFIRM, THAT HOSPITAL WARDS ACROSS THE COUNTRY ARE NOW OVERCROWDED WITH PATIENTS COMPLAINING OF THE SAME FEW SYMPTOMS... FROM SUDDEN MIGRAINES AND SEVERE PAIN, TO COMPLETE LOSS OF MOTOR FUNCTIONS.
"MOST OF THE ILL ARE REPORTED TO BE IN THE EMPLOY OF THE UNITED STATES GOVERNMENT, SPECIFICALLY THE MILITARY, OR CIVILIANS LIVING NEAR MILITARY BASES. THE WORST OF THEM ARE UNABLE TO MOVE, AND SOME EVEN UNABLE TO SPEAK.
"AS IF THIS WASN'T ENOUGH TO THROW THE NATION INTO UPHEAVAL, POWER OUTAGES ARE RUNNING RAMPANT FROM COAST TO COAST. AS HARD AS IT IS TO TIE THE EVENTS TOGETHER, ONE IS HESITANT TO WRITE THEM OFF AS A COINCIDENCE.
"BUT IT DOESN'T STOP THERE. WE HAVE RECEIVED RECENT REPORTS FROM MULTIPLE SOURCES THAT ALL COMMUNICATION WITH WASHINGTON D.C., SAVE FOR THE MOST BASIC PHONE SERVICES, HAS BEEN CUT OFF. WE TAKE YOU NOW TO OUR CORRESPONDENT ALLYSON KNUE, WHO IS JUST OUTSIDE THE NATION'S CAPTIOL INTERVIEWING CONCERNED CITIZENS."
"THANKS, DAN. THIS HAS BEEN A STRANGE DAY, INDEED. I AM STANDING AT WHAT APPEARS TO BE THE CUT OFF POINT FOR ALL CELLULAR COMMUNICATION IN THE D.C. AREA. IN FACT, AS YOU ALREADY KNOW, DAN, DUE TO THE INCREASING AMOUNT OF POWER OUTAGES, THAT'S NOT THE ONLY THING IN DISARRAY..."
"I'M SORRY TO INTERRUPT, ALLYSON, BUT WE'RE RECEIVING ANOTHER REPORT. FOOTAGE OF THIS STRANGE PHENOMENON HAS BEEN OBTAINED FROM FT. MEADE, MARYLAND, NEAR THE BALTIMORE AREA.

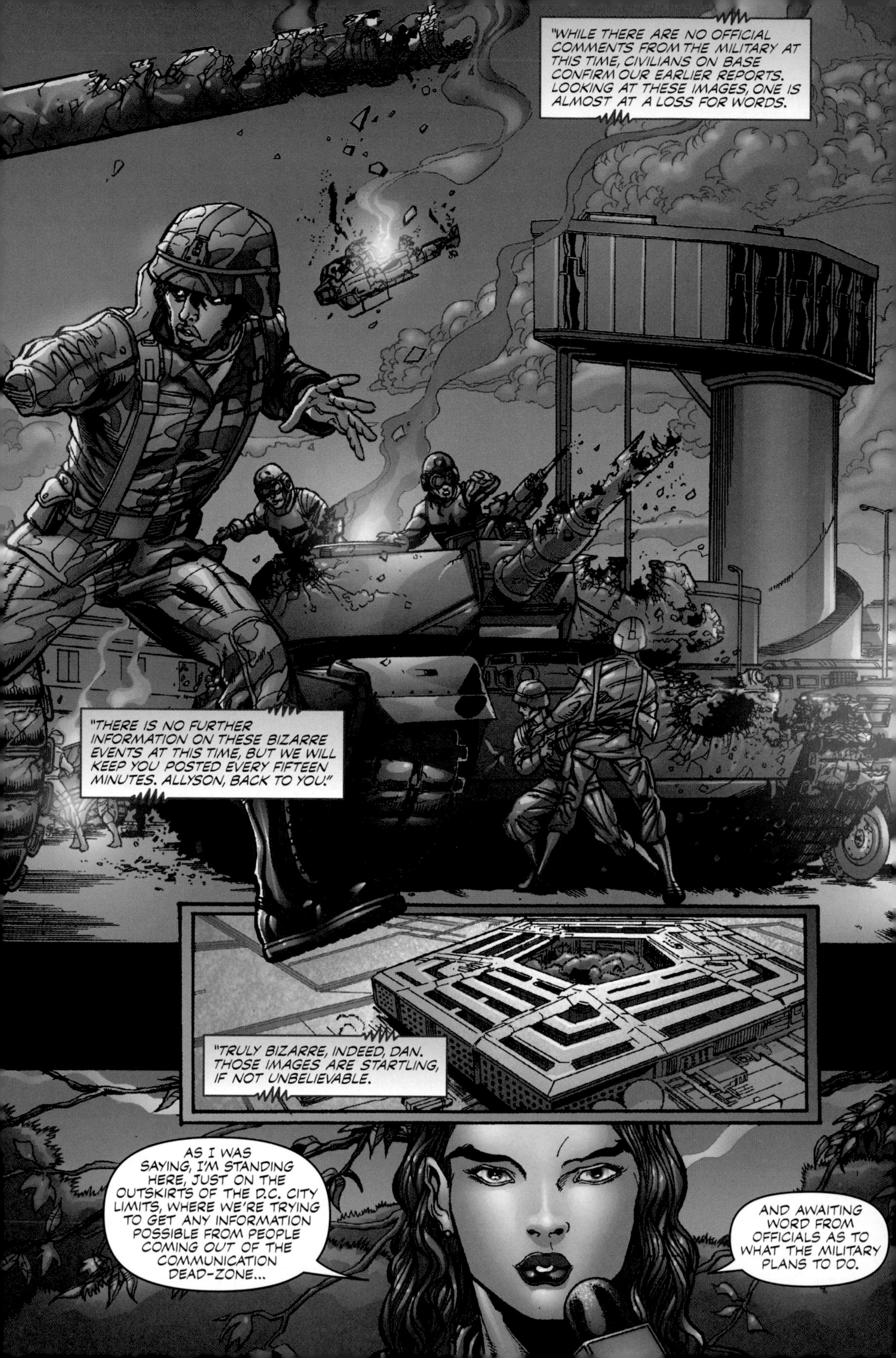
"WHILE THERE ARE NO OFFICIAL COMMENTS FROM THE MILITARY AT THIS TIME, CIVILIANS ON BASE CONFIRM OUR EARLIER REPORTS. LOOKING AT THESE IMAGES, ONE IS ALMOST AT A LOSS FOR WORDS.
"THERE IS NO FURTHER INFORMATION ON THESE BIZARRE EVENTS AT THIS TIME, BUT WE WILL KEEP YOU POSTED EVERY FIFTEEN MINUTES. ALLYSON, BACK TO YOU."
"TRULY BIZARRE, INDEED, DAN. THOSE IMAGES ARE STARTLING, IF NOT UNBELIEVABLE.
AS I WAS SAYING, I'M STANDING HERE, JUST ON THE OUTSKIRTS OF THE D.C. CITY LIMITS, WHERE WE'RE TRYING TO GET ANY INFORMATION POSSIBLE FROM PEOPLE COMING OUT OF THE COMMUNICATION DEAD-ZONE...
AND AWAITING WORD FROM OFFICIALS AS TO WHAT THE MILITARY PLANS TO DO.

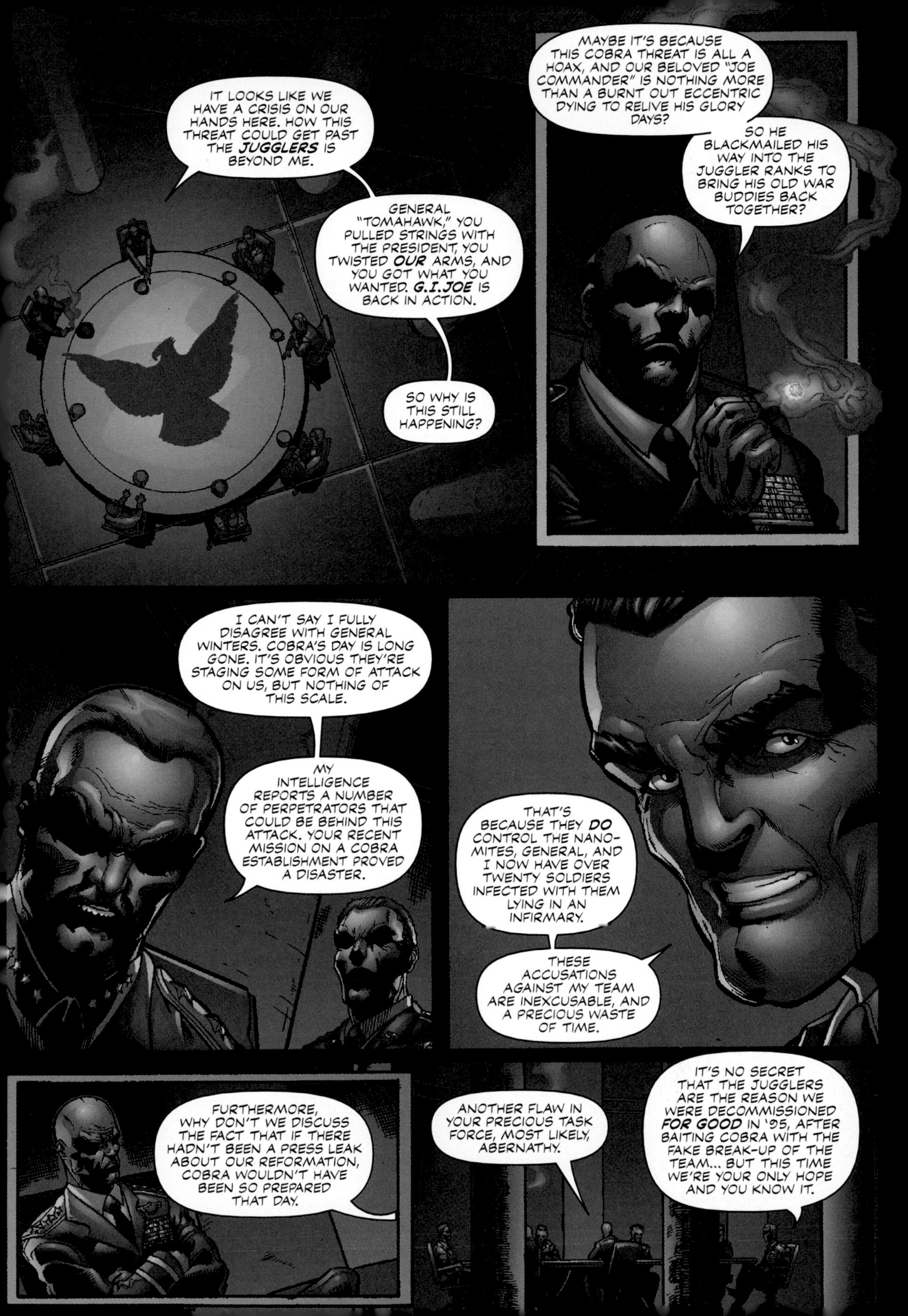
IT LOOKS LIKE WE HAVE A CRISIS ON OUR HANDS HERE. HOW THIS THREAT COULD GET PAST THE ***JUGGLERS*** IS BEYOND ME.
GENERAL "TOMAHAWK," YOU PULLED STRINGS WITH THE PRESIDENT, YOU TWISTED ***OUR*** ARMS, AND YOU GOT WHAT YOU WANTED. ***G.I.JOE*** IS BACK IN ACTION.
SO WHY IS THIS STILL HAPPENING?
MAYBE IT'S BECAUSE THIS COBRA THREAT IS ALL A HOAX, AND OUR BELOVED "JOE COMMANDER" IS NOTHING MORE THAN A BURNT OUT ECCENTRIC DYING TO RELIVE HIS GLORY DAYS?
SO HE BLACKMAILED HIS WAY INTO THE JUGGLER RANKS TO BRING HIS OLD WAR BUDDIES BACK TOGETHER?
I CAN'T SAY I FULLY DISAGREE WITH GENERAL WINTERS. COBRA'S DAY IS LONG GONE. IT'S OBVIOUS THEY'RE STAGING SOME FORM OF ATTACK ON US, BUT NOTHING OF THIS SCALE.
MY INTELLIGENCE REPORTS A NUMBER OF PERPETRATORS THAT COULD BE BEHIND THIS ATTACK. YOUR RECENT MISSION ON A COBRA ESTABLISHMENT PROVED A DISASTER.
THAT'S BECAUSE THEY ***DO*** CONTROL THE NANO-MITES, GENERAL, AND I NOW HAVE OVER TWENTY SOLDIERS INFECTED WITH THEM LYING IN AN INFIRMARY.
THESE ACCUSATIONS AGAINST MY TEAM ARE INEXCUSABLE, AND A PRECIOUS WASTE OF TIME.
FURTHERMORE, WHY DON'T WE DISCUSS THE FACT THAT IF THERE HADN'T BEEN A PRESS LEAK ABOUT OUR REFORMATION, COBRA WOULDN'T HAVE BEEN SO PREPARED THAT DAY.
ANOTHER FLAW IN YOUR PRECIOUS TASK FORCE, MOST LIKELY, ABERNATHY.
IT'S NO SECRET THAT THE JUGGLERS ARE THE REASON WE WERE DECOMMISSIONED ***FOR GOOD*** IN '95, AFTER BAITING COBRA WITH THE FAKE BREAK-UP OF THE TEAM... BUT THIS TIME WE'RE YOUR ONLY HOPE AND YOU KNOW IT.

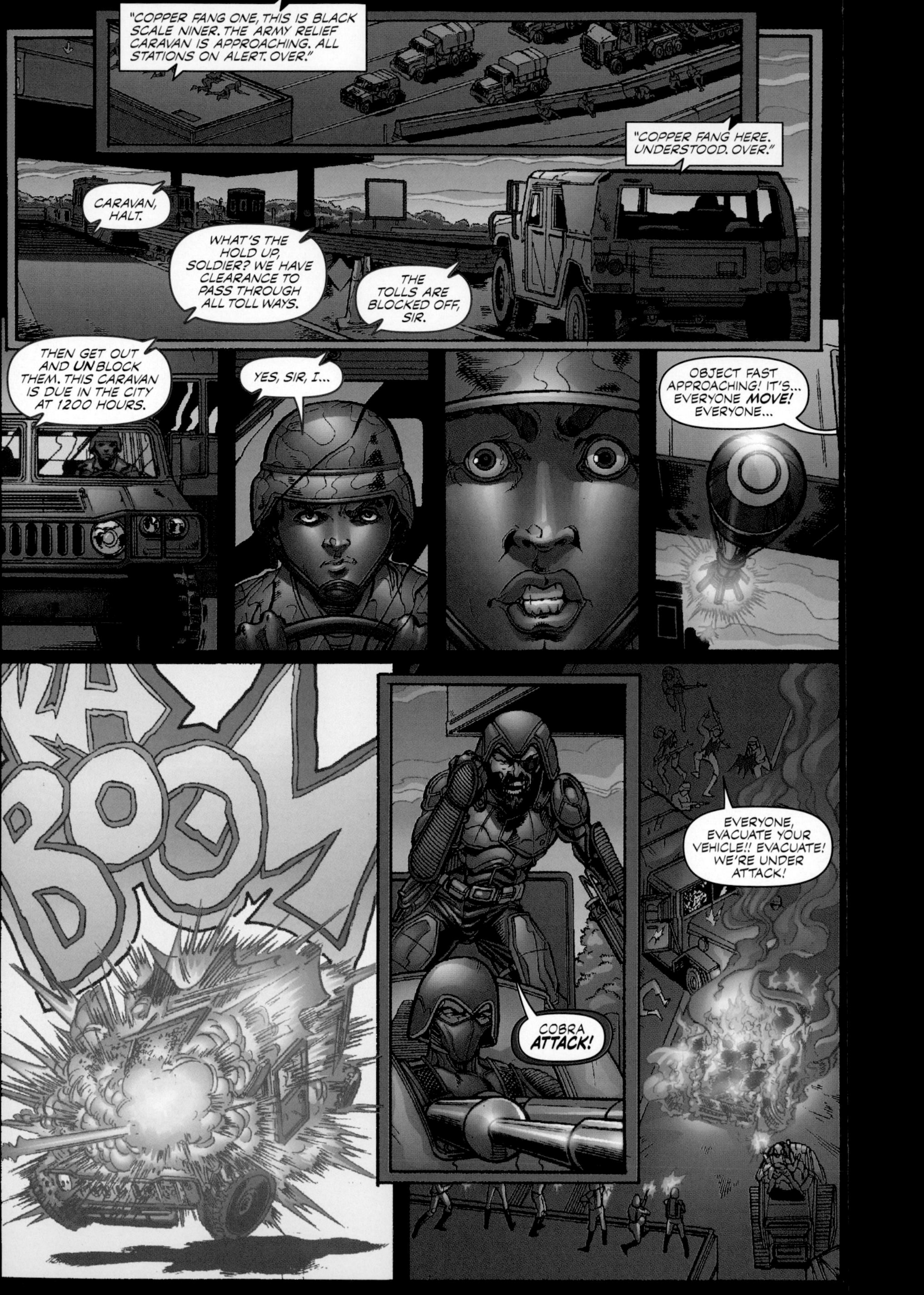
"COPPER FANG ONE, THIS IS BLACK SCALE NINER. THE ARMY RELIEF CARAVAN IS APPROACHING. ALL STATIONS ON ALERT. OVER."
"COPPER FANG HERE. UNDERSTOOD. OVER."
CARAVAN, HALT.
WHAT'S THE HOLD UP, SOLDIER? WE HAVE CLEARANCE TO PASS THROUGH ALL TOLL WAYS.
THE TOLLS ARE BLOCKED OFF, SIR.
THEN GET OUT AND UNBLOCK THEM. THIS CARAVAN IS DUE IN THE CITY AT 1200 HOURS.
YES, SIR, I...
OBJECT FAST APPROACHING! IT'S... EVERYONE MOVE! EVERYONE...
BOOM
COBRA ATTACK!
EVERYONE, EVACUATE YOUR VEHICLE!! EVACUATE! WE'RE UNDER ATTACK!

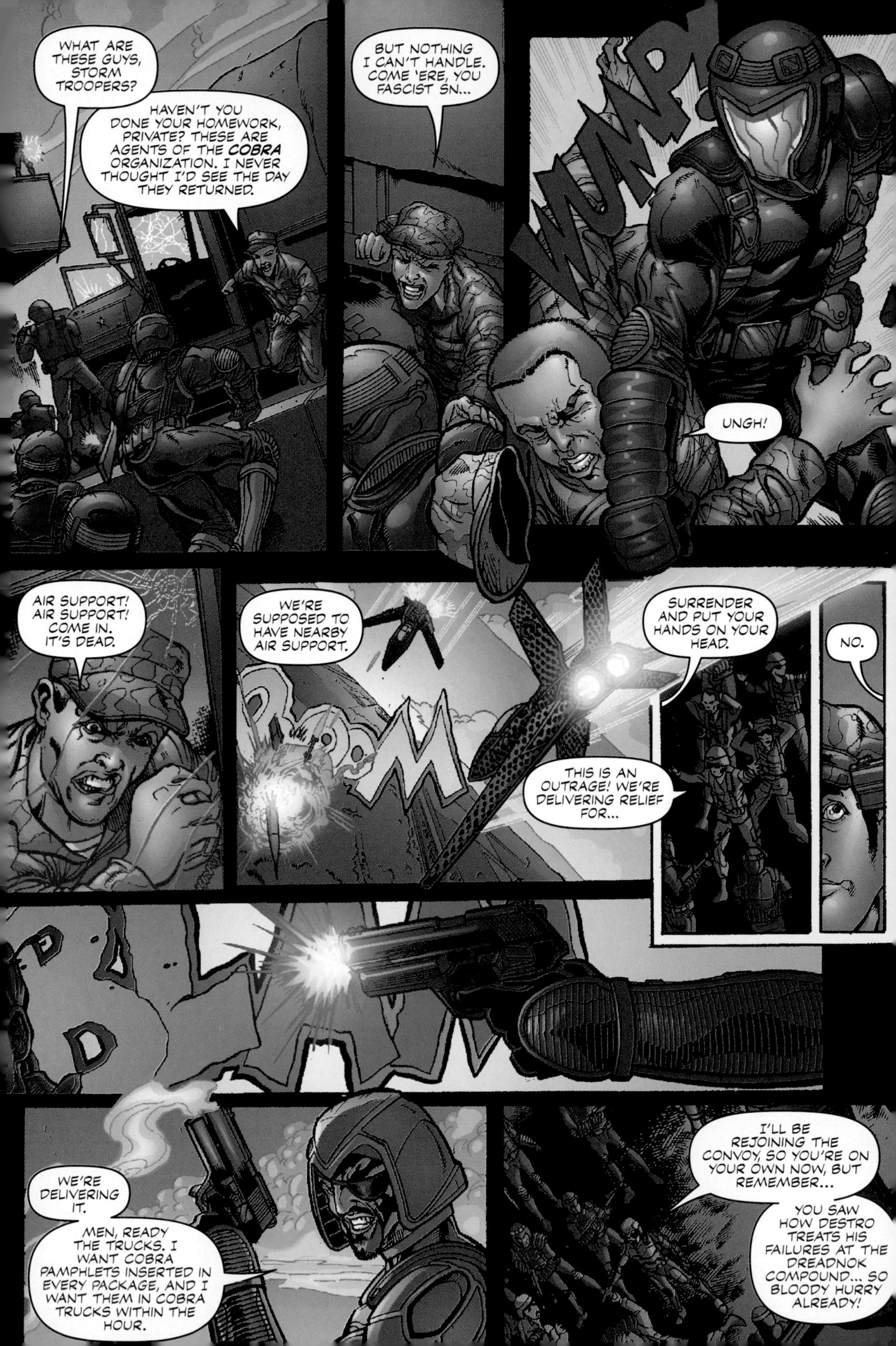

WHAT ARE THESE GUYS, STORM TROOPERS?
HAVEN'T YOU DONE YOUR HOMEWORK, PRIVATE? THESE ARE AGENTS OF THE **COBRA** ORGANIZATION. I NEVER THOUGHT I'D SEE THE DAY THEY RETURNED.
BUT NOTHING I CAN'T HANDLE. COME 'ERE, YOU FASCIST SN...
WUMP!
UNGH!
AIR SUPPORT! AIR SUPPORT! COME IN. IT'S DEAD.
WE'RE SUPPOSED TO HAVE NEARBY AIR SUPPORT.
SURRENDER AND PUT YOUR HANDS ON YOUR HEAD.
THIS IS AN OUTRAGE! WE'RE DELIVERING RELIEF FOR...
NO.
WE'RE DELIVERING IT.
MEN, READY THE TRUCKS. I WANT COBRA PAMPHLETS INSERTED IN EVERY PACKAGE, AND I WANT THEM IN COBRA TRUCKS WITHIN THE HOUR.
I'LL BE REJOINING THE CONVOY, SO YOU'RE ON YOUR OWN NOW, BUT REMEMBER...
YOU SAW HOW DESTRO TREATS HIS FAILURES AT THE DREADNOK COMPOUND... SO BLOODY HURRY ALREADY!

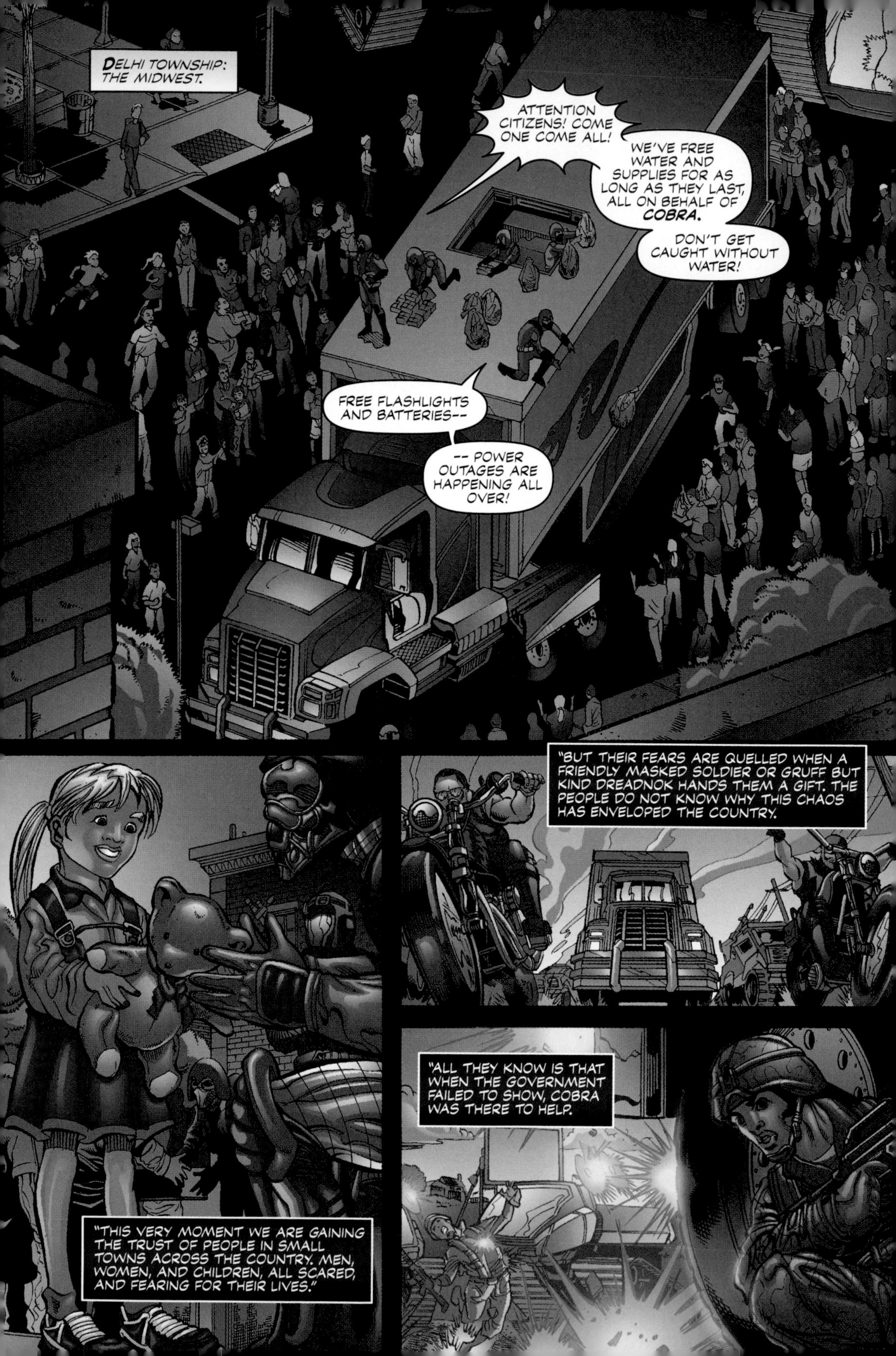
DELHI TOWNSHIP: THE MIDWEST.
ATTENTION CITIZENS! COME ONE COME ALL!
WE'VE FREE WATER AND SUPPLIES FOR AS LONG AS THEY LAST, ALL ON BEHALF OF COBRA.
DON'T GET CAUGHT WITHOUT WATER!
FREE FLASHLIGHTS AND BATTERIES--
-- POWER OUTAGES ARE HAPPENING ALL OVER!
"THIS VERY MOMENT WE ARE GAINING THE TRUST OF PEOPLE IN SMALL TOWNS ACROSS THE COUNTRY. MEN, WOMEN, AND CHILDREN, ALL SCARED, AND FEARING FOR THEIR LIVES."
"BUT THEIR FEARS ARE QUELLED WHEN A FRIENDLY MASKED SOLDIER OR GRUFF BUT KIND DREADNOK HANDS THEM A GIFT. THE PEOPLE DO NOT KNOW WHY THIS CHAOS HAS ENVELOPED THE COUNTRY.
"ALL THEY KNOW IS THAT WHEN THE GOVERNMENT FAILED TO SHOW, COBRA WAS THERE TO HELP.

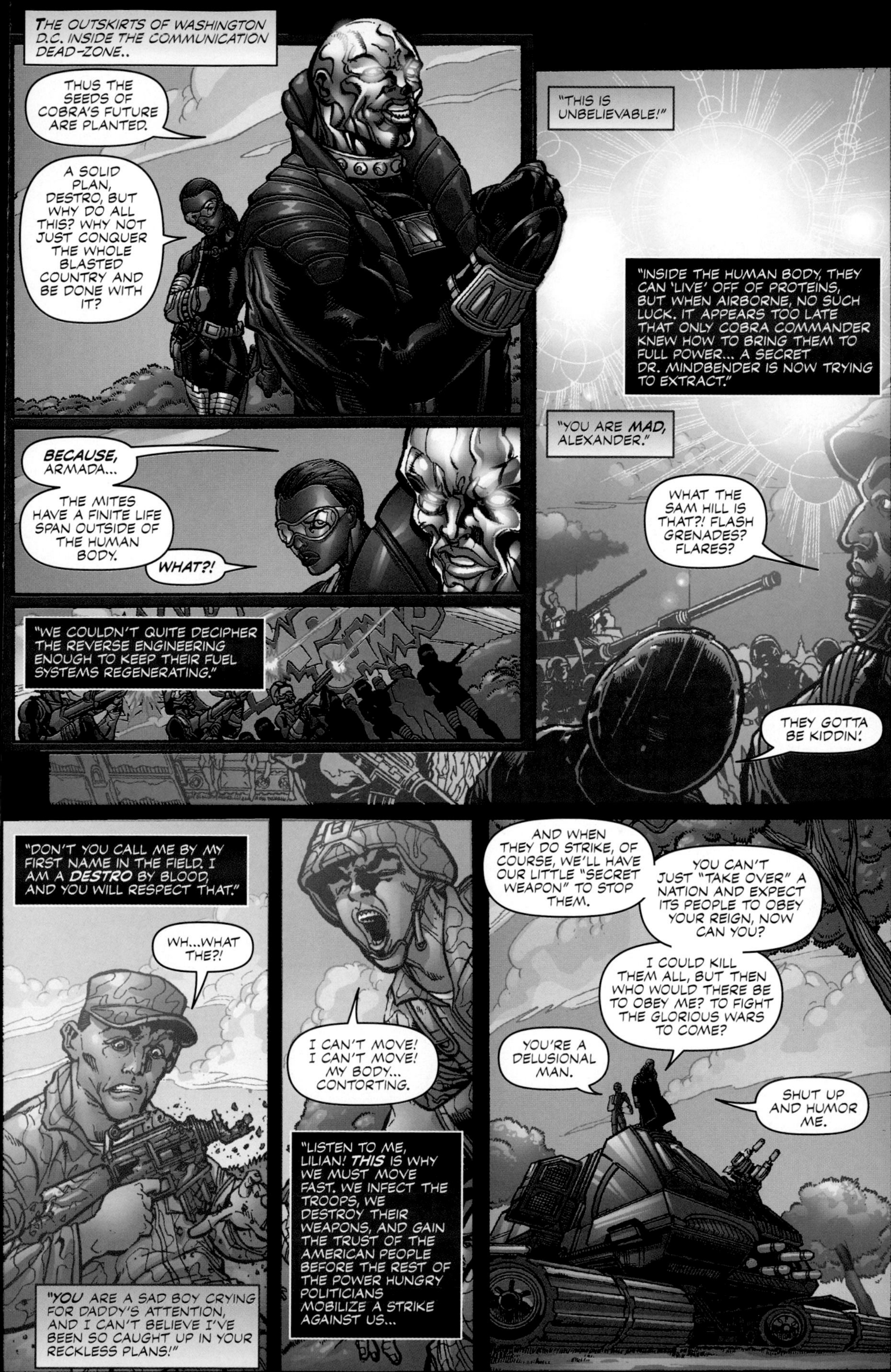
THE OUTSKIRTS OF WASHINGTON D.C. INSIDE THE COMMUNICATION DEAD-ZONE..
THUS THE SEEDS OF COBRA'S FUTURE ARE PLANTED.
A SOLID PLAN, DESTRO, BUT WHY DO ALL THIS? WHY NOT JUST CONQUER THE WHOLE BLASTED COUNTRY AND BE DONE WITH IT?
BECAUSE, ARMADA...
THE MITES HAVE A FINITE LIFE SPAN OUTSIDE OF THE HUMAN BODY.
WHAT?!
"WE COULDN'T QUITE DECIPHER THE REVERSE ENGINEERING ENOUGH TO KEEP THEIR FUEL SYSTEMS REGENERATING."
"THIS IS UNBELIEVABLE!"
"INSIDE THE HUMAN BODY, THEY CAN 'LIVE' OFF OF PROTEINS, BUT WHEN AIRBORNE, NO SUCH LUCK. IT APPEARS TOO LATE THAT ONLY COBRA COMMANDER KNEW HOW TO BRING THEM TO FULL POWER... A SECRET DR. MINDBENDER IS NOW TRYING TO EXTRACT."
"YOU ARE MAD, ALEXANDER."
WHAT THE SAM HILL IS THAT?! FLASH GRENADES? FLARES?
THEY GOTTA BE KIDDIN'.
"DON'T YOU CALL ME BY MY FIRST NAME IN THE FIELD. I AM A DESTRO BY BLOOD, AND YOU WILL RESPECT THAT."
WH...WHAT THE?!
"YOU ARE A SAD BOY CRYING FOR DADDY'S ATTENTION, AND I CAN'T BELIEVE I'VE BEEN SO CAUGHT UP IN YOUR RECKLESS PLANS!"
I CAN'T MOVE! I CAN'T MOVE! MY BODY... CONTORTING.
"LISTEN TO ME, LILIAN! THIS IS WHY WE MUST MOVE FAST. WE INFECT THE TROOPS, WE DESTROY THEIR WEAPONS, AND GAIN THE TRUST OF THE AMERICAN PEOPLE BEFORE THE REST OF THE POWER HUNGRY POLITICIANS MOBILIZE A STRIKE AGAINST US...
AND WHEN THEY DO STRIKE, OF COURSE, WE'LL HAVE OUR LITTLE "SECRET WEAPON" TO STOP THEM.
YOU CAN'T JUST "TAKE OVER" A NATION AND EXPECT ITS PEOPLE TO OBEY YOUR REIGN, NOW CAN YOU?
I COULD KILL THEM ALL, BUT THEN WHO WOULD THERE BE TO OBEY ME? TO FIGHT THE GLORIOUS WARS TO COME?
YOU'RE A DELUSIONAL MAN.
SHUT UP AND HUMOR ME.

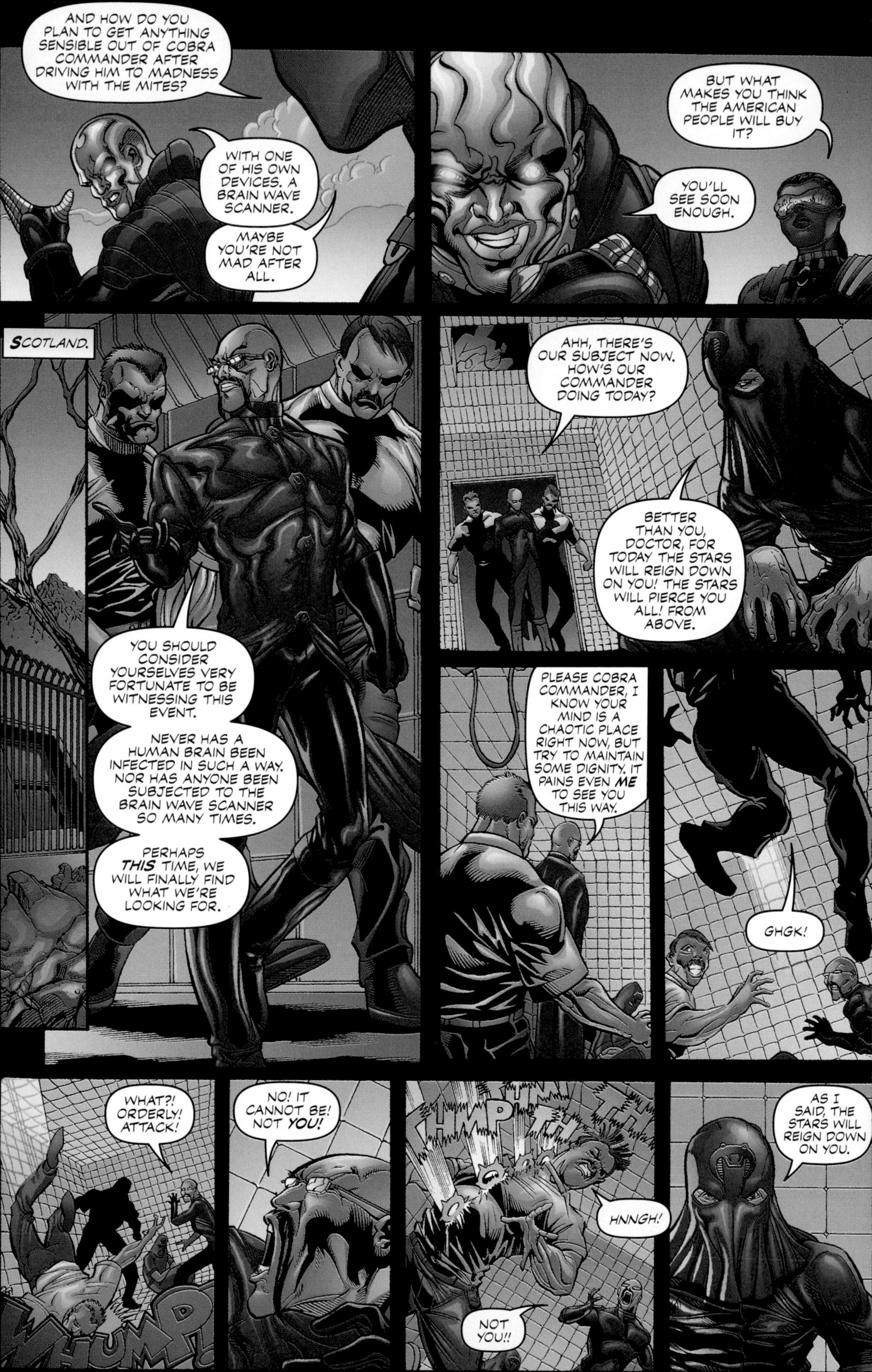
AND HOW DO YOU PLAN TO GET ANYTHING SENSIBLE OUT OF COBRA COMMANDER AFTER DRIVING HIM TO MADNESS WITH THE MITES?
WITH ONE OF HIS OWN DEVICES. A BRAIN WAVE SCANNER.
MAYBE YOU'RE NOT MAD AFTER ALL.
BUT WHAT MAKES YOU THINK THE AMERICAN PEOPLE WILL BUY IT?
YOU'LL SEE SOON ENOUGH.
SCOTLAND.
YOU SHOULD CONSIDER YOURSELVES VERY FORTUNATE TO BE WITNESSING THIS EVENT.
NEVER HAS A HUMAN BRAIN BEEN INFECTED IN SUCH A WAY. NOR HAS ANYONE BEEN SUBJECTED TO THE BRAIN WAVE SCANNER SO MANY TIMES.
PERHAPS THIS TIME, WE WILL FINALLY FIND WHAT WE'RE LOOKING FOR.
AHH, THERE'S OUR SUBJECT NOW. HOW'S OUR COMMANDER DOING TODAY?
BETTER THAN YOU, DOCTOR, FOR TODAY THE STARS WILL REIGN DOWN ON YOU! THE STARS WILL PIERCE YOU ALL! FROM ABOVE.
PLEASE COBRA COMMANDER, I KNOW YOUR MIND IS A CHAOTIC PLACE RIGHT NOW, BUT TRY TO MAINTAIN SOME DIGNITY. IT PAINS EVEN ME TO SEE YOU THIS WAY.
GHGK!
WHAT?! ORDERLY! ATTACK!
WHUMP
NO! IT CANNOT BE! NOT YOU!
THMPTH
HNNGH!
NOT YOU!!
AS I SAID, THE STARS WILL REIGN DOWN ON YOU.

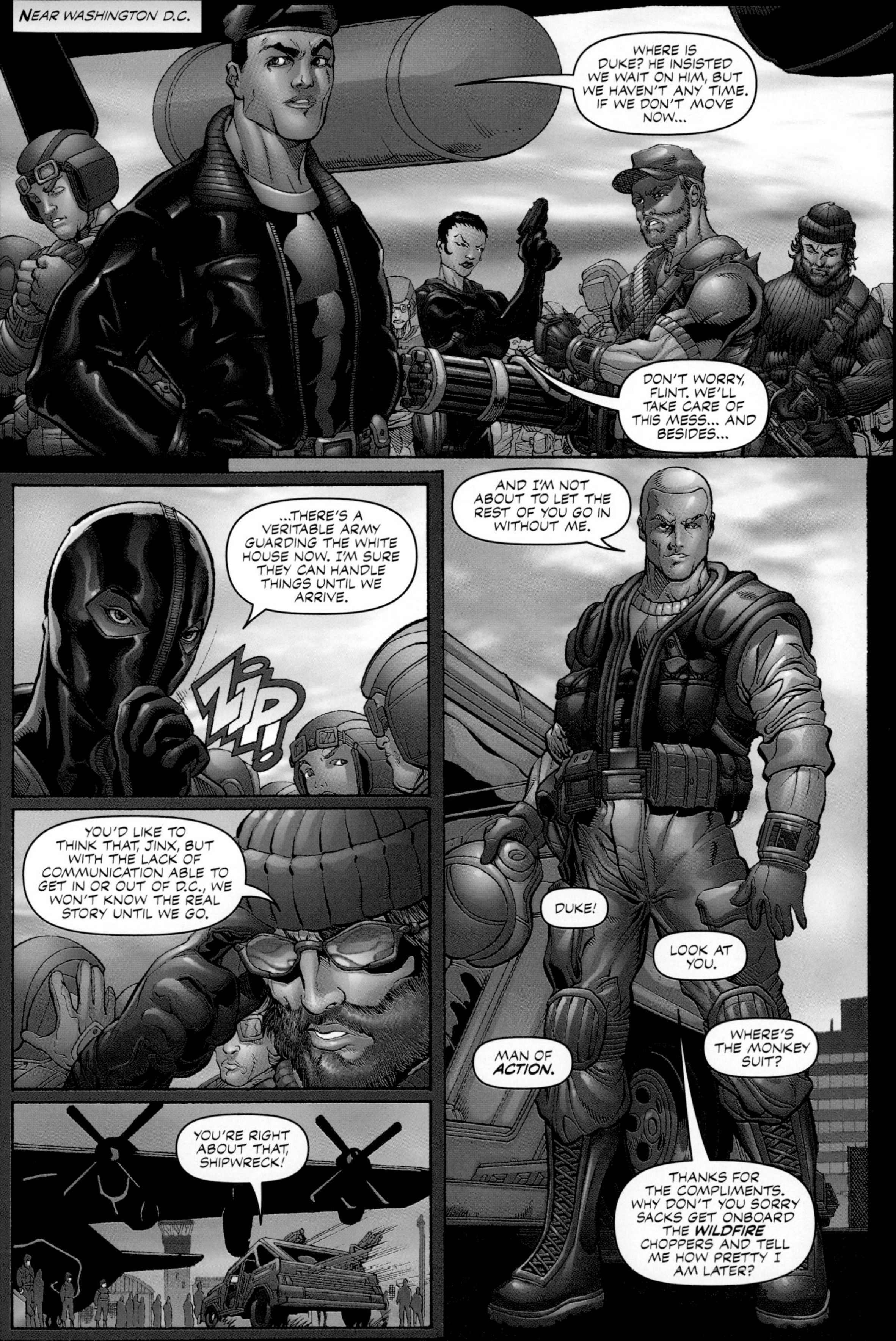
NEAR WASHINGTON D.C.
WHERE IS DUKE? HE INSISTED WE WAIT ON HIM, BUT WE HAVEN'T ANY TIME. IF WE DON'T MOVE NOW...
DON'T WORRY, FLINT. WE'LL TAKE CARE OF THIS MESS... AND BESIDES...
...THERE'S A VERITABLE ARMY GUARDING THE WHITE HOUSE NOW. I'M SURE THEY CAN HANDLE THINGS UNTIL WE ARRIVE.
ZIP!
YOU'D LIKE TO THINK THAT, JINX, BUT WITH THE LACK OF COMMUNICATION ABLE TO GET IN OR OUT OF D.C., WE WON'T KNOW THE REAL STORY UNTIL WE GO.
YOU'RE RIGHT ABOUT THAT, SHIPWRECK!
AND I'M NOT ABOUT TO LET THE REST OF YOU GO IN WITHOUT ME.
DUKE!
LOOK AT YOU.
MAN OF ACTION.
WHERE'S THE MONKEY SUIT?
THANKS FOR THE COMPLIMENTS. WHY DON'T YOU SORRY SACKS GET ONBOARD THE WILDFIRE CHOPPERS AND TELL ME HOW PRETTY I AM LATER?

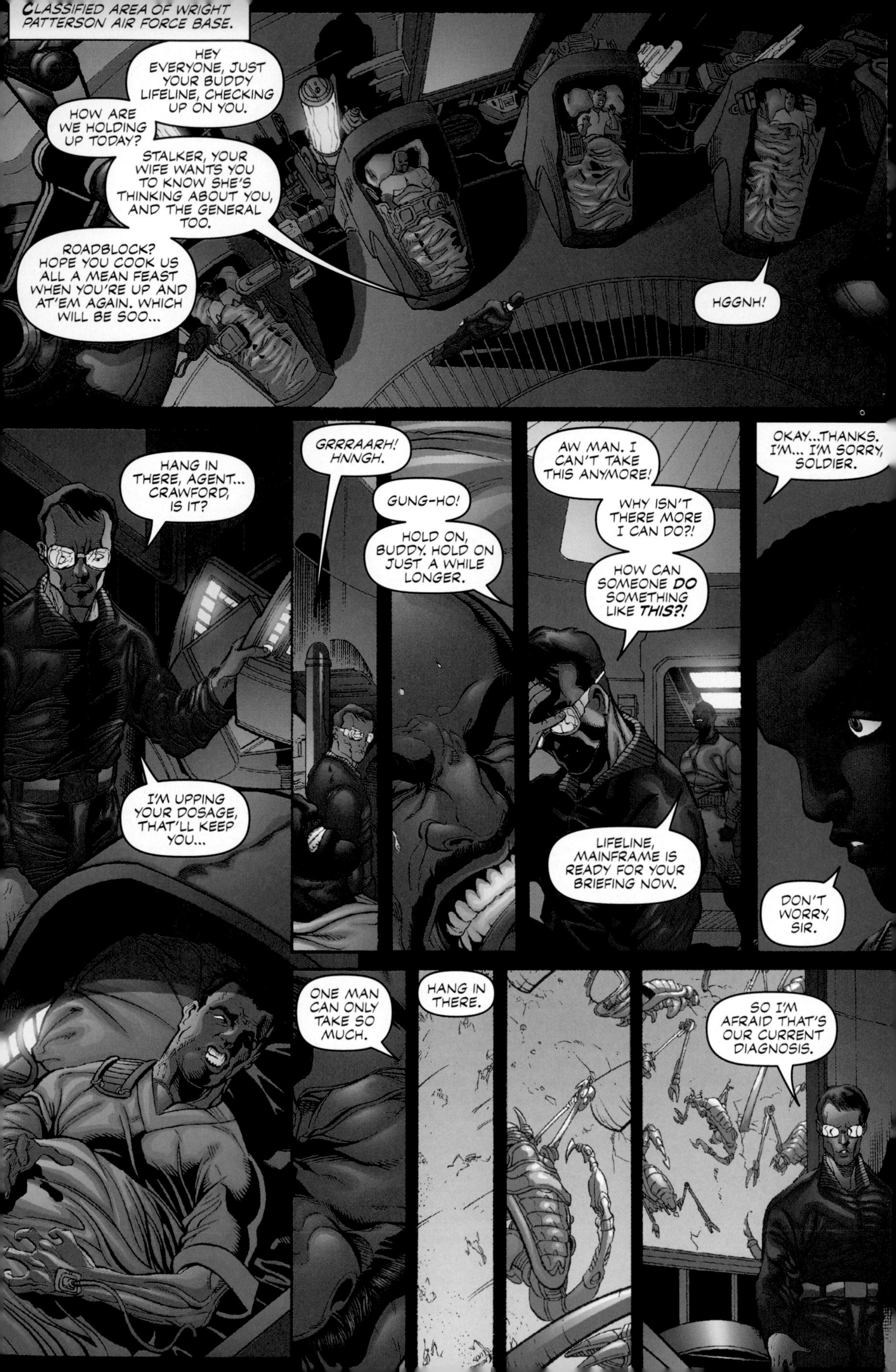
CLASSIFIED AREA OF WRIGHT PATTERSON AIR FORCE BASE.
HEY EVERYONE, JUST YOUR BUDDY LIFELINE, CHECKING UP ON YOU.
HOW ARE WE HOLDING UP TODAY?
STALKER, YOUR WIFE WANTS YOU TO KNOW SHE'S THINKING ABOUT YOU, AND THE GENERAL TOO.
ROADBLOCK? HOPE YOU COOK US ALL A MEAN FEAST WHEN YOU'RE UP AND AT'EM AGAIN. WHICH WILL BE SOO...
HGGNH!
HANG IN THERE, AGENT... CRAWFORD, IS IT?
I'M UPPING YOUR DOSAGE, THAT'LL KEEP YOU...
GRRRAARH! HNNGH.
GUNG-HO!
HOLD ON, BUDDY. HOLD ON JUST A WHILE LONGER.
AW MAN. I CAN'T TAKE THIS ANYMORE!
WHY ISN'T THERE MORE I CAN DO?!
HOW CAN SOMEONE DO SOMETHING LIKE THIS?!
LIFELINE, MAINFRAME IS READY FOR YOUR BRIEFING NOW.
OKAY...THANKS. I'M... I'M SORRY, SOLDIER.
DON'T WORRY, SIR.
ONE MAN CAN ONLY TAKE SO MUCH.
HANG IN THERE.
SO I'M AFRAID THAT'S OUR CURRENT DIAGNOSIS.

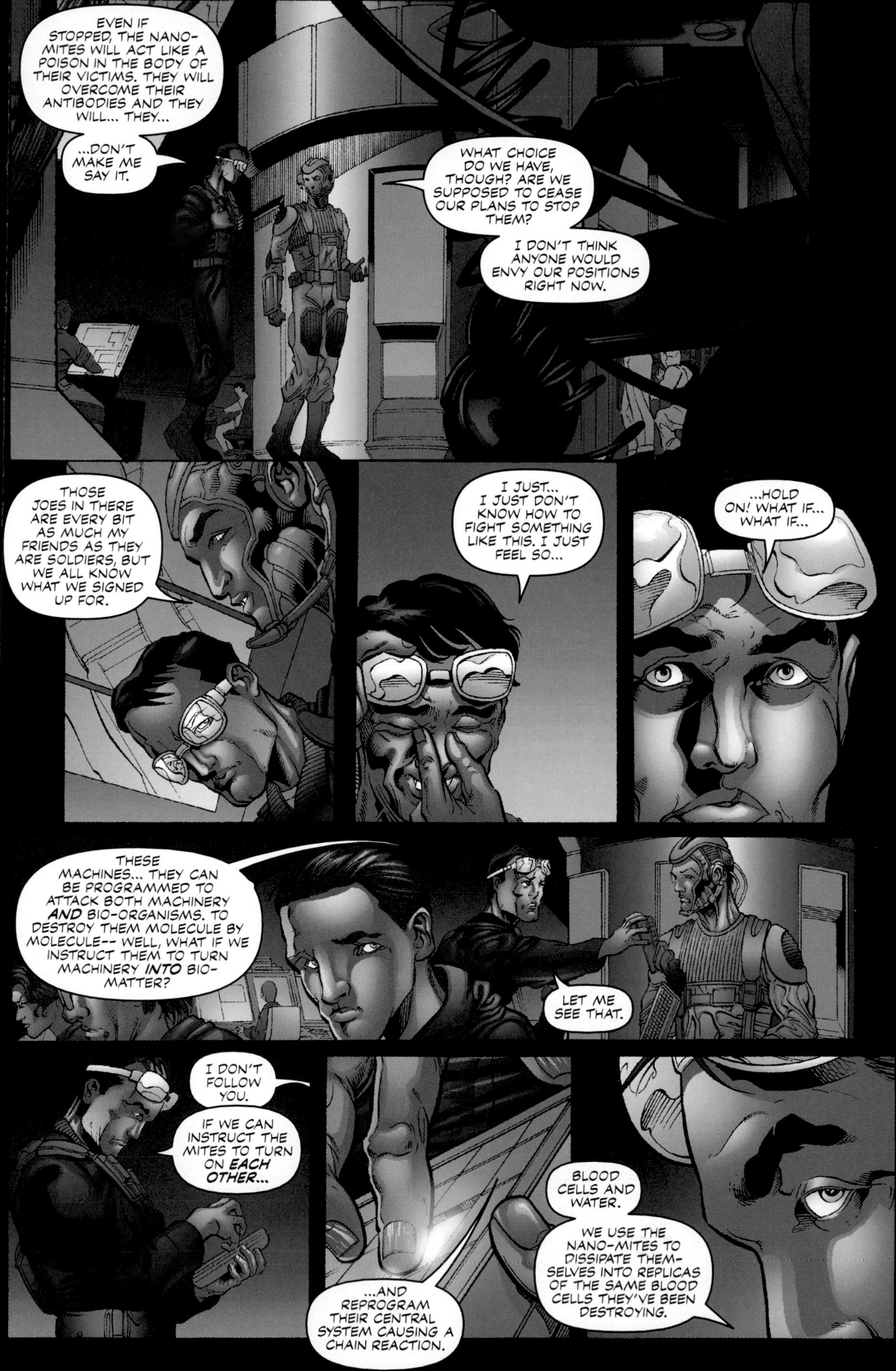
EVEN IF STOPPED, THE NANO-MITES WILL ACT LIKE A POISON IN THE BODY OF THEIR VICTIMS. THEY WILL OVERCOME THEIR ANTIBODIES AND THEY WILL... THEY...
...DON'T MAKE ME SAY IT.
WHAT CHOICE DO WE HAVE, THOUGH? ARE WE SUPPOSED TO CEASE OUR PLANS TO STOP THEM?
I DON'T THINK ANYONE WOULD ENVY OUR POSITIONS RIGHT NOW.
THOSE JOES IN THERE ARE EVERY BIT AS MUCH MY FRIENDS AS THEY ARE SOLDIERS, BUT WE ALL KNOW WHAT WE SIGNED UP FOR.
I JUST... I JUST DON'T KNOW HOW TO FIGHT SOMETHING LIKE THIS. I JUST FEEL SO...
...HOLD ON! WHAT IF... WHAT IF...
THESE MACHINES... THEY CAN BE PROGRAMMED TO ATTACK BOTH MACHINERY **AND** BIO-ORGANISMS. TO DESTROY THEM MOLECULE BY MOLECULE-- WELL, WHAT IF WE INSTRUCT THEM TO TURN MACHINERY **INTO** BIO-MATTER?
LET ME SEE THAT.
I DON'T FOLLOW YOU.
IF WE CAN INSTRUCT THE MITES TO TURN ON **EACH OTHER...**
...AND REPROGRAM THEIR CENTRAL SYSTEM CAUSING A CHAIN REACTION.
BLOOD CELLS AND WATER.
WE USE THE NANO-MITES TO DISSIPATE THEM-SELVES INTO REPLICAS OF THE SAME BLOOD CELLS THEY'VE BEEN DESTROYING.

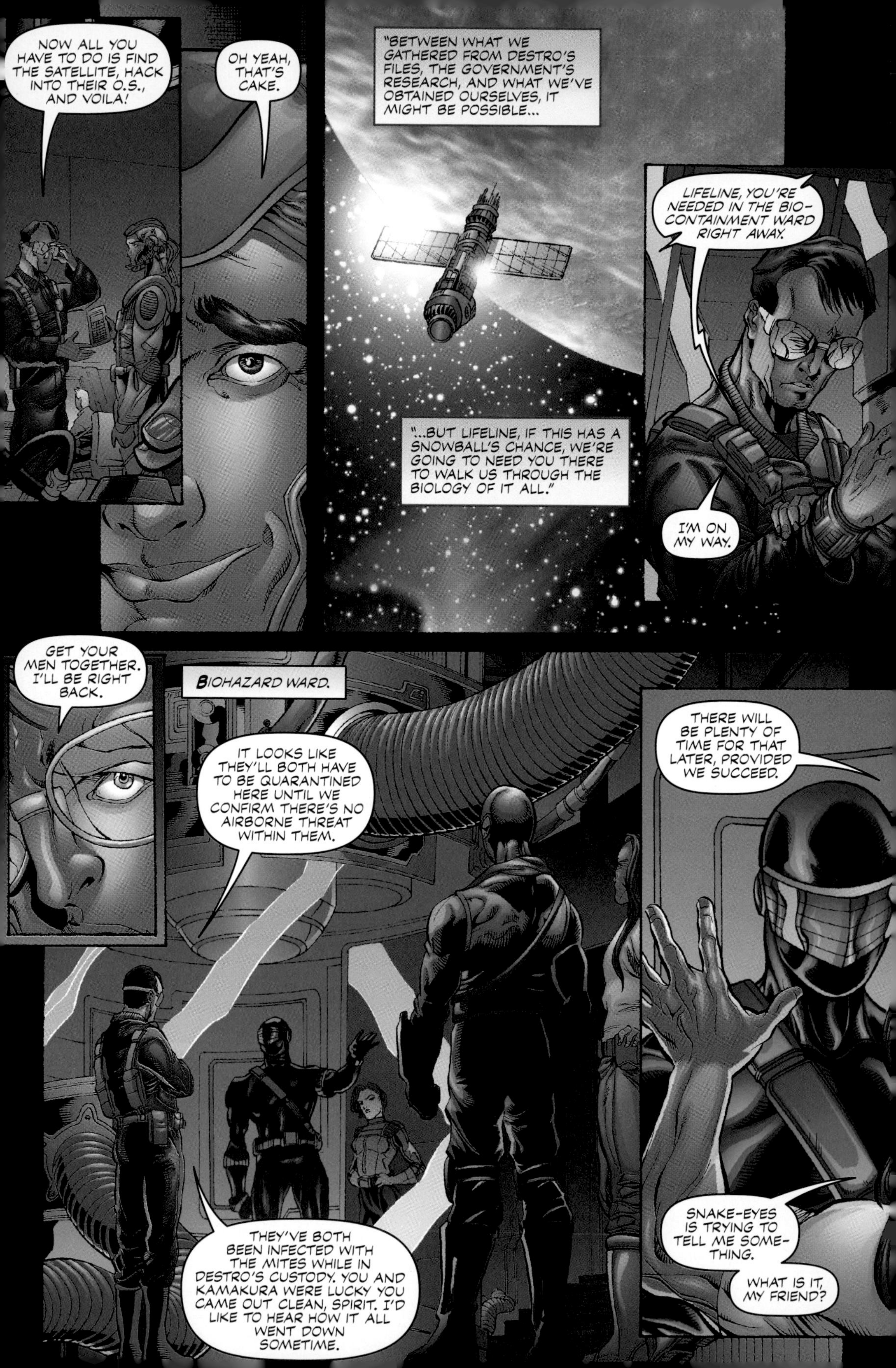
NOW ALL YOU HAVE TO DO IS FIND THE SATELLITE, HACK INTO THEIR O.S., AND VOILA!
OH YEAH, THAT'S CAKE.
"BETWEEN WHAT WE GATHERED FROM DESTRO'S FILES, THE GOVERNMENT'S RESEARCH, AND WHAT WE'VE OBTAINED OURSELVES, IT MIGHT BE POSSIBLE...
"...BUT LIFELINE, IF THIS HAS A SNOWBALL'S CHANCE, WE'RE GOING TO NEED YOU THERE TO WALK US THROUGH THE BIOLOGY OF IT ALL."
LIFELINE, YOU'RE NEEDED IN THE BIO-CONTAINMENT WARD RIGHT AWAY.
I'M ON MY WAY.
GET YOUR MEN TOGETHER. I'LL BE RIGHT BACK.
BIOHAZARD WARD.
IT LOOKS LIKE THEY'LL BOTH HAVE TO BE QUARANTINED HERE UNTIL WE CONFIRM THERE'S NO AIRBORNE THREAT WITHIN THEM.
THEY'VE BOTH BEEN INFECTED WITH THE MITES WHILE IN DESTRO'S CUSTODY. YOU AND KAMAKURA WERE LUCKY YOU CAME OUT CLEAN, SPIRIT. I'D LIKE TO HEAR HOW IT ALL WENT DOWN SOMETIME.
THERE WILL BE PLENTY OF TIME FOR THAT LATER, PROVIDED WE SUCCEED.
SNAKE-EYES IS TRYING TO TELL ME SOME-THING.
WHAT IS IT, MY FRIEND?

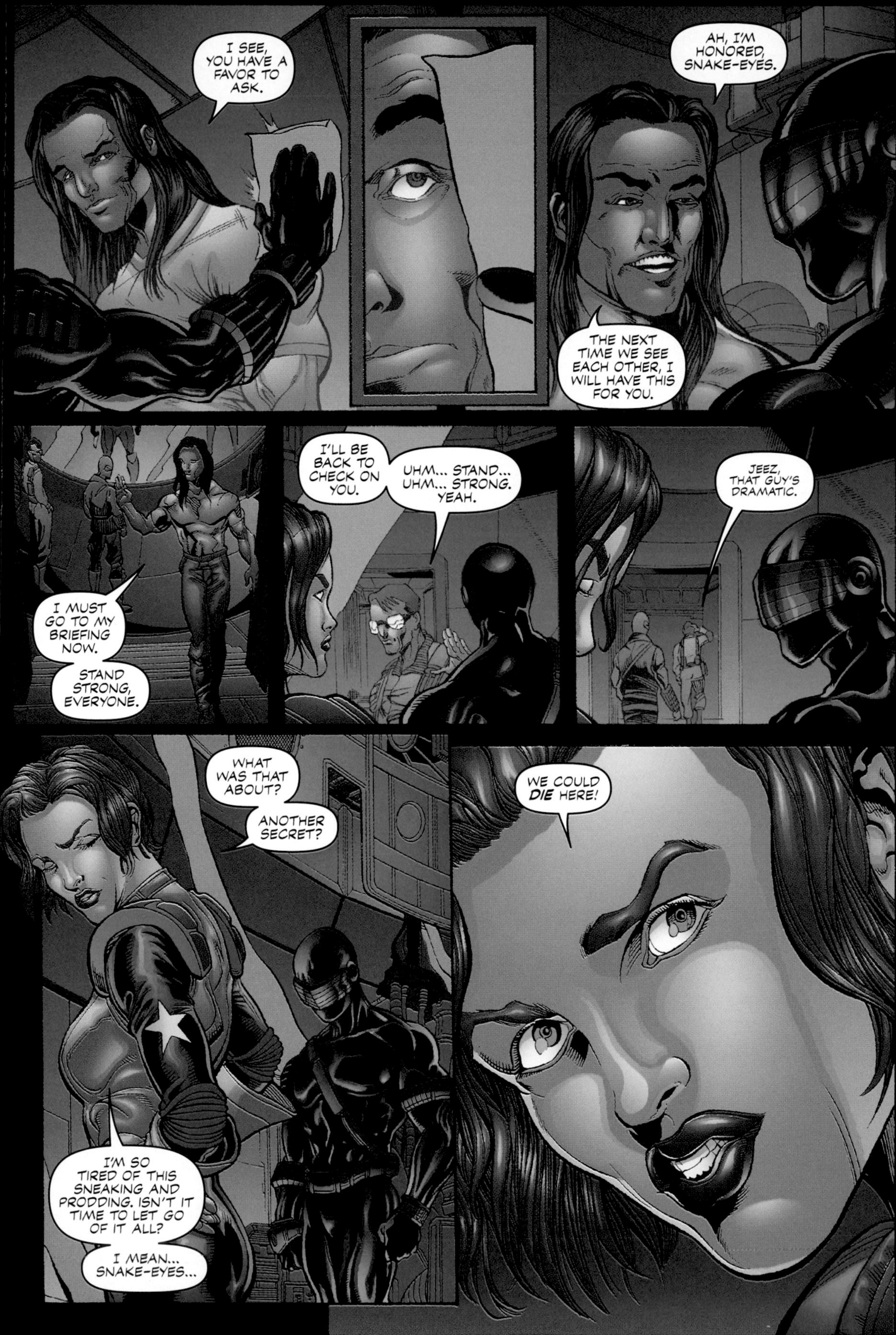
I SEE, YOU HAVE A FAVOR TO ASK.
AH, I'M HONORED, SNAKE-EYES.
THE NEXT TIME WE SEE EACH OTHER, I WILL HAVE THIS FOR YOU.
I MUST GO TO MY BRIEFING NOW.
STAND STRONG, EVERYONE.
I'LL BE BACK TO CHECK ON YOU.
UHM... STAND... UHM... STRONG. YEAH.
JEEZ, THAT GUY'S DRAMATIC.
WHAT WAS THAT ABOUT?
ANOTHER SECRET?
I'M SO TIRED OF THIS SNEAKING AND PRODDING. ISN'T IT TIME TO LET GO OF IT ALL?
I MEAN... SNAKE-EYES...
WE COULD *DIE* HERE!

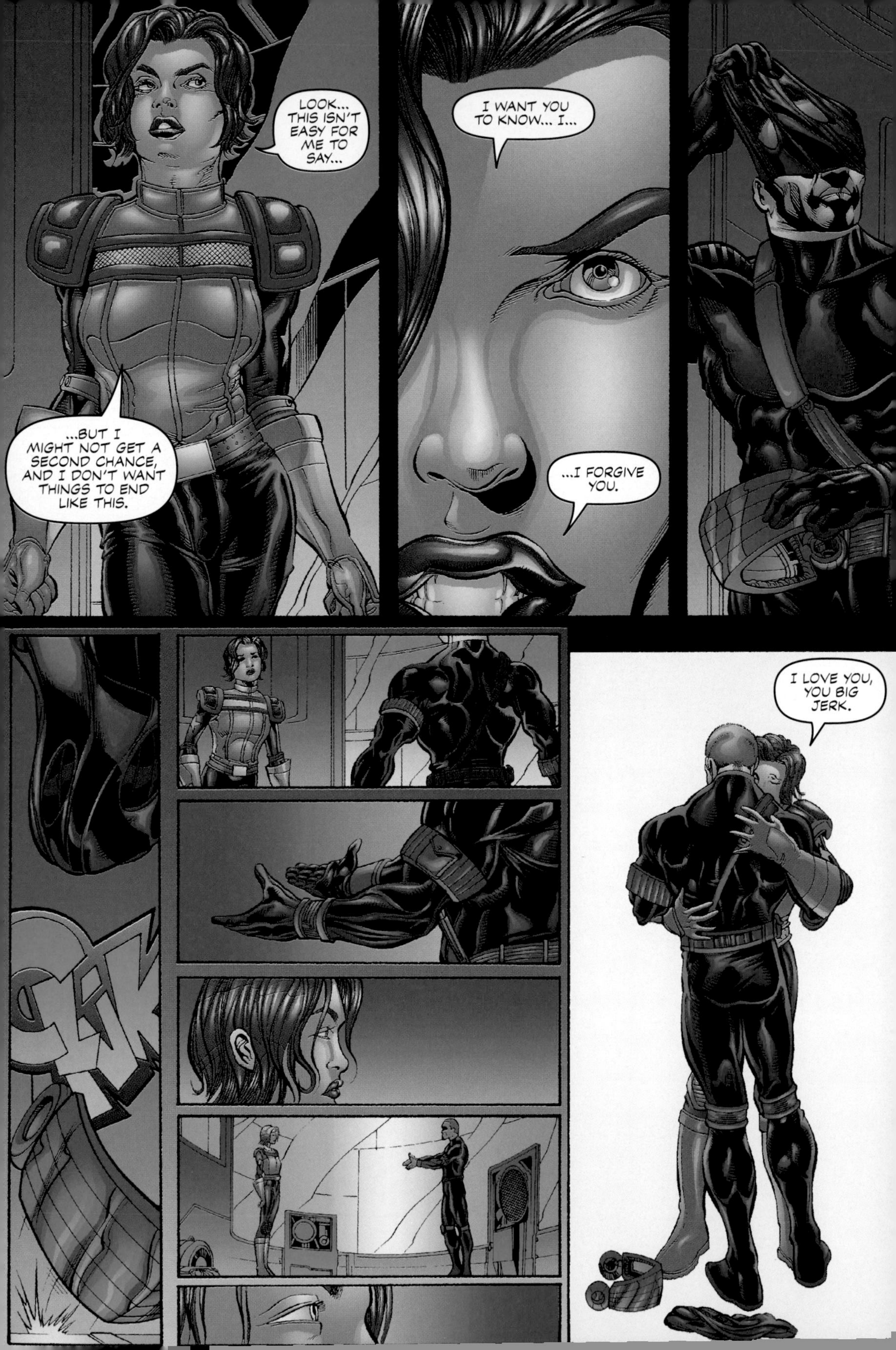
LOOK... THIS ISN'T EASY FOR ME TO SAY...
...BUT I MIGHT NOT GET A SECOND CHANCE, AND I DON'T WANT THINGS TO END LIKE THIS.
I WANT YOU TO KNOW... I...
...I FORGIVE YOU.
I LOVE YOU, YOU BIG JERK.

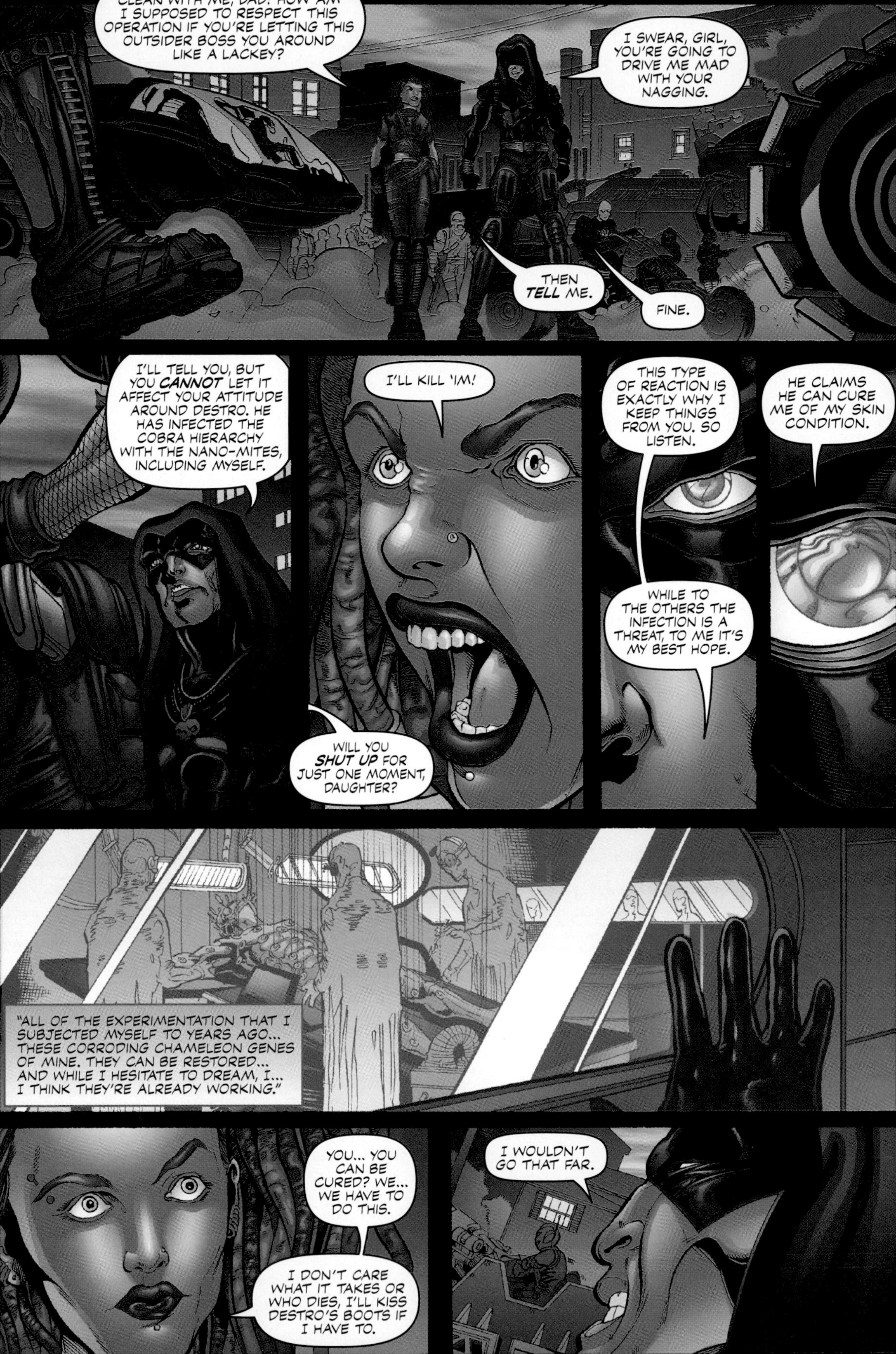

YOU'VE GOTTA COME CLEAN WITH ME, DAD! HOW AM I SUPPOSED TO RESPECT THIS OPERATION IF YOU'RE LETTING THIS OUTSIDER BOSS YOU AROUND LIKE A LACKEY?
I SWEAR, GIRL, YOU'RE GOING TO DRIVE ME MAD WITH YOUR NAGGING.
THEN TELL ME.
FINE.
I'LL TELL YOU, BUT YOU CANNOT LET IT AFFECT YOUR ATTITUDE AROUND DESTRO. HE HAS INFECTED THE COBRA HIERARCHY WITH THE NANO-MITES, INCLUDING MYSELF.
I'LL KILL 'IM!
WILL YOU SHUT UP FOR JUST ONE MOMENT, DAUGHTER?
THIS TYPE OF REACTION IS EXACTLY WHY I KEEP THINGS FROM YOU. SO LISTEN.
WHILE TO THE OTHERS THE INFECTION IS A THREAT, TO ME IT'S MY BEST HOPE.
HE CLAIMS HE CAN CURE ME OF MY SKIN CONDITION.
"ALL OF THE EXPERIMENTATION THAT I SUBJECTED MYSELF TO YEARS AGO... THESE CORRODING CHAMELEON GENES OF MINE. THEY CAN BE RESTORED... AND WHILE I HESITATE TO DREAM, I... I THINK THEY'RE ALREADY WORKING."
YOU... YOU CAN BE CURED? WE... WE HAVE TO DO THIS.
I DON'T CARE WHAT IT TAKES OR WHO DIES, I'LL KISS DESTRO'S BOOTS IF I HAVE TO.
I WOULDN'T GO THAT FAR.

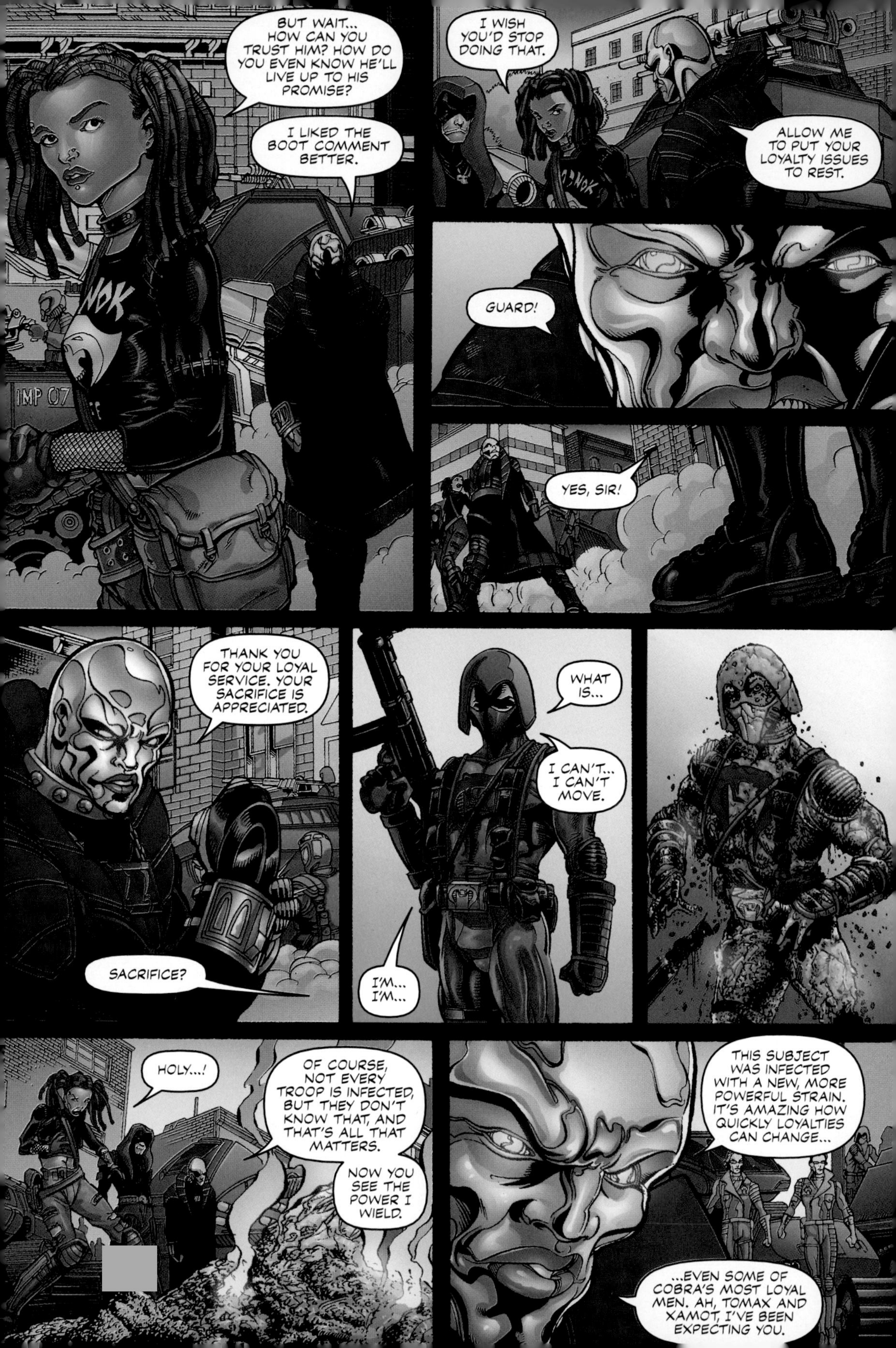
BUT WAIT... HOW CAN YOU TRUST HIM? HOW DO YOU EVEN KNOW HE'LL LIVE UP TO HIS PROMISE?
I LIKED THE BOOT COMMENT BETTER.
IMP 07
I WISH YOU'D STOP DOING THAT.
ALLOW ME TO PUT YOUR LOYALTY ISSUES TO REST.
GUARD!
YES, SIR!
THANK YOU FOR YOUR LOYAL SERVICE. YOUR SACRIFICE IS APPRECIATED.
SACRIFICE?
WHAT IS...
I CAN'T... I CAN'T MOVE.
I'M... I'M...
HOLY...!
OF COURSE, NOT EVERY TROOP IS INFECTED, BUT THEY DON'T KNOW THAT, AND THAT'S ALL THAT MATTERS.
NOW YOU SEE THE POWER I WIELD.
THIS SUBJECT WAS INFECTED WITH A NEW, MORE POWERFUL STRAIN. IT'S AMAZING HOW QUICKLY LOYALTIES CAN CHANGE...
...EVEN SOME OF COBRA'S MOST LOYAL MEN. AH, TOMAX AND XAMOT, I'VE BEEN EXPECTING YOU.

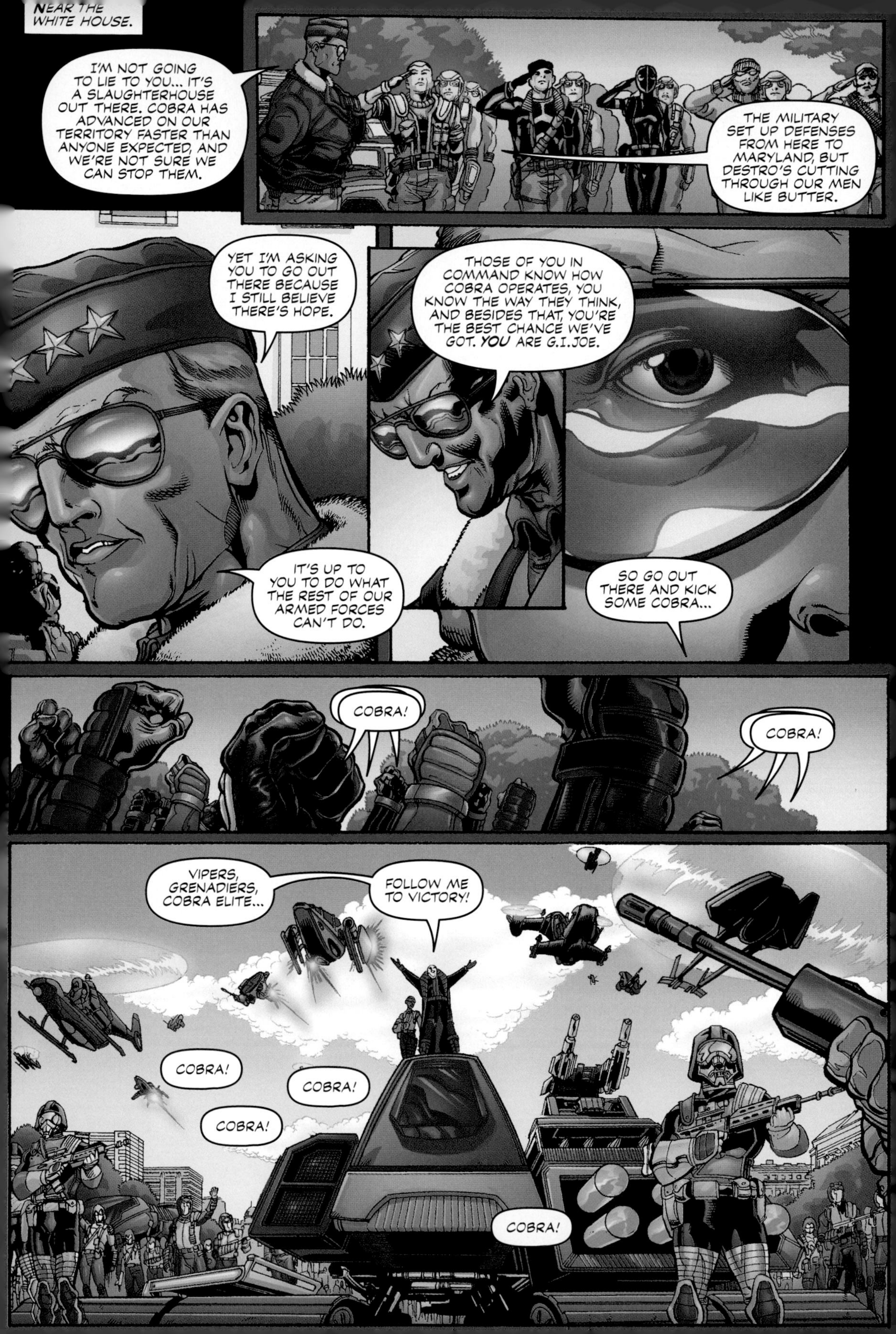
NEAR THE WHITE HOUSE.
I'M NOT GOING TO LIE TO YOU... IT'S A SLAUGHTERHOUSE OUT THERE. COBRA HAS ADVANCED ON OUR TERRITORY FASTER THAN ANYONE EXPECTED, AND WE'RE NOT SURE WE CAN STOP THEM.
THE MILITARY SET UP DEFENSES FROM HERE TO MARYLAND, BUT DESTRO'S CUTTING THROUGH OUR MEN LIKE BUTTER.
YET I'M ASKING YOU TO GO OUT THERE BECAUSE I STILL BELIEVE THERE'S HOPE.
THOSE OF YOU IN COMMAND KNOW HOW COBRA OPERATES, YOU KNOW THE WAY THEY THINK, AND BESIDES THAT, YOU'RE THE BEST CHANCE WE'VE GOT. YOU ARE G.I. JOE.
IT'S UP TO YOU TO DO WHAT THE REST OF OUR ARMED FORCES CAN'T DO.
SO GO OUT THERE AND KICK SOME COBRA...
COBRA!
COBRA!
VIPERS, GRENADIERS, COBRA ELITE...
FOLLOW ME TO VICTORY!
COBRA!
COBRA!
COBRA!
COBRA!

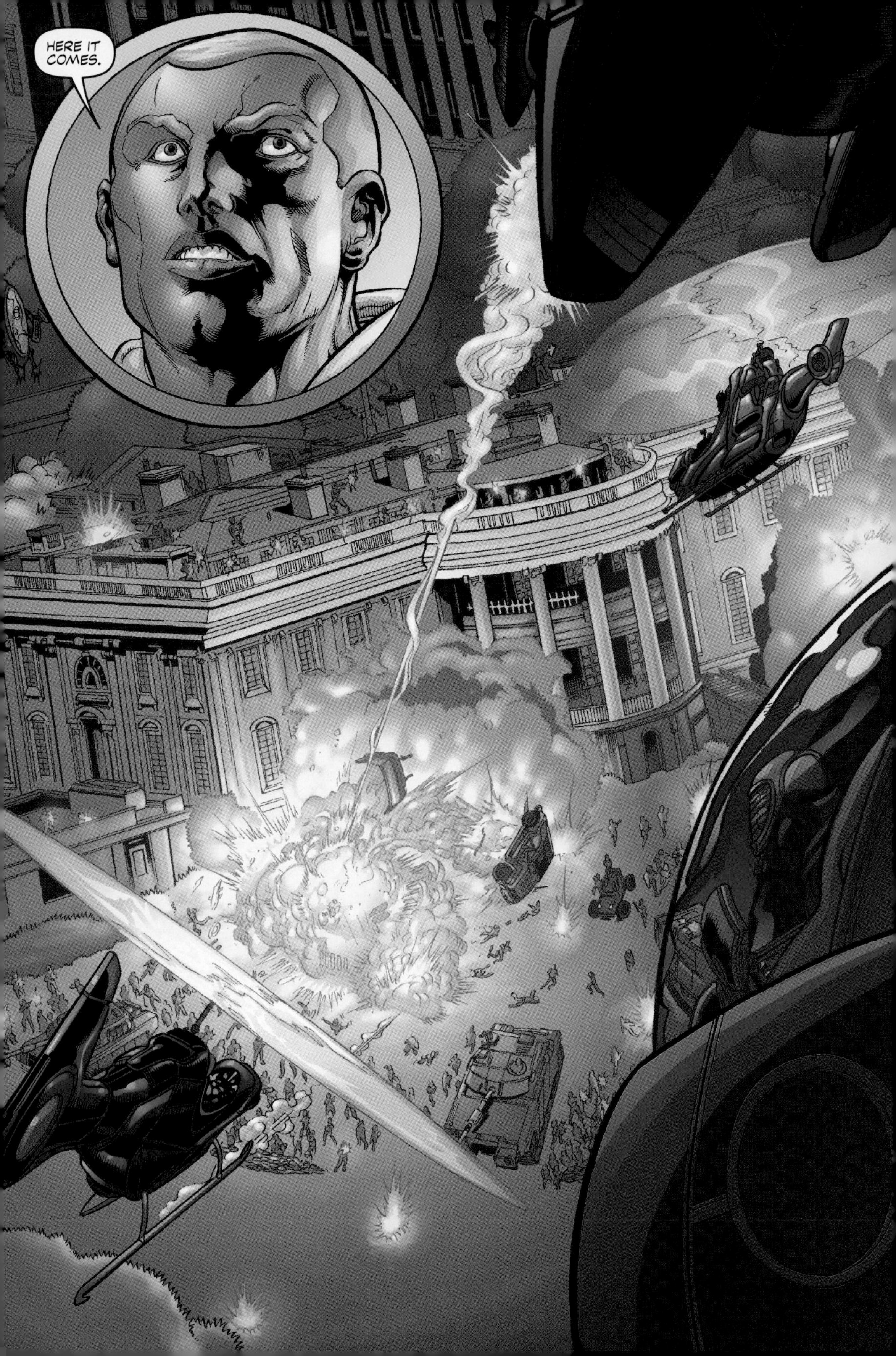
HERE IT COMES.

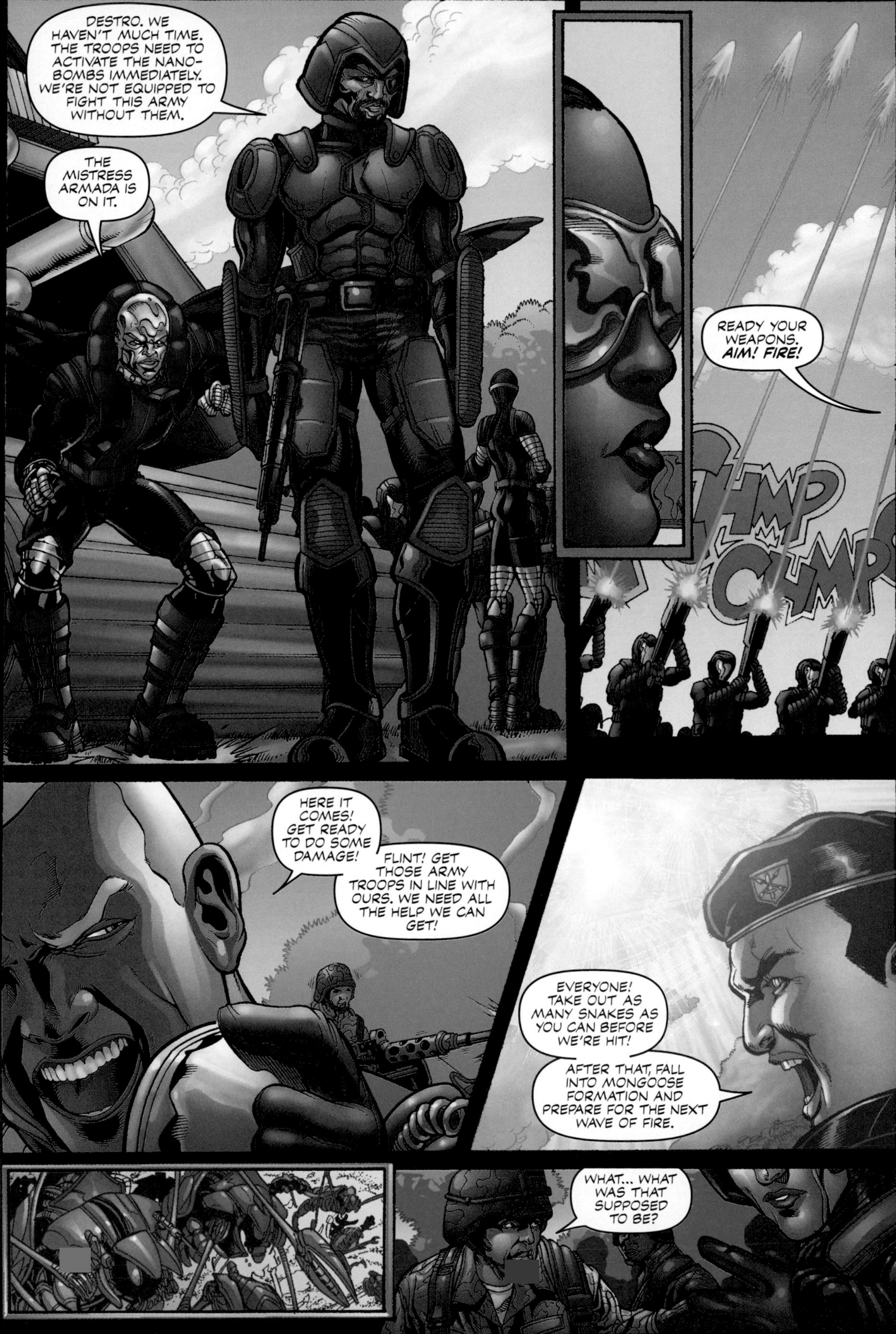
DESTRO. WE HAVEN'T MUCH TIME. THE TROOPS NEED TO ACTIVATE THE NANO-BOMBS IMMEDIATELY. WE'RE NOT EQUIPPED TO FIGHT THIS ARMY WITHOUT THEM.
THE MISTRESS ARMADA IS ON IT.
READY YOUR WEAPONS. *AIM! FIRE!*
CHMP
HERE IT COMES! GET READY TO DO SOME DAMAGE!
FLINT! GET THOSE ARMY TROOPS IN LINE WITH OURS. WE NEED ALL THE HELP WE CAN GET!
EVERYONE! TAKE OUT AS MANY SNAKES AS YOU CAN BEFORE WE'RE HIT!
AFTER THAT, FALL INTO MONGOOSE FORMATION AND PREPARE FOR THE NEXT WAVE OF FIRE.
WHAT... WHAT WAS THAT SUPPOSED TO BE?

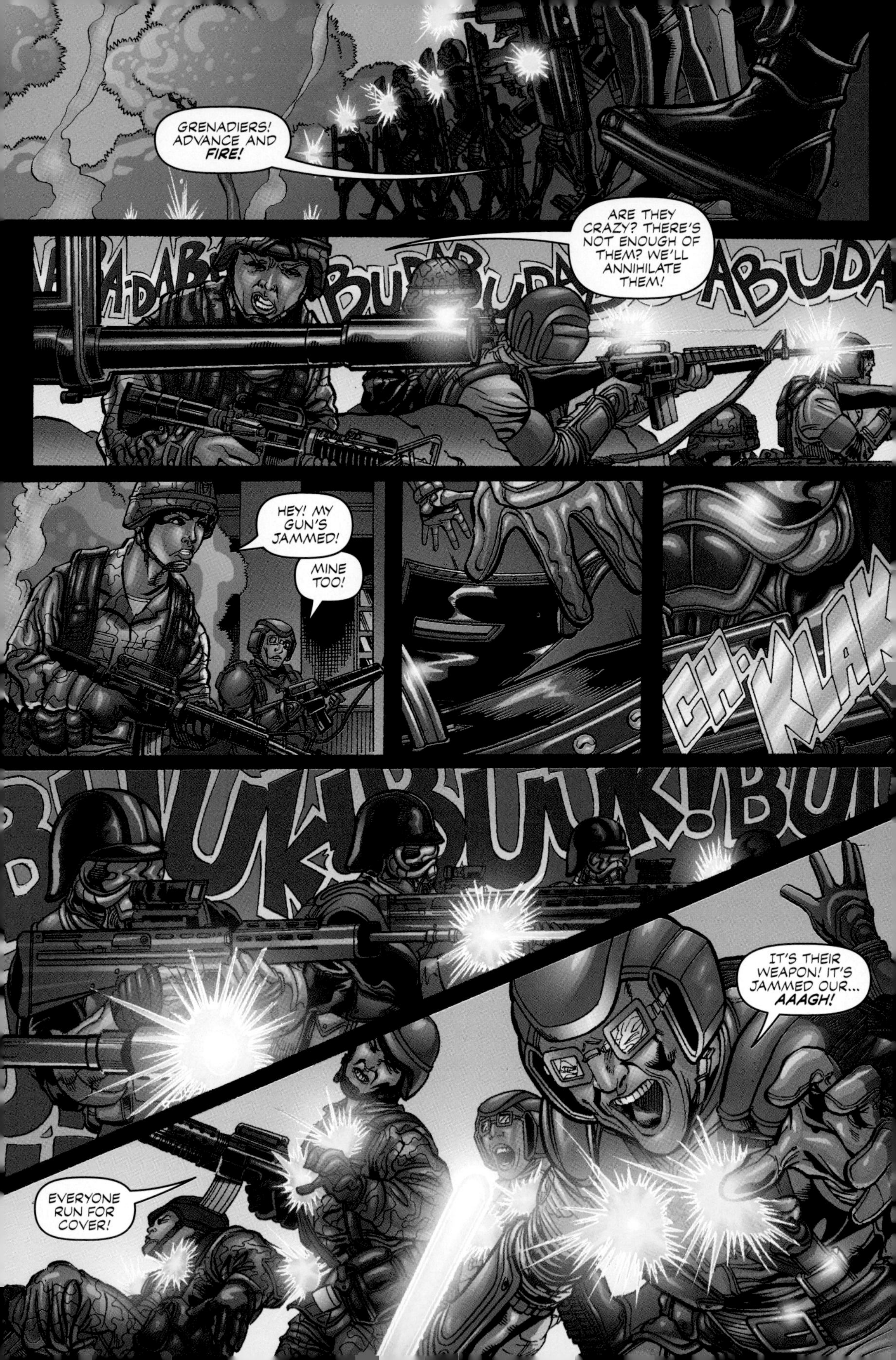
GRENADIERS! ADVANCE AND FIRE!
ARE THEY CRAZY? THERE'S NOT ENOUGH OF THEM? WE'LL ANNIHILATE THEM!
HEY! MY GUN'S JAMMED!
MINE TOO!
IT'S THEIR WEAPON! IT'S JAMMED OUR... AAAGH!
EVERYONE RUN FOR COVER!

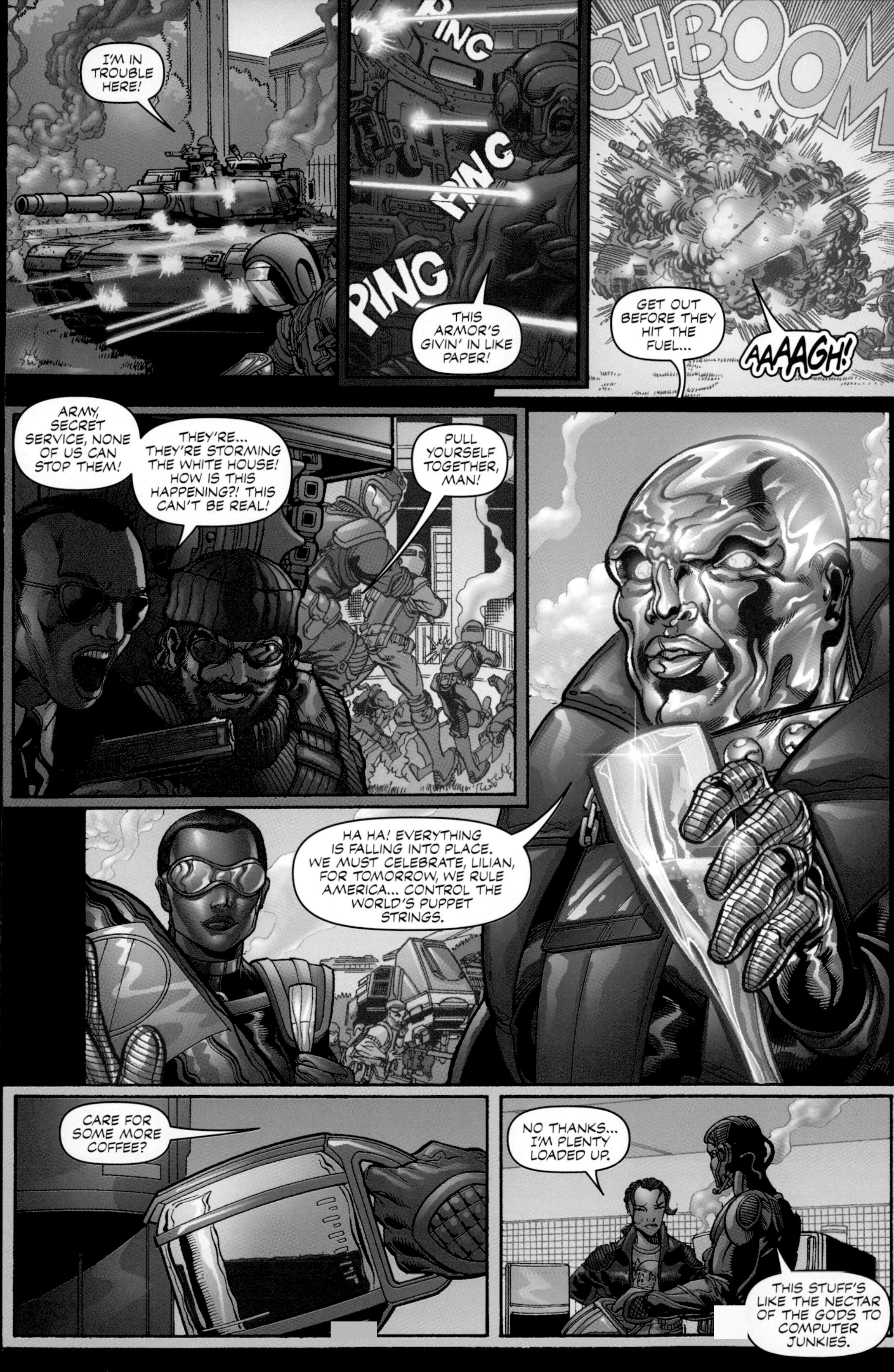
I'M IN TROUBLE HERE!
PING
PING
PING
PING
THIS ARMOR'S GIVIN' IN LIKE PAPER!
CHBOOM
GET OUT BEFORE THEY HIT THE FUEL...
AAAAGH!
ARMY, SECRET SERVICE, NONE OF US CAN STOP THEM!
THEY'RE... THEY'RE STORMING THE WHITE HOUSE! HOW IS THIS HAPPENING?! THIS CAN'T BE REAL!
PULL YOURSELF TOGETHER, MAN!
HA HA! EVERYTHING IS FALLING INTO PLACE. WE MUST CELEBRATE, LILIAN, FOR TOMORROW, WE RULE AMERICA... CONTROL THE WORLD'S PUPPET STRINGS.
CARE FOR SOME MORE COFFEE?
NO THANKS... I'M PLENTY LOADED UP.
THIS STUFF'S LIKE THE NECTAR OF THE GODS TO COMPUTER JUNKIES.

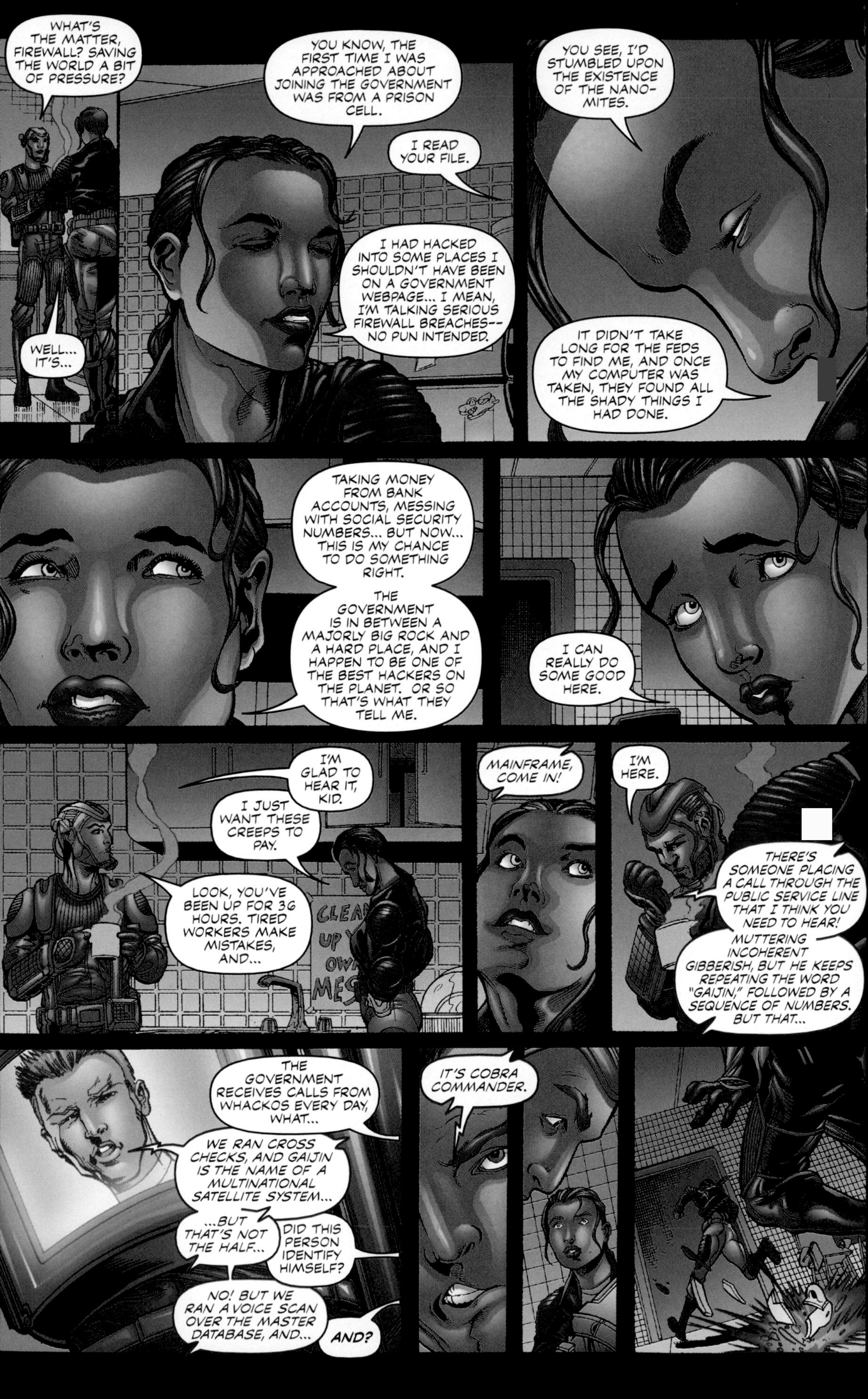
WHAT'S THE MATTER, FIREWALL? SAVING THE WORLD A BIT OF PRESSURE?
WELL... IT'S...
YOU KNOW, THE FIRST TIME I WAS APPROACHED ABOUT JOINING THE GOVERNMENT WAS FROM A PRISON CELL.
I READ YOUR FILE.
I HAD HACKED INTO SOME PLACES I SHOULDN'T HAVE BEEN ON A GOVERNMENT WEBPAGE... I MEAN, I'M TALKING SERIOUS FIREWALL BREACHES-- NO PUN INTENDED.
YOU SEE, I'D STUMBLED UPON THE EXISTENCE OF THE NANO-MITES.
IT DIDN'T TAKE LONG FOR THE FEDS TO FIND ME, AND ONCE MY COMPUTER WAS TAKEN, THEY FOUND ALL THE SHADY THINGS I HAD DONE.
TAKING MONEY FROM BANK ACCOUNTS, MESSING WITH SOCIAL SECURITY NUMBERS... BUT NOW... THIS IS MY CHANCE TO DO SOMETHING RIGHT.
THE GOVERNMENT IS IN BETWEEN A MAJORLY BIG ROCK AND A HARD PLACE, AND I HAPPEN TO BE ONE OF THE BEST HACKERS ON THE PLANET. OR SO THAT'S WHAT THEY TELL ME.
I CAN REALLY DO SOME GOOD HERE.
I'M GLAD TO HEAR IT, KID.
I JUST WANT THESE CREEPS TO PAY.
LOOK, YOU'VE BEEN UP FOR 36 HOURS. TIRED WORKERS MAKE MISTAKES, AND...
MAINFRAME, COME IN!
I'M HERE.
THERE'S SOMEONE PLACING A CALL THROUGH THE PUBLIC SERVICE LINE THAT I THINK YOU NEED TO HEAR!
MUTTERING INCOHERENT GIBBERISH, BUT HE KEEPS REPEATING THE WORD "GAIJIN," FOLLOWED BY A SEQUENCE OF NUMBERS. BUT THAT...
THE GOVERNMENT RECEIVES CALLS FROM WHACKOS EVERY DAY, WHAT...
WE RAN CROSS CHECKS, AND GAIJIN IS THE NAME OF A MULTINATIONAL SATELLITE SYSTEM...
...BUT THAT'S NOT THE HALF...
DID THIS PERSON IDENTIFY HIMSELF?
NO! BUT WE RAN A VOICE SCAN OVER THE MASTER DATABASE, AND...
AND?
IT'S COBRA COMMANDER.

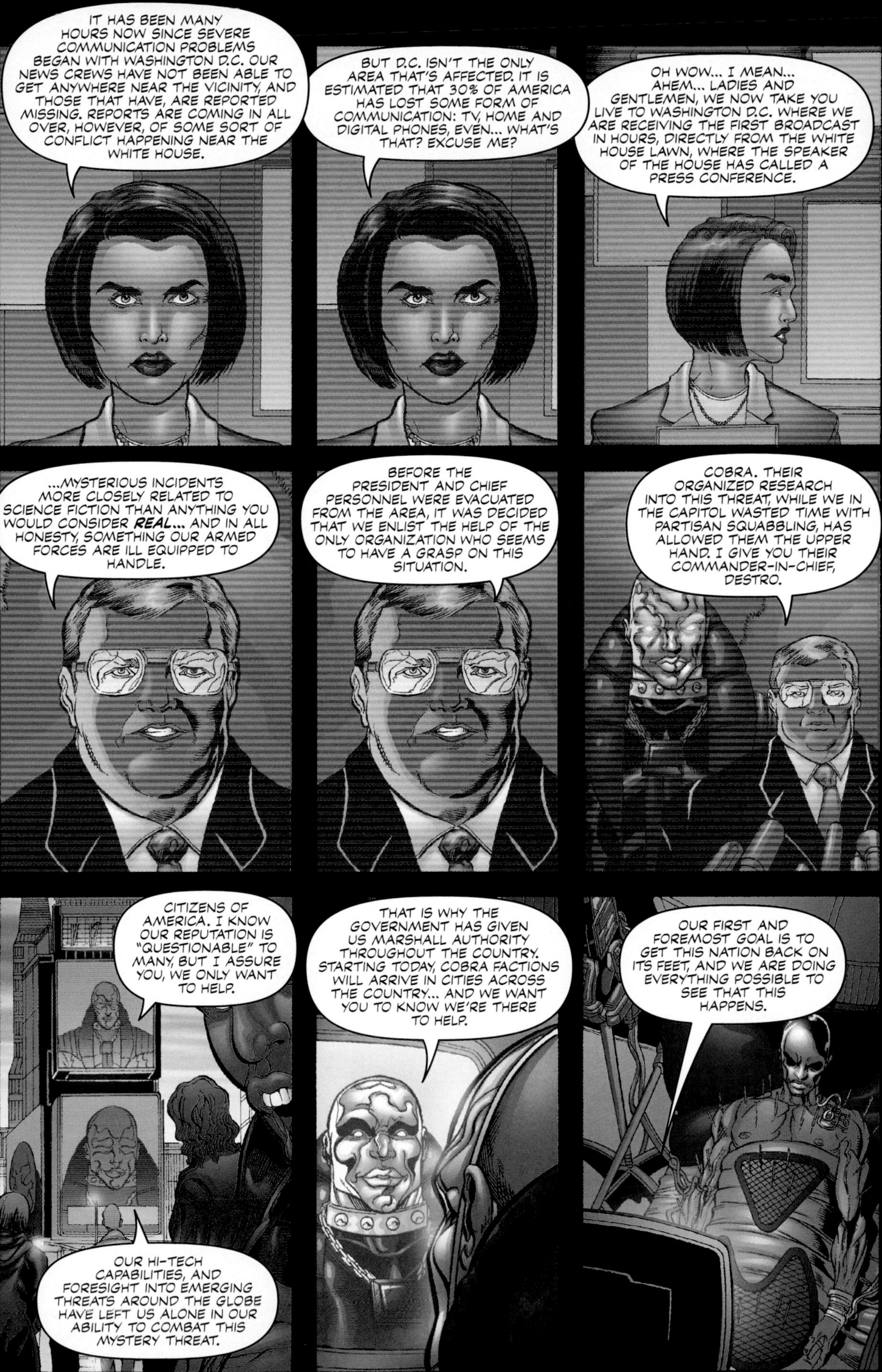
IT HAS BEEN MANY HOURS NOW SINCE SEVERE COMMUNICATION PROBLEMS BEGAN WITH WASHINGTON D.C. OUR NEWS CREWS HAVE NOT BEEN ABLE TO GET ANYWHERE NEAR THE VICINITY, AND THOSE THAT HAVE, ARE REPORTED MISSING. REPORTS ARE COMING IN ALL OVER, HOWEVER, OF SOME SORT OF CONFLICT HAPPENING NEAR THE WHITE HOUSE.
BUT D.C. ISN'T THE ONLY AREA THAT'S AFFECTED. IT IS ESTIMATED THAT 30% OF AMERICA HAS LOST SOME FORM OF COMMUNICATION: TV, HOME AND DIGITAL PHONES, EVEN... WHAT'S THAT? EXCUSE ME?
OH WOW... I MEAN... AHEM... LADIES AND GENTLEMEN, WE NOW TAKE YOU LIVE TO WASHINGTON D.C. WHERE WE ARE RECEIVING THE FIRST BROADCAST IN HOURS, DIRECTLY FROM THE WHITE HOUSE LAWN, WHERE THE SPEAKER OF THE HOUSE HAS CALLED A PRESS CONFERENCE.
...MYSTERIOUS INCIDENTS MORE CLOSELY RELATED TO SCIENCE FICTION THAN ANYTHING YOU WOULD CONSIDER REAL... AND IN ALL HONESTY, SOMETHING OUR ARMED FORCES ARE ILL EQUIPPED TO HANDLE.
BEFORE THE PRESIDENT AND CHIEF PERSONNEL WERE EVACUATED FROM THE AREA, IT WAS DECIDED THAT WE ENLIST THE HELP OF THE ONLY ORGANIZATION WHO SEEMS TO HAVE A GRASP ON THIS SITUATION.
COBRA. THEIR ORGANIZED RESEARCH INTO THIS THREAT, WHILE WE IN THE CAPITOL WASTED TIME WITH PARTISAN SQUABBLING, HAS ALLOWED THEM THE UPPER HAND. I GIVE YOU THEIR COMMANDER-IN-CHIEF, DESTRO.
CITIZENS OF AMERICA. I KNOW OUR REPUTATION IS "QUESTIONABLE" TO MANY, BUT I ASSURE YOU, WE ONLY WANT TO HELP.
OUR HI-TECH CAPABILITIES, AND FORESIGHT INTO EMERGING THREATS AROUND THE GLOBE HAVE LEFT US ALONE IN OUR ABILITY TO COMBAT THIS MYSTERY THREAT.
THAT IS WHY THE GOVERNMENT HAS GIVEN US MARSHALL AUTHORITY THROUGHOUT THE COUNTRY. STARTING TODAY, COBRA FACTIONS WILL ARRIVE IN CITIES ACROSS THE COUNTRY... AND WE WANT YOU TO KNOW WE'RE THERE TO HELP.
OUR FIRST AND FOREMOST GOAL IS TO GET THIS NATION BACK ON ITS FEET, AND WE ARE DOING EVERYTHING POSSIBLE TO SEE THAT THIS HAPPENS.

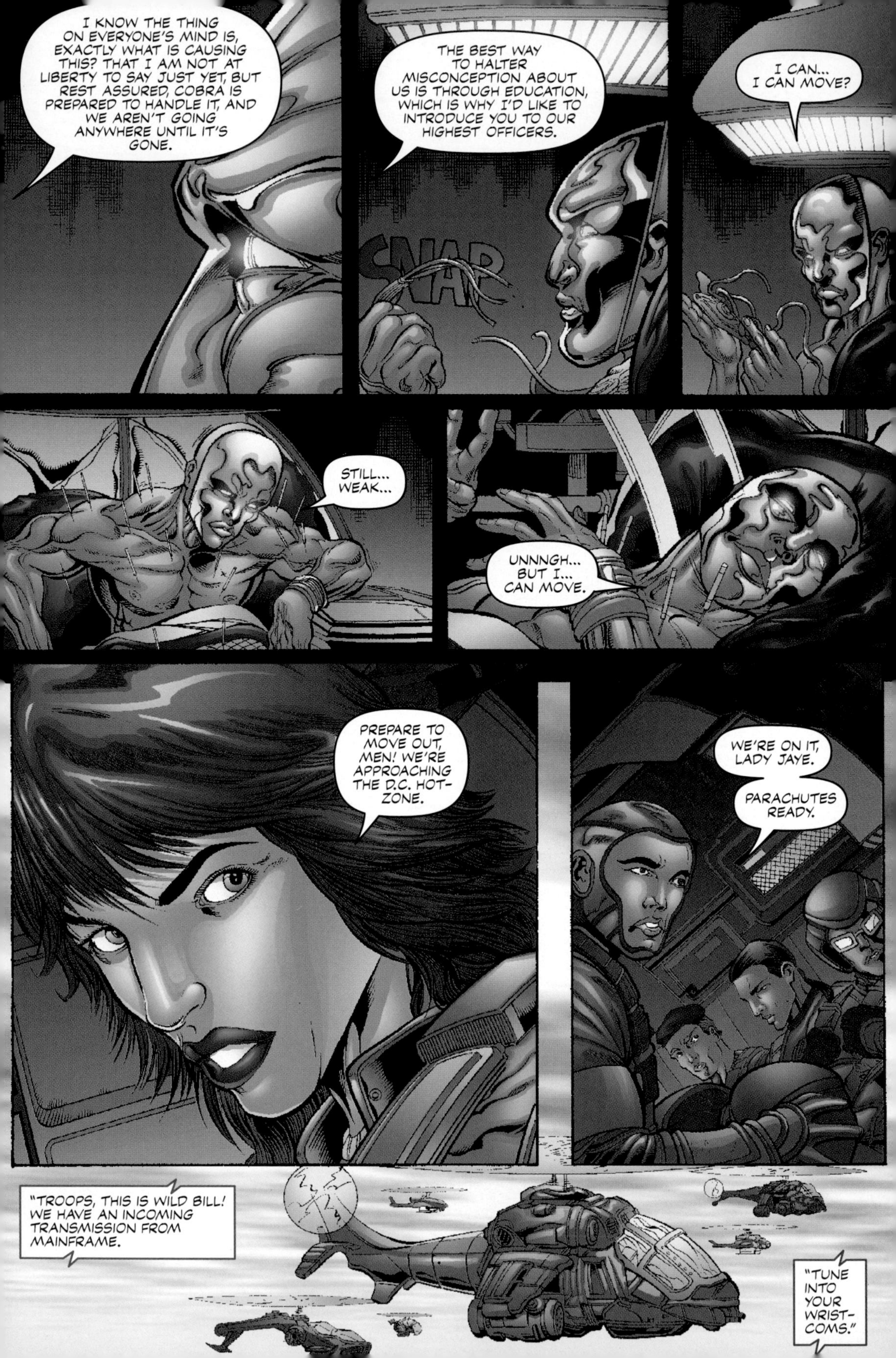
I KNOW THE THING ON EVERYONE'S MIND IS, EXACTLY WHAT IS CAUSING THIS? THAT I AM NOT AT LIBERTY TO SAY JUST YET, BUT REST ASSURED, COBRA IS PREPARED TO HANDLE IT, AND WE AREN'T GOING ANYWHERE UNTIL IT'S GONE.
THE BEST WAY TO HALTER MISCONCEPTION ABOUT US IS THROUGH EDUCATION, WHICH IS WHY I'D LIKE TO INTRODUCE YOU TO OUR HIGHEST OFFICERS.
SNAP
I CAN... I CAN MOVE?
STILL... WEAK...
UNNNGH... BUT I... CAN MOVE.
PREPARE TO MOVE OUT, MEN! WE'RE APPROACHING THE D.C. HOT-ZONE.
WE'RE ON IT, LADY JAYE.
PARACHUTES READY.
"TROOPS, THIS IS WILD BILL! WE HAVE AN INCOMING TRANSMISSION FROM MAINFRAME.
"TUNE INTO YOUR WRIST-COMS."

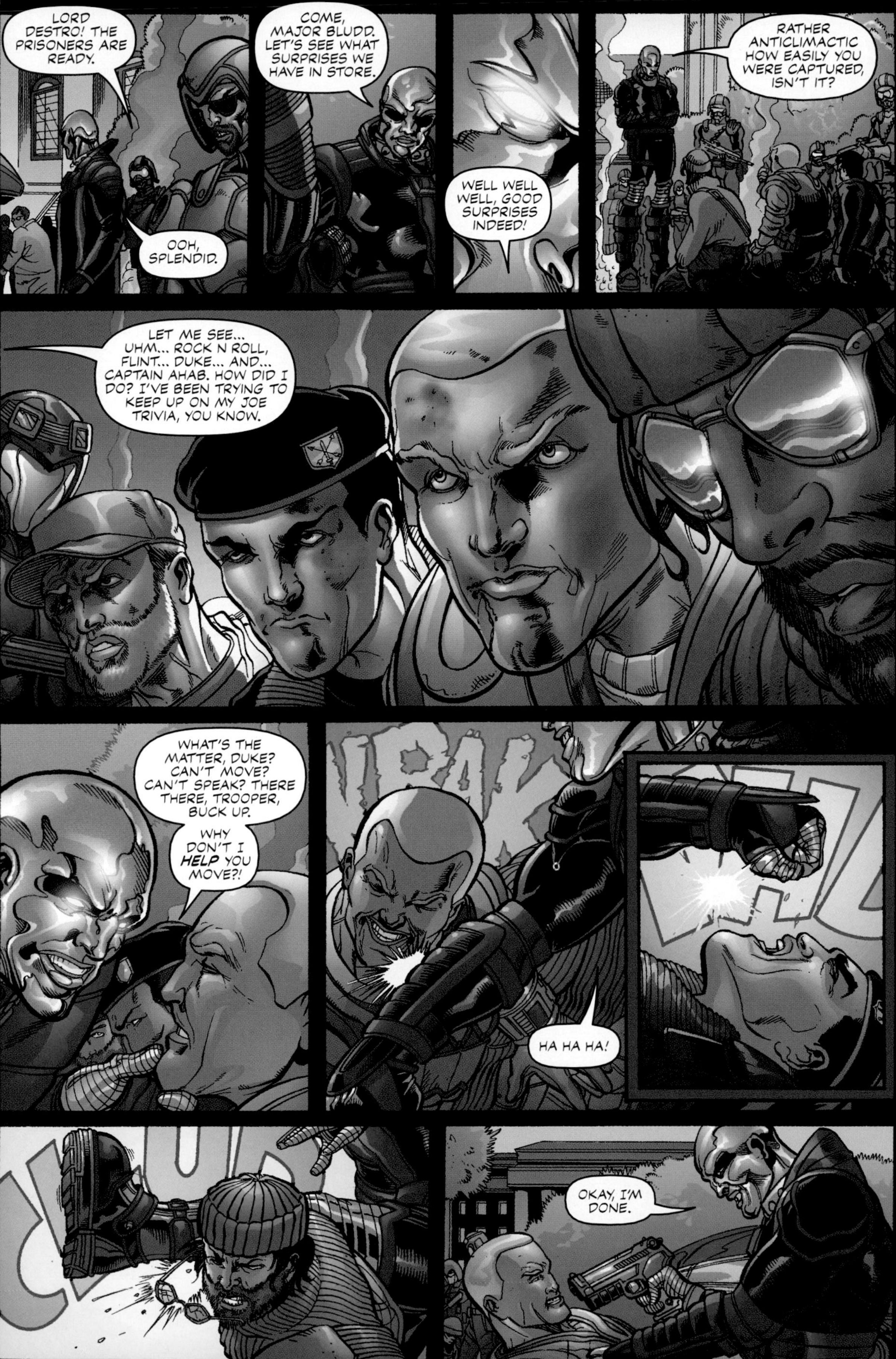
LORD DESTRO! THE PRISONERS ARE READY.
OOH, SPLENDID.
COME, MAJOR BLUDD. LET'S SEE WHAT SURPRISES WE HAVE IN STORE.
WELL WELL WELL, GOOD SURPRISES INDEED!
RATHER ANTICLIMACTIC HOW EASILY YOU WERE CAPTURED, ISN'T IT?
LET ME SEE... UHM... ROCK N ROLL, FLINT... DUKE... AND... CAPTAIN AHAB. HOW DID I DO? I'VE BEEN TRYING TO KEEP UP ON MY JOE TRIVIA, YOU KNOW.
WHAT'S THE MATTER, DUKE? CAN'T MOVE? CAN'T SPEAK? THERE THERE, TROOPER, BUCK UP.
WHY DON'T I **HELP** YOU MOVE?!
HA HA HA!
OKAY, I'M DONE.

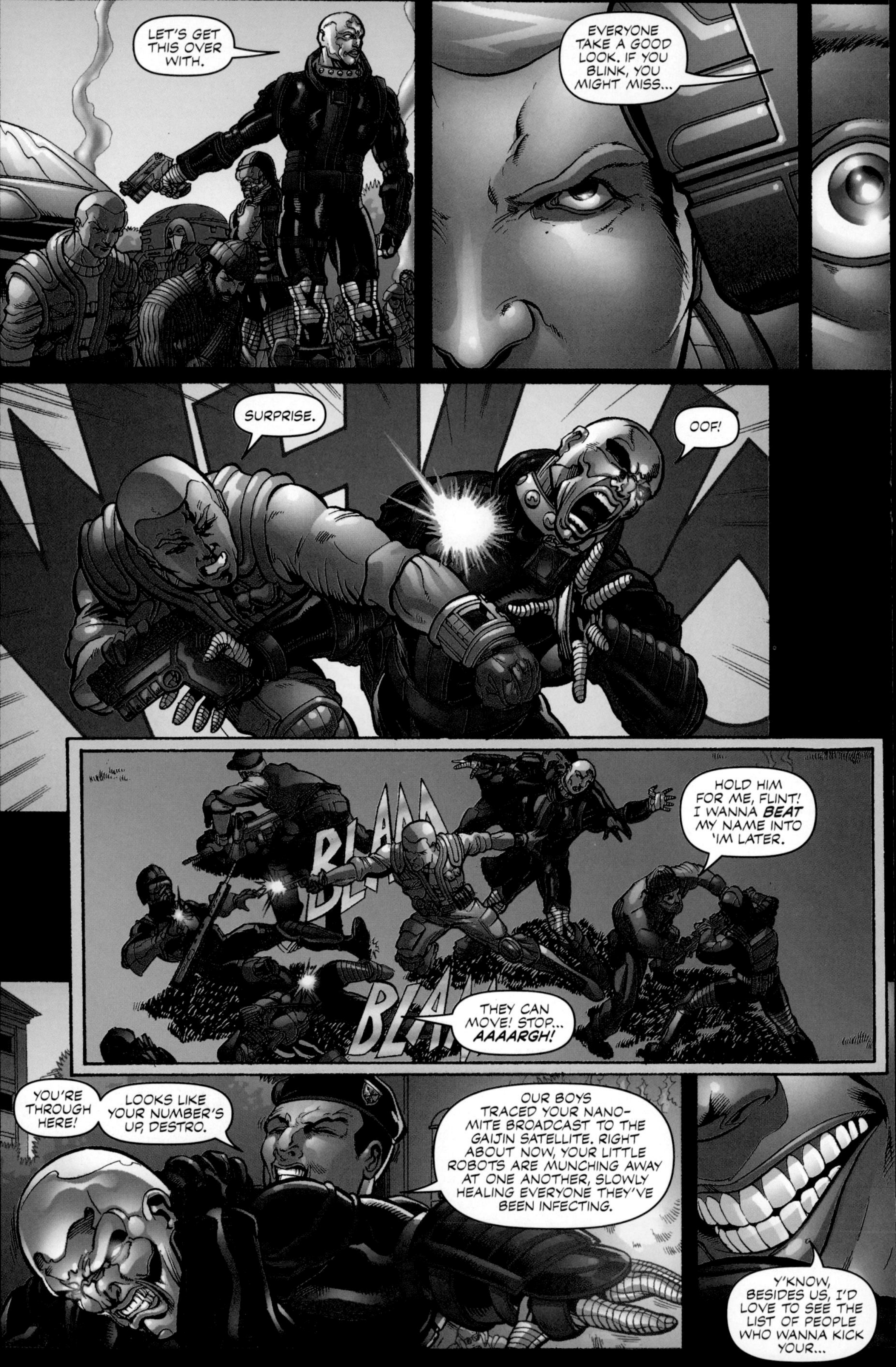
LET'S GET THIS OVER WITH.
EVERYONE TAKE A GOOD LOOK. IF YOU BLINK, YOU MIGHT MISS...
SURPRISE.
OOF!
HOLD HIM FOR ME, FLINT! I WANNA BEAT MY NAME INTO 'IM LATER.
THEY CAN MOVE! STOP... AAAARGH!
YOU'RE THROUGH HERE!
LOOKS LIKE YOUR NUMBER'S UP, DESTRO.
OUR BOYS TRACED YOUR NANO-MITE BROADCAST TO THE GAIJIN SATELLITE. RIGHT ABOUT NOW, YOUR LITTLE ROBOTS ARE MUNCHING AWAY AT ONE ANOTHER, SLOWLY HEALING EVERYONE THEY'VE BEEN INFECTING.
Y'KNOW, BESIDES US, I'D LOVE TO SEE THE LIST OF PEOPLE WHO WANNA KICK YOUR...

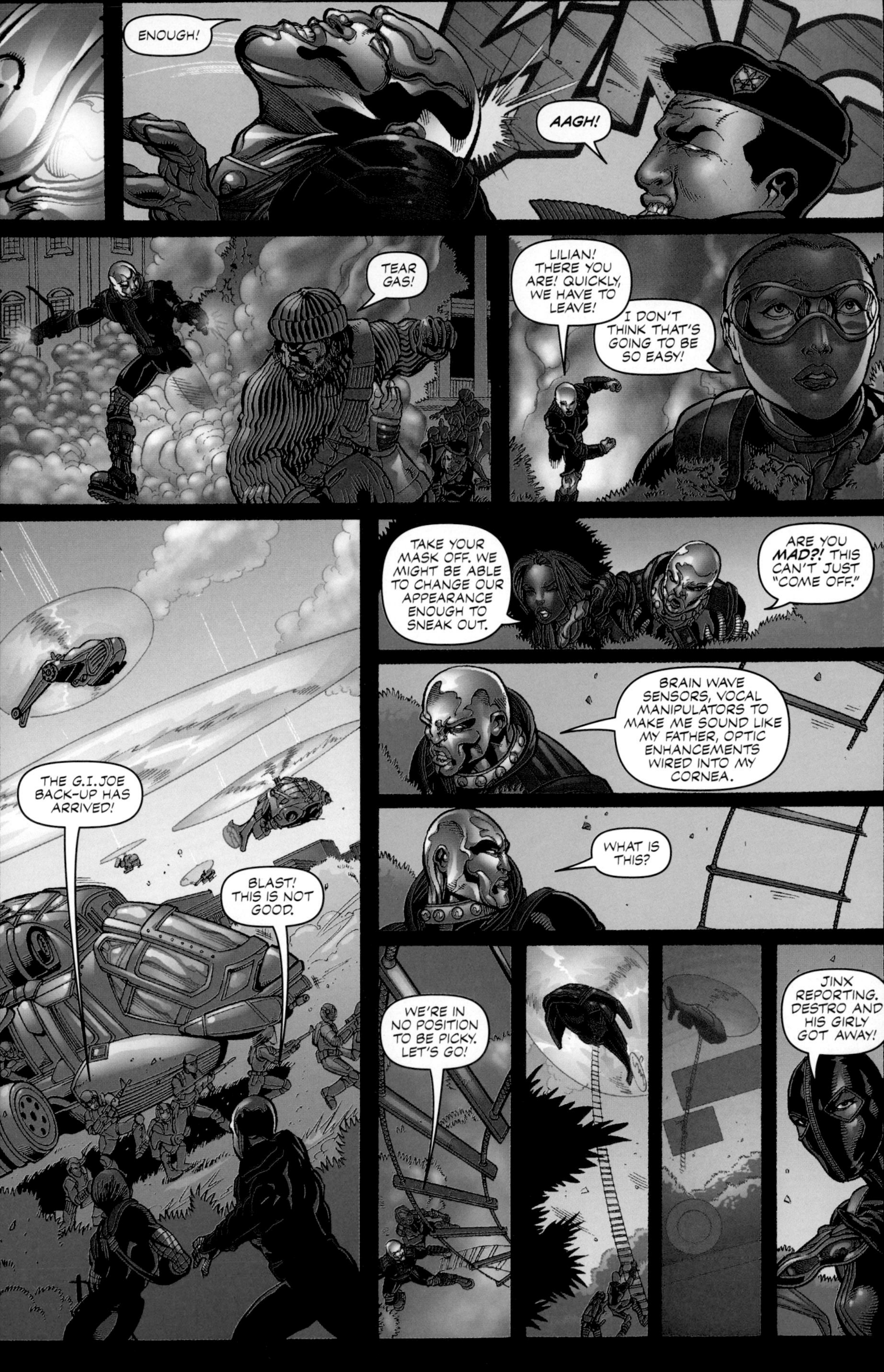
ENOUGH!
AAGH!
TEAR GAS!
LILIAN! THERE YOU ARE! QUICKLY, WE HAVE TO LEAVE!
I DON'T THINK THAT'S GOING TO BE SO EASY!
THE G.I.JOE BACK-UP HAS ARRIVED!
BLAST! THIS IS NOT GOOD.
TAKE YOUR MASK OFF. WE MIGHT BE ABLE TO CHANGE OUR APPEARANCE ENOUGH TO SNEAK OUT.
ARE YOU MAD?! THIS CAN'T JUST "COME OFF."
BRAIN WAVE SENSORS, VOCAL MANIPULATORS TO MAKE ME SOUND LIKE MY FATHER, OPTIC ENHANCEMENTS WIRED INTO MY CORNEA.
WHAT IS THIS?
WE'RE IN NO POSITION TO BE PICKY. LET'S GO!
JINX REPORTING. DESTRO AND HIS GIRLY GOT AWAY!

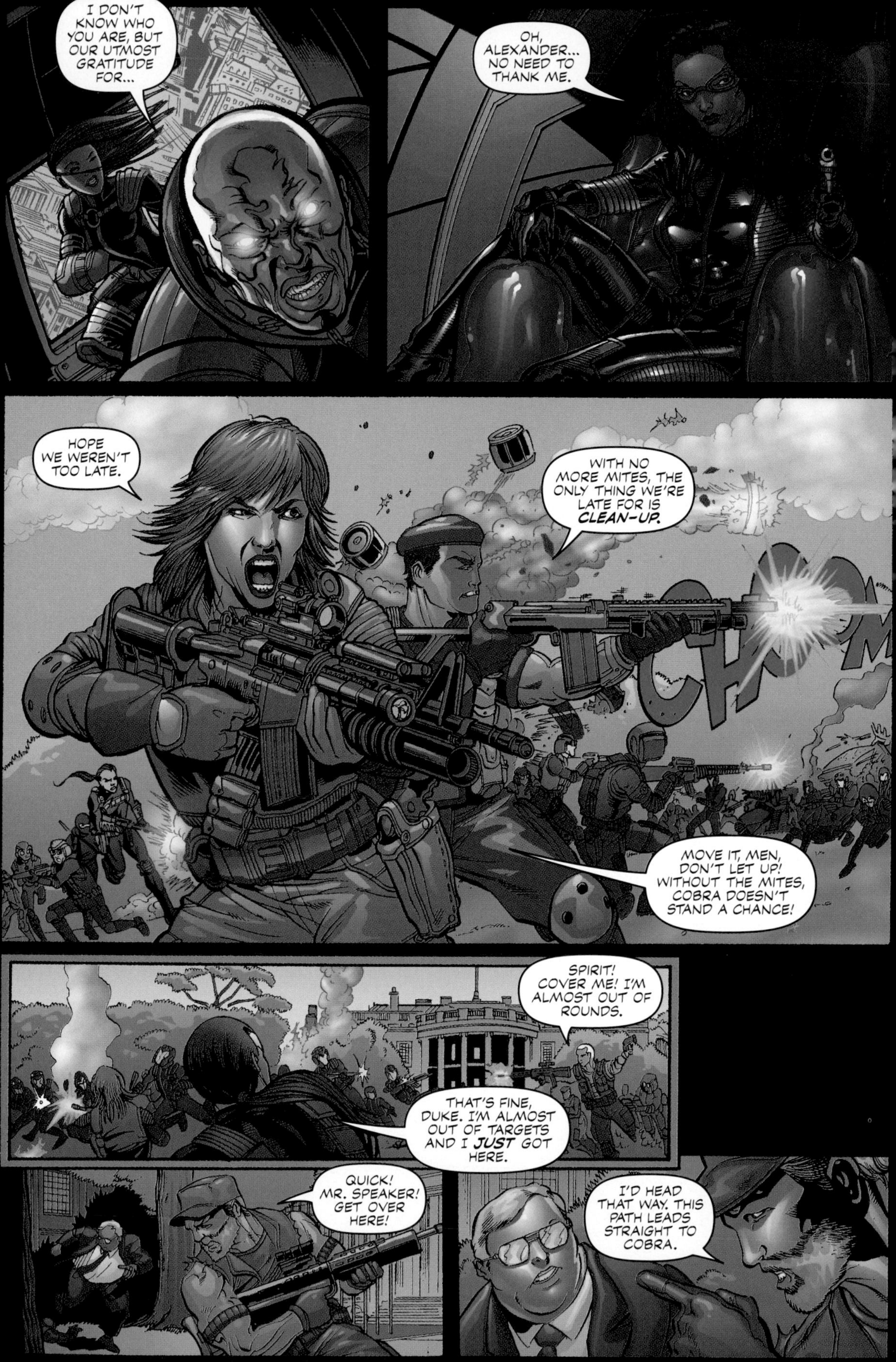
I DON'T KNOW WHO YOU ARE, BUT OUR UTMOST GRATITUDE FOR...
OH, ALEXANDER... NO NEED TO THANK ME.
HOPE WE WEREN'T TOO LATE.
WITH NO MORE MITES, THE ONLY THING WE'RE LATE FOR IS CLEAN-UP.
MOVE IT, MEN, DON'T LET UP! WITHOUT THE MITES, COBRA DOESN'T STAND A CHANCE!
SPIRIT! COVER ME! I'M ALMOST OUT OF ROUNDS.
THAT'S FINE, DUKE. I'M ALMOST OUT OF TARGETS AND I JUST GOT HERE.
QUICK! MR. SPEAKER! GET OVER HERE!
I'D HEAD THAT WAY. THIS PATH LEADS STRAIGHT TO COBRA.

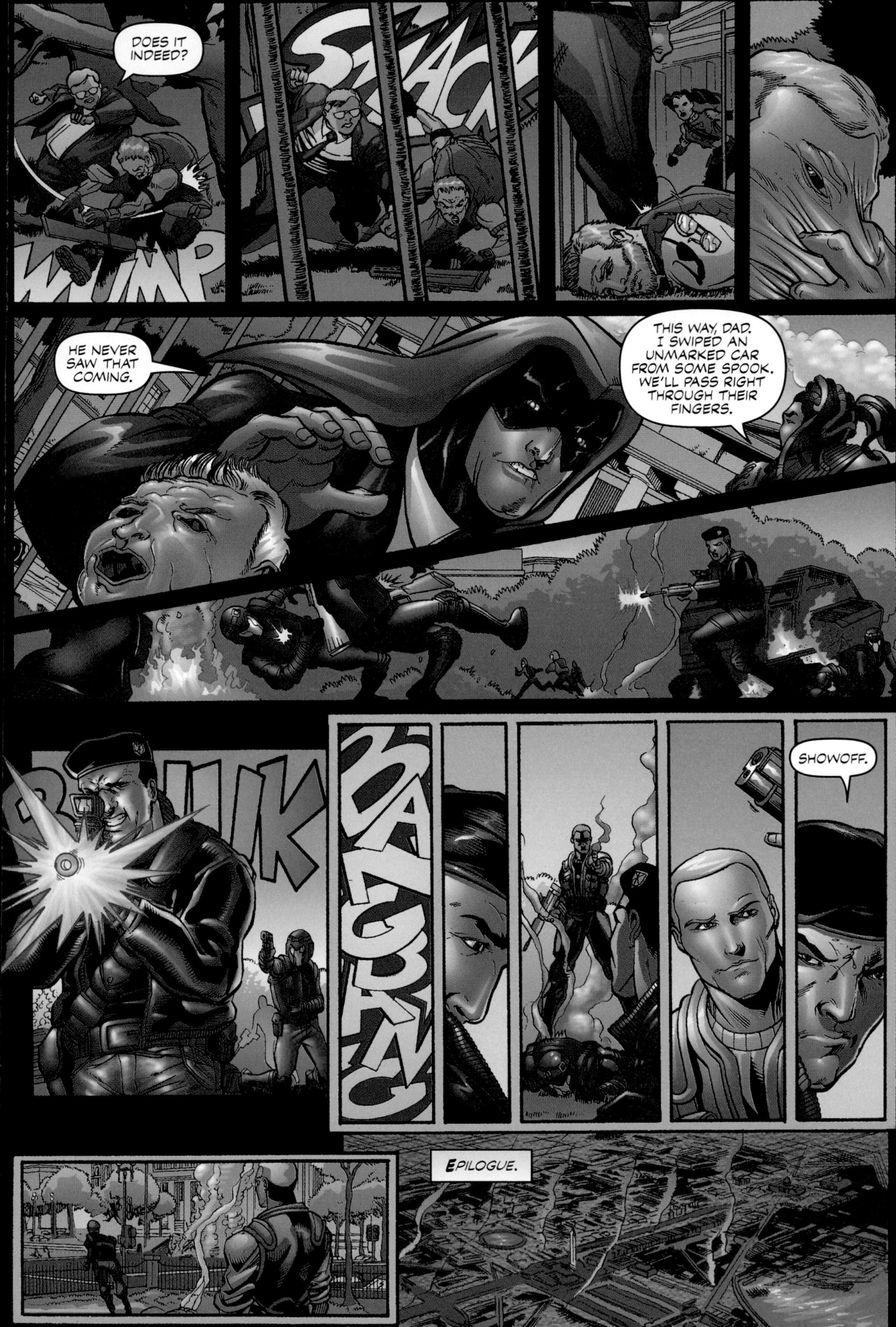
DOES IT INDEED?
WUMP
SMACK
HE NEVER SAW THAT COMING.
THIS WAY, DAD. I SWIPED AN UNMARKED CAR FROM SOME SPOOK. WE'LL PASS RIGHT THROUGH THEIR FINGERS.
BLAMBANG
SHOWOFF.
EPILOGUE.

"THE LAST OF COBRA'S TROOPS WERE CAPTURED YESTERDAY AFTERNOON, AS THE G.I.JOE TASK FORCE MADE A SURPRISE ATTACK ON THE TERRORIST ARMY. WHILE NONE OF THE COBRA HIERARCHY WERE CAUGHT, IT IS BELIEVED THEIR ARMY HAS BEEN SERIOUSLY DIMINISHED BY THE CAPTURES."

"THE SPEAKER OF THE HOUSE WAS FOUND LAST NIGHT ON THE BASEMENT FLOOR OF THE CAPITOL BUILDING, APPARENTLY BOUND, GAGGED, AND LOCKED IN A JANITORIAL CLOSET BY COBRA OFFICERS. DOCTORS SAY THE SPEAKER RECEIVED MINOR CUTS AND BRUISES, BUT IS IN FINE CONDITION."

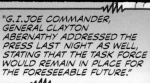

"G.I.JOE COMMANDER, GENERAL CLAYTON ABERNATHY ADDRESSED THE PRESS LAST NIGHT AS WELL, STATING THAT THE TASK FORCE WOULD REMAIN IN PLACE FOR THE FORESEEABLE FUTURE."

"ON ANOTHER NOTE, SOME CITIZENS ARE PROTESTING THE ARREST OF THE COBRA GUARD, CLAIMING THAT WHEN THE U.S. FAILED TO HELP, COBRA WAS THERE. JOIN US AT 10:00 FOR A SPECIAL REPORT."

TWO WEEKS LATER.

THIS IS *ALL YOUR FAULT.* I *TOLD* YOU YOU WERE GOING TOO FAR.

DON'T TRY TO BLAME ME. YOU WERE WITH ME EVERY STEP OF THE...

SHH... I HEAR SOMETHING.

IS... IS SOMEONE THERE? PLEASE, HELP! WE NEED WATER! FOOD! PLEASE.

YOU'LL BE GETTING NEITHER.

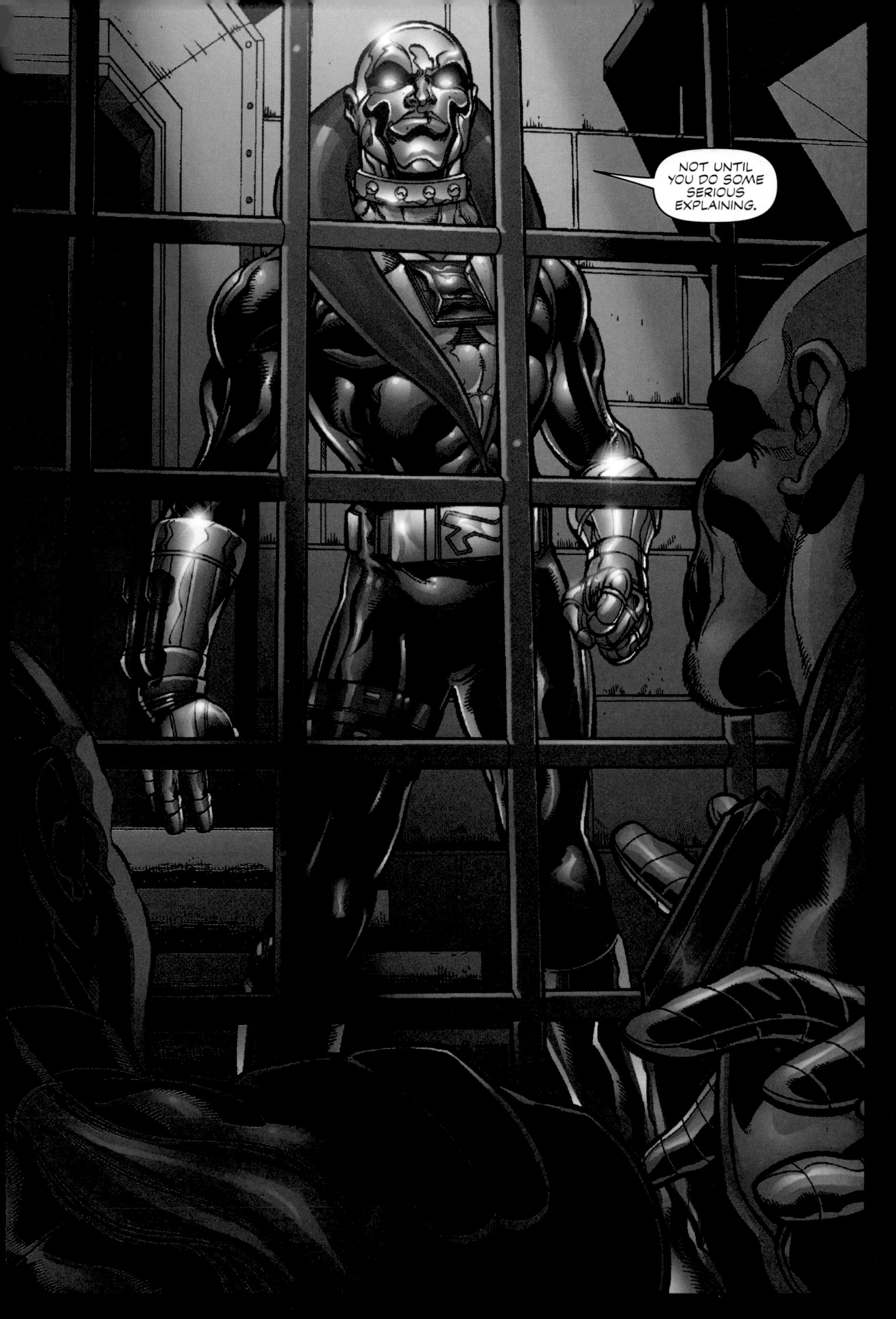
NOT UNTIL YOU DO SOME SERIOUS EXPLAINING.

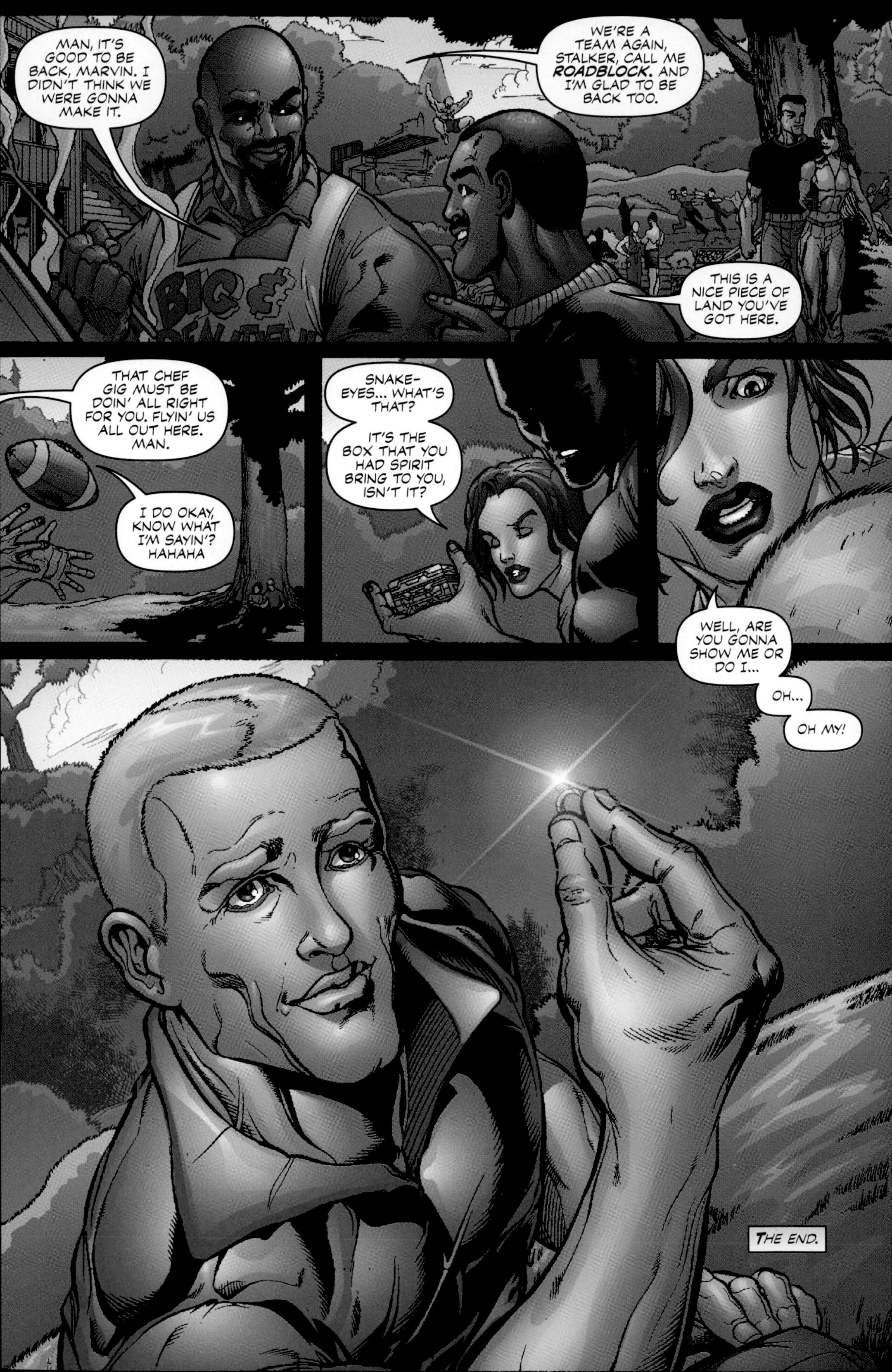
MAN, IT'S GOOD TO BE BACK, MARVIN. I DIDN'T THINK WE WERE GONNA MAKE IT.
WE'RE A TEAM AGAIN, STALKER, CALL ME ROADBLOCK. AND I'M GLAD TO BE BACK TOO.
THIS IS A NICE PIECE OF LAND YOU'VE GOT HERE.
THAT CHEF GIG MUST BE DOIN' ALL RIGHT FOR YOU. FLYIN' US ALL OUT HERE. MAN.
I DO OKAY, KNOW WHAT I'M SAYIN'? HAHAHA
SNAKE-EYES... WHAT'S THAT?
IT'S THE BOX THAT YOU HAD SPIRIT BRING TO YOU, ISN'T IT?
WELL, ARE YOU GONNA SHOW ME OR DO I...
OH...
OH MY!
THE END.

PRODUCTION ART GALLERY

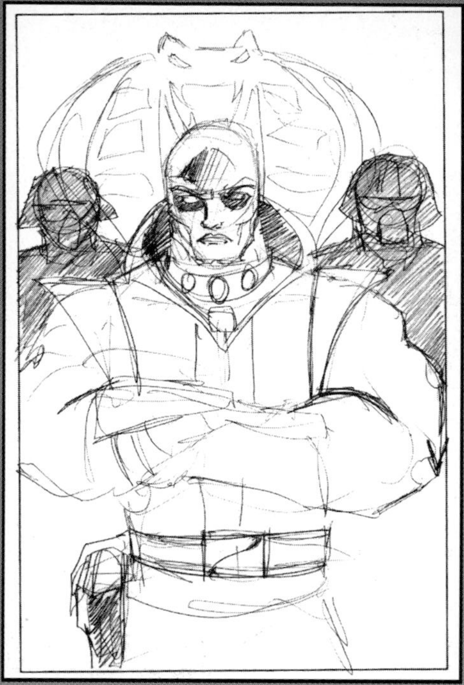

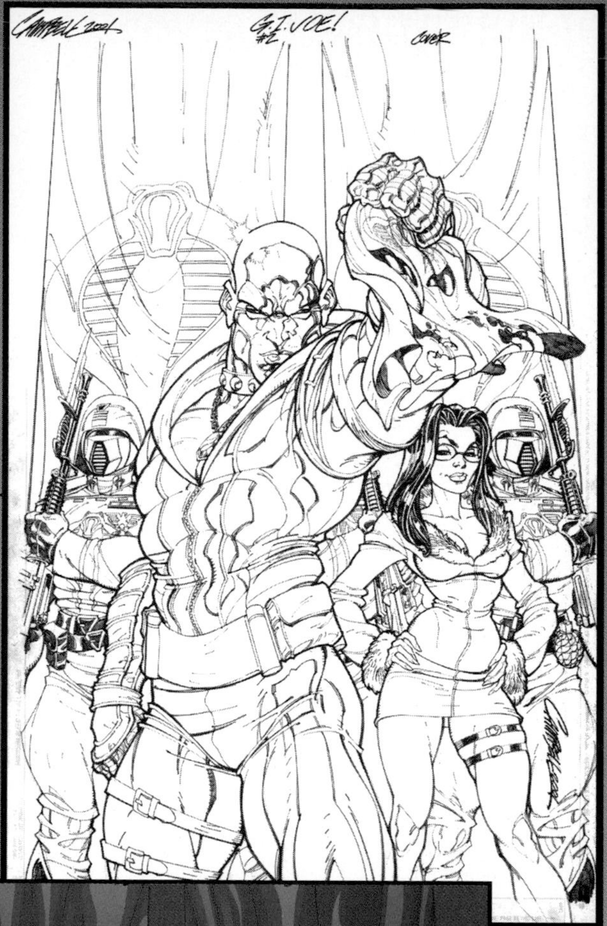
G.I. JOE!
#2
COVER

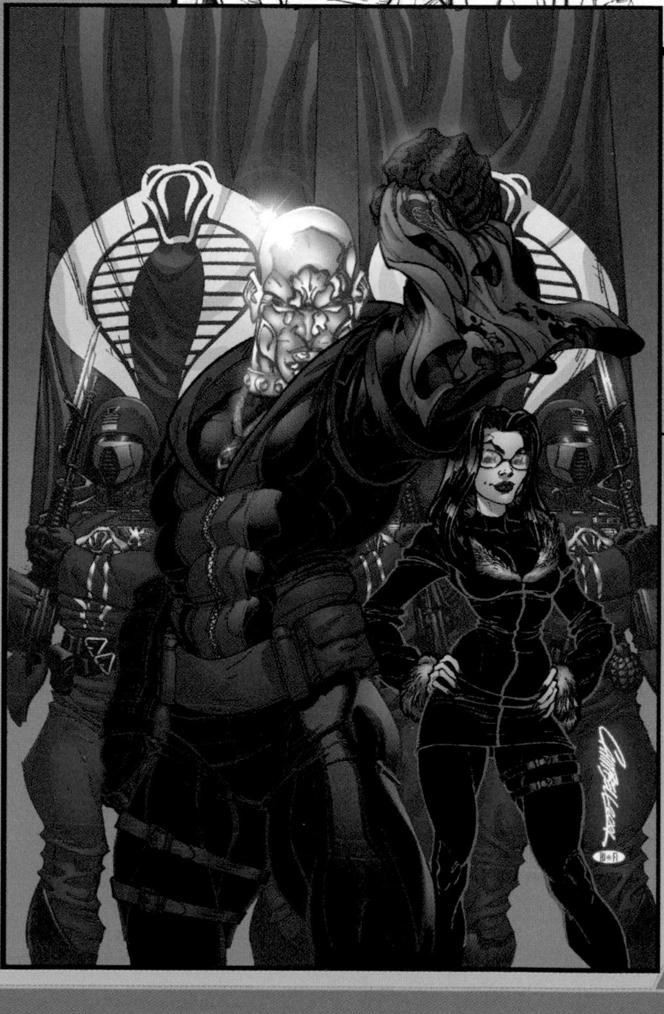

Pencils to Color:
G.I. JOE issue #2
Cover

PRODUCTION ART GALLERY

A G.I.JOE page: From Layout to Color

Layout

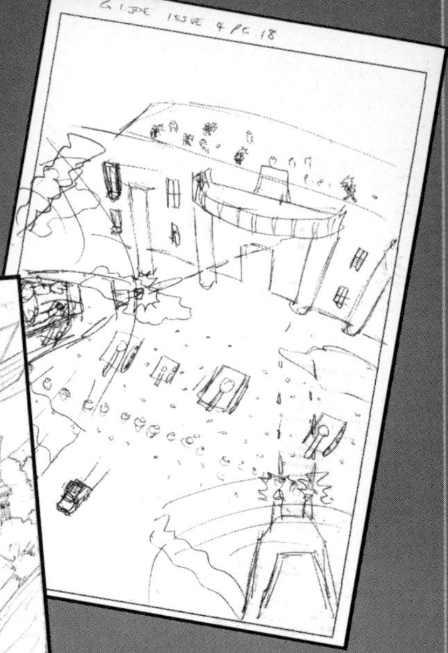
G.I.JOE ISSUE 4 PG 18

Pencils

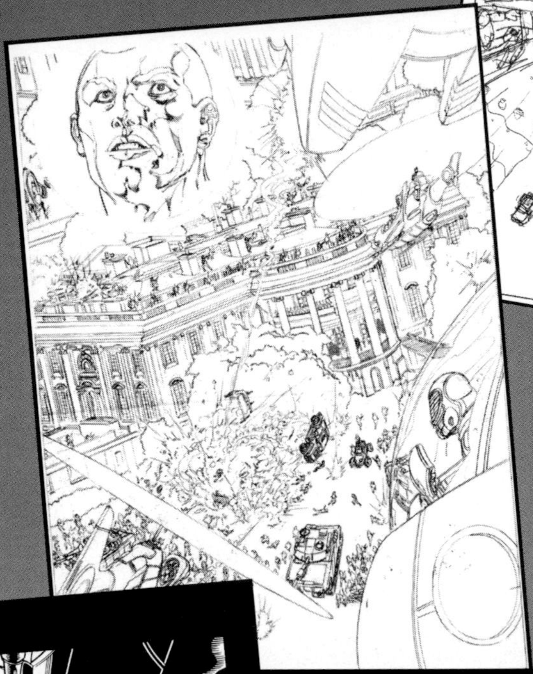

Inks

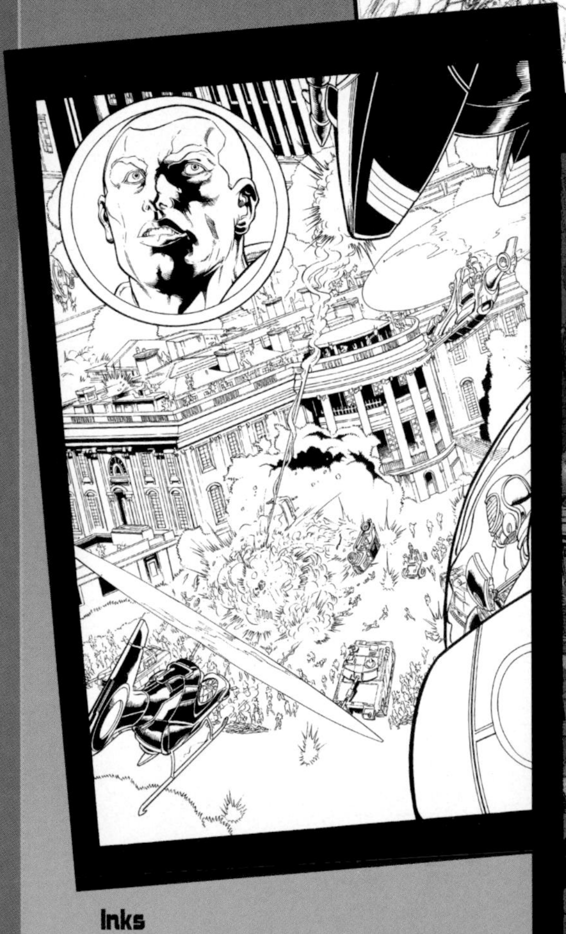

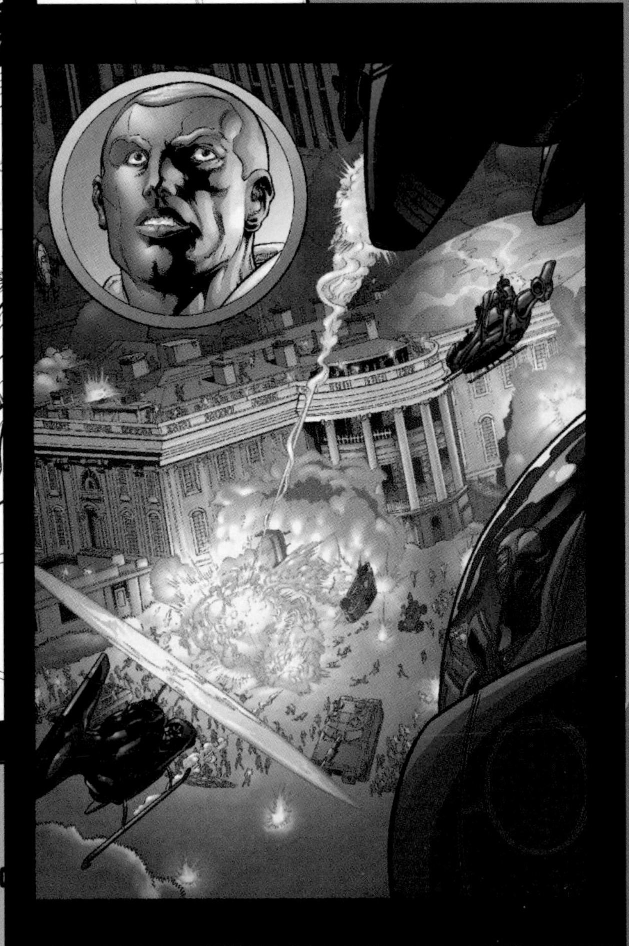